Schools and Special Needs

Issues of Innovation and Inclusion

Alan Dyson and Alan Millward

P·C·P

Paul Chapman
Publishing Ltd

Paul Chapman Publishing Ltd
A SAGE Publications Company
6 Bonhill Street
London EC2A 4PU

SAGE Publications Inc.
2455 Teller Road
Thousand Oaks, California 91320

SAGE Publications India Pvt Ltd
32, M-Block Market
Greater Kailash-I
New Delhi 110 048

British Library Cataloguing in Publication data

A catalogue record for this book is available from the British
Library

ISBN 0 7619 6441 X
ISBN 0 7619 6442 8 (pbk)

Library of Congress catalog record available

Typeset by Dorwyn Ltd, Hampshire
Printed in Great Britain by Athenaeum Press, Gateshead

Contents

Preface

This book is about how mainstream schools respond to the diverse learning characteristics of the students who attend them. In particular, it is about the ways in which schools have used the concepts and practices of 'special needs education' to respond to that diversity and about how some schools have sought to move beyond the boundaries of those concepts and practices by developing what we have latterly learned to call 'inclusive' approaches.

At its core are case studies of four English comprehensive schools which were pursuing innovative approaches to special needs education – approaches that moved them in the direction of greater inclusion. The book explores both the successes of those schools and the problems and tensions they encountered. However, it seeks to be more than simply a descriptive account of practices and occurrences in these schools. Drawing on and critiquing the work of Mel Ainscow and Tom Skrtic, it is also centrally concerned with understanding these schools from a theoretical standpoint. In this way, it hopes to move beyond the particularity of the four schools to issues, patterns and principles which underpin responses to diversity in all schools and, perhaps in all education systems.

In contrast to much current literature on 'inclusive education', the book is not straightforwardly optimistic in tone. The authors find themselves unconvinced by suggestions that 'inclusion' is a simple concept unequivocally yielding unproblematic practices. They remain sceptical about claims that 'inclusion' marks, in any simple way, a step forward in the uninterrupted progress of, or beyond, special needs education. On the other hand, neither do they wish to present an essentially conservative argument for the maintenance of a non-inclusive *status quo*. Instead, 'inclusion' is seen from a historical perspective. It is, the book argues, the currently-favoured resolution of dilemmas and contradictions which are much older than itself and which will, in the fullness of time, diminish, fragment and ultimately replace 'inclusion' with new – though not necessarily 'better' – responses to diversity. This process, the book argues, is unavoidable but is not entirely beyond the control of practitioners, policy-makers and other stakeholders in education. Crucially, therefore, the book is concerned with helping all those involved in constructing educational responses to diversity to understand the dilemmas and contradictions they face a little more clearly, in the hope of informing a fuller and better-informed debate about how they might be resolved.

A note on language

The language which surrounds educational responses to diversity is often confused and conflicting. The term 'special educational needs', for instance, can be seen to carry with it unwanted categorisations and implications of within-learner deficit. Equally, terms such as 'inclusion', 'inclusive education' and 'inclusive schools' tend to have only the most general of meanings unless and until they are defined precisely.

Writing about these topics is, therefore, difficult and the temptation is to surround every term with apostrophes, as above, in order to indicate a resistance to its unwanted meanings. However, our policy throughout this book is to use 'inclusion', 'special educational needs' and their derivatives largely without such health warnings. Our defence is that we make some attempt to define the former with care, whilst the latter is, if nothing else, an administrative category which has reasonable clarity of meaning as such in the English education system.

However, this does signal a further difficulty. The book focuses on English comprehensive schools and therefore we use the terminology of the English system throughout. This means, for instance, that we refer to 'ordinary' or 'mainstream' schools rather than to 'regular' schools and that we do not offer definitions of common terms such as 'SENCO' or 'Code of Practice stages' each time they occur. For our non-English readers, we have provided a brief explanatory glossary. For our non-English but UK readers, we can confirm that our references to the 'English system' indicate our acknowledgement of the important differences between that system and those of the other parts of the UK, rather than an assumption that English practices are the norm elsewhere.

Acknowledgements

This book would not have been possible without the patience, tolerance and openness of the heads, teachers and other staff of 'Lakeside', 'Moorgate', 'St Joseph's' and 'Seaview' schools. Their willingness to accept our presence and to engage with us in debates on our findings was an indication of their commitment to the continuing development of their responses to student diversity.

The research out of which this book grew was supported by the Economic and Social Research Council as award number R000236254. We are grateful for that support. We are also grateful for the substantial input which our former colleagues, Catherine Clark and Sue Robson, made to that research and for the work on this manuscript undertaken by our current colleagues, Frances Gallannaugh and Christine Redden.

Finally, we would like to acknowledge the helpful comments made by Mel Ainscow on an earlier draft of Chapter 2. Our debate with his work – and that of Tom Skrtic – is an acknowledgement of their major contribution to current thinking. We hope, therefore, that our critique does justice to that contribution and is not too 'black and white'.

Glossary

This glossary is intended primarily for readers who are not familiar with the English school system.

A-level 'Advanced' level: an academically-oriented examination taken by some students at age 18.

City and Guilds An organisation offering accreditation for vocationally oriented courses, sometimes taken, at the time of our fieldwork, as an alternative to GCSEs.

Code of Practice The *Code of Practice on the Assessment and Identification of Special Educational Needs* (DfE, 1994) set out official guidance to schools and LEAs on the procedures they should follow in assessing students' special educational needs. Its main feature was to mark the severity of students' needs in terms of a series of five **stages**. Students with the greatest needs are placed at stage 5 and receive a **statement** of special educational needs (something like an IEP in the USA), offering legal guarantees for the provision made to meet their needs. All students with special educational needs have to be recorded in the school's special educational needs **register**. A revision of the Code is due to take effect in 2001.

Comprehensive school A school for secondary aged (i.e. 11–16/18 years) pupils which does not select by 'ability'. In most parts of England, comprehensive schools replaced a system which selected the highest-attaining students into **grammar** schools and placed the remainder in **secondary modern** schools during the 1970s. However, remnants of the selective system remain in some parts of the country.

FTE 'Full-time equivalents': a measure of staff time as a fraction or multiple of a full-time member of staff.

GCSE 'General Certificate of Secondary Education': the major set of examinations taken by most (but not all) students at the end of statutory schooling (i.e. age 16). The highest grade is **A***. Pass grades are regarded as **A*–G** and 'good' passes are regarded as **A*–C**. The proportion of students achieving these grades in each school is reported publicly each year and the media frequently draw up '**league tables**' of school performance.

Heads of Year   Secondary schools in England typically group their students horizontally (i.e. by age) for teaching purposes. All the students in a particular year group are the responsibility of the **head of year** (also known as **year head** or **year tutor**). Typically, these managers have a largely pastoral responsibility and are aided by a team of **form tutors** working with groups of *c*.30 students each. Increasingly, year heads have taken on a responsibility for monitoring students' academic attainment (sometimes acquiring new titles such as St Joseph's **learning co-ordinators**). In some schools (such as Moorgate), students are grouped vertically (i.e. in mixed-age groups) in a **house** system for pastoral purposes.

Individual Education Plan (IEP)   A teaching plan for a student with special educational needs, usually drawn up by the school's SENCO in collaboration with other teachers. The IEP has no legal force (unlike the statement) but there is a clear expectation that parents will be involved in its formulation and that it will be reviewed regularly. All students placed at stage 2 or above of the Code of Practice are expected to have an IEP.

INSET   In-Service Education and Training: professional development activities, often organised by schools and their LEAs

Key Stages (KSs)   The National Curriculum is organised in terms of programmes for Key Stage 1 (years 1 and 2, effectively, age 5–7), Key Stage 2 (years 3–6, age 7–11), Key Stage 3 (years 7–9, age 11–14) and Key Stage 4 (years 10 and 11, age 14–16). After KS4, some students stay on into the **sixth form** for a further two years.

Local Education Authority (LEA)   The body responsible for administering education in a particular area. LEA areas vary in size from medium-size towns to large cities or shire counties.

LMS   'Local Management of Schools': the system of delegating budgets and many other aspects of management from LEAs to schools.

Learning Support Assistants (LSAs)   Adults working alongside teachers in classrooms, particularly with students with special educational needs. LSAs are not usually qualified teachers and may have low levels of training.

Ofsted   The 'Office for Standards in Education' is the body responsible for official inspections in the education system. School inspections at the time of our fieldwork took place every four years and the inspection reports were publicly available. **HMI** (Her Majesty's Inspectors) form part of Ofsted.

Pupil Referral Unit (PRU)   An institution providing education for students who have been excluded from their schools for disciplinary reasons.

Sets and streams   Types of student grouping for teaching purposes. A **stream** is a teaching group which has been created on the assumption that all its members function at a similar level and which stays together for all or most subjects. A **set** is like a stream except that it only stays together for one subject. Other subject departments may create their own sets or place students in so-called **'mixed-ability'** groups.

Special educational needs (SEN)   In the English system, some 18 per cent of students are regarded as having 'special educational needs', though only a small proportion of these will be placed in special schools or other special settings. It is not necessary for students to be allocated to any disability category in order to be regarded as having special educational needs. Technically, the term 'special needs' refers to a wider range of non-educational needs. In practice, however, the two are often used interchangeably.

Special Educational Needs Co-ordinator (SENCO)   The SENCO is the teacher in a school who has responsibility for co-ordinating the school's response to students with special educational needs. Often, SENCOs in comprehensive schools have some training in special needs education and undertake a good deal of special needs teaching. However, it is quite possible for SENCOs not to be special needs education specialists and/or for them to have other roles (e.g. as members of senior management teams) in the school.

Special Educational Needs Support Services   Most LEAs maintain peripatetic teaching services for students with special educational needs which supplement the provision that schools can make from their own resources. They are also sometimes known as **'Learning Support Services'**.

Support teachers   Support teachers are trained teachers who work in ordinary classrooms with students with special educational needs. They may be members of LEA support services, or be trained special needs specialists on the school's own staff, or be subject teachers working in this role for a few hours each week.

1

Inclusion in an English Context

The advent of inclusion

In October 1997, the recently-installed Labour government in England
issued a Green Paper on special needs education which contained the
following statement:

> We want to see more pupils with SEN included within main-
> stream primary and secondary schools. We support the United
> Nations Educational, Scientific and Cultural Organisation (UN-
> ESCO) Salamanca World Statement on Special Needs Education
> 1994. This calls on governments to adopt the principle of inclusive
> education, enrolling all children in regular schools, unless there
> are compelling reasons for doing otherwise. This implies a pro-
> gressive extension of the capacity of mainstream schools to pro-
> vide for children with a wide range of needs.
>
> (DfEE, 1997a, p.44)

This was the first time that any British government had committed
itself to creating an avowedly inclusive education system and marked
the extent to which inclusion had become, in the space of a few years,
the dominant issue in special needs education in this country.

The government's commitment was significant in two respects.
First, it signalled an intention to shake special needs provision out of
the somewhat complacent state in which, it is arguable, it had rested
for the past two decades. The Warnock Report of 1978 (DES, 1978),
implemented in large part by the 1981 Education Act, had given England a liberal special education system which made it possible for
additional resources and specialist services to be provided for meeting
children's 'special educational needs' without recourse to special
school placement. This in turn meant that it was relatively straightforward for students with special educational needs to be 'integrated'
from special schools into mainstream schools. The consequence was
that England moved to a position in the middle rank of European

1

countries in terms of its commitment to integration (Vislie, 1995). Whilst it was not as fully integrated as, say, the Scandinavian countries, neither was it anywhere near as segregated as its near neighbours, the Netherlands or France.

Insofar as integration did develop in the period between 1978 and 1997, it did so in a somewhat *ad hoc* manner. The 1981 Act was, in terms of integration, an enabling piece of legislation and central government avoided giving any strong steer to placement policies, seeing these as essentially a matter for local education authorities (LEAs). Whilst, therefore, some LEAs embraced integration enthusiastically (see, for instance, Jones, 1983), others retained substantial infrastructures of segregated provision. The result was that the 1981 Act produced no dramatic shift towards a more fully integrated system (Swann, 1985, 1988, 1992). The 1997 Green Paper, therefore, marked an important change in direction, not only in its explicit dissatisfaction with the *status quo*, but also in its view that inclusion is a matter in which central government should be directly concerned.

The second significance of the 1997 Green Paper was its explicit alignment of policy in England with international trends in special education. The Salamanca Statement (UNESCO, 1994) to which the Green Paper refers had been formulated three years earlier by delegates from 92 governments and 25 international organisations and committed the international education community to the development of inclusive schools. It dramatically illustrated the extent to which inclusion had indeed become a 'global agenda' (Pijl, Meijer and Hegarty, 1997). However, English special education policy, although influenced by the Scandinavian example and by US legislation (notably, PL94–142) around the time of Warnock, had not previously been noted for its borrowings from policy developments elsewhere. The explicit adoption of an international declaration on a specific aspect of education policy was, therefore, unusual – as, indeed, was the importing into a government policy document of a term, 'inclusion', which had its origins elsewhere and which, at the time, was still largely unfamiliar to teachers and other members of the special needs community in England.

Inclusion and the national context

It is, indeed, this phenomenon of an apparently imported policy which should make us cautious in attempting to understand inclusion in the English context. Superficially, the meaning of inclusion is relatively straightforward. The New Zealand scholar, Keith Ballard, for instance, defines inclusion in the following way:

Inclusive education means education that is non-discriminatory in terms of disability, culture, gender or other aspects of students or staff that are assigned significance by a society. It involves all students in a community, with no exceptions and irrespective of their intellectual, physical, sensory or other differences, having equal rights to access the culturally valued curriculum of their society as full-time valued members of age-appropriate main-stream classrooms. Inclusion emphasizes diversity over assimila-tion, striving to avoid the colonization of minority experiences by dominant modes of thought and action.

(Ballard, 1997, pp. 244–245)

However, the English scholar Tony Booth (1995) warns that this ap-parently simple concept of inclusion is both extremely slippery and highly context-specific. Ballard's definition of inclusion, for instance, reflects both his own commitment to disability issues, the particular significance of cultural diversity – notably the place of Maori culture in a society dominated by people of European origin – in New Zea-land and the impact of that country's heavily rights-oriented approach to social issues in general and the framing of legislation in particular (see, for instance, Ballard, 1994, 1995, 1996, 1999; Ballard and Mac-donald, 1998). Similarly, the Salamanca Statement reflects the fact that many of the 92 participating governments came from relatively poorer countries. It is, therefore, at least as much concerned with finding ways and means of providing basic education for a wide range of marginalised groups (street children, working children, children from ethnic minorities, children from remote areas and so on) as it is with the transfer of students from special to mainstream schools in rela-tively well-resourced and sophisticated education systems.

Even more significantly, from an English point of view, inclusion is a term which seems to have its origins in the USA in the late 1980s and which grew in strength during the early 1990s (Fuchs and Fuchs, 1994; Skrtic, 1995b). Certainly, a substantial volume of literature has been generated in the USA and has impacted on the English context; the relationship between the work of Tom Skrtic in the USA and Mel Ainscow in England, which we shall discuss in the next chapter, is merely one instance of this impact. However, the American notion of inclusion grew out of a social policy history which is significantly different from that in England (Ware, 1998). If nothing else, the issue of race in the US has generated a notion of civil rights which is not shared in this country. Moreover, the US education system differs from that in England in ways which are directly relevant to the mean-ing of inclusion (Pijl, 1994b). The proportion of students identified as in need of special education, the formal assessment procedure, the reliance on categorical forms of provision, the grade system, the regular education testing and assessment systems, the relationship between the individual school on the one hand and local, state and federal government on the other are all different in significant ways from their equivalents here.

It follows that, although it is possible to agree across national boundaries what inclusion means in general terms, the reality in each national system will be determined by the history, culture and politics of that system (Daniels and Garner, 1999). It is, therefore, dangerous to see the recent adoption of the inclusion agenda by the UK government as a straightforward alignment with a policy direction that is both globally understood and relatively straightforward. Instead, we must ask what inclusion looks like in England and out of what historical background it emerges if we are to understand its meaning in our own context. It is not the purpose of this chapter to rehearse the recent history of English special needs education in full (Clark *et al.*, 1997, and Stakes and Hornby, 1997, provide some of the detail that is missing here), but there are at least two salient features of that history which have a direct bearing on the meaning of inclusion in England – the role of mainstream schools in special needs provision and the 'liberal' tradition in English special needs education.

The role of the mainstream school

Although, historically, England has long maintained a substantial infrastructure of segregated special education, it also has a long tradition of expecting mainstream schools to make some form of provision that was recognisably 'special'. The 1944 Education Act is best remembered for establishing a system of separate schooling for children of different aptitudes and abilities, paralleled by a segregated special education system with different types of schools for children in each of eleven categories of 'handicap'. However, the Act also placed a duty on LEAs to ascertain the needs of children for special education and anticipated that such 'treatment' would be provided in many cases in mainstream schools.

Although the response to this aspect of the 1944 Act seems to have been patchy, it nonetheless initiated a trend for mainstream schools to explore ways of making special needs provision and for legislation and guidance at national and local level to expect that such provision would be the norm. The Warnock Report (DES, 1978) continued this trend by indicating that, while some 18 per cent of school students would have special needs at any one time, the great majority of these would have their needs met in mainstream schools. More recently, the government's special educational needs Code of Practice (DfE, 1994) has formalised the expectation that schools will have staff with designated responsibility for co-ordinating special needs provision, that they will deploy rigorous assessment procedures to identify needs and that they will meet those needs for the most part within the ordinary classroom and out of their own resources. Placement in special schools, therefore, is seen as very much a last resort.

Within this context, neither the integration movement of the 1970s nor the inclusion movement of the 1990s constituted quite the shock to the system that might otherwise have been the case. Rather than requiring schools to set up entirely new forms of provision, they have, for the most part, simply encouraged schools to extend their existing provision to accommodate students with somewhat more pronounced difficulties. Whilst, therefore, there have been some high-profile projects and initiatives in inclusion (see, for instance, Jordan and Goodey, 1996), a good deal of inclusive practice has been developed quietly, over a period of years, without even the need to set up special facilities and units in mainstream schools.

The liberal principle

This history of special needs education in mainstream schools points to the extent to which the English education system has, at least in respect of special needs, been driven by relatively liberal principles (Clark *et al.*, 1997). Whilst it is important not to underestimate the extent to which these principles have been contested or have failed to generate genuinely *radical* approaches (see, for instance, Barton, 1997; Booth, Ainscow and Dyson, 1998; Riddell and Brown, 1994; Rouse and Florian, 1997, amongst many others), there are, nonetheless, historical trends in English special needs education which are very much in tune with what we have recently learned to call inclusion.

The 'liberal principles' we refer to are not so coherent or well defined as to constitute a thoroughgoing ideological position. Nonetheless, the English education system generally and its special needs provision in particular have, we suggest, been informed by notions of equity, the value of the individual and the right of all individuals to participate in shared communities, curricula and learning experiences. The expectation in education legislation and guidance that students with special needs would normally be educated in mainstream schools can be seen as a manifestation of these principles and the Warnock Report's famous declaration that:

The purpose of education for all children is the same; the goals are
the same

(DES, 1978, 1.4)

is the *locus classicus* of their formal expression.

These liberal principles have, at the very least, acted as a counter-
balance to the undoubted exclusionary pressures which exist in the system. More than this, however, they have led to an ongoing exploration of
the extent to which students with special needs might be educated, not
merely in the same institution as their peers, but alongside them in
ordinary classrooms and within a common curriculum. In the post-
Second World War years, for instance, special education in mainstream
schools seems to have consisted predominantly of grouping students by
their supposed ability and placing the lowest attainers in the lowest
'streams'. Even this practice, however, could be read as an attempt to
make specialist provision without the need to segregate students into
special schools (Tansley and Gulliford, 1960). Moreover, it was frequently
supplemented for students with less global difficulties by remedial teaching in clinics, or delivered by specialists on the school staff or by peripatetic teachers, which involved the segregation of students from their
classmates for only limited amounts of time (Sampson, 1975).

In the 1960s and, increasingly, in the 1970s, these forms of provision
were subjected to growing criticism, partly on the grounds of their inef-
fectiveness, but partly also from a liberal position which saw them as
segregatory, stigmatising and, ultimately, limiting of the educational- and
life-opportunities to which students with special needs had access (Carroll, 1972; Collins, 1972; Galletley, 1976; Galloway and Goodwin, 1979;
Golby and Gulliver, 1979; Lovell, Johnson and Platts, 1962). These critiques led to experiments with what originally was known as 'remedial
work across the curriculum' (Gulliford, 1979) but subsequently developed into the 'whole school approach'. The implementation of the
whole school approach proved, in practice, to be both patchy and problematic (Bines, 1986; Clark *et al.*, 1997; Croll and Moses, 1985). However,
its basic premise was simple. It was based, in Dessent's words, on the
'devolution of special needs resources and responsibilities to all teachers
and to all curriculum areas' (Dessent, 1987, p. 25).

In other words, special needs provision would no longer be something that was separate from mainstream education, conducted outside the ordinary classroom and the responsibility of 'special'
teachers. Instead, it would be the responsibility of the 'whole school',
taking place within ordinary classrooms and delivered by ordinary
teachers. The mechanisms whereby this was to be brought about were
threefold (Clark *et al.*, 1997):

- a change in curriculum and pedagogy in ordinary classrooms so that they became accessible to the full range of students in the school;
- the provision of additional teacher-support in classrooms both for students experiencing difficulties and for their teachers; and
- the reconstruction of the remedial teacher's role into that of the 'special educational needs co-ordinator' with responsibility, not for delivering specialist teaching to an identified minority of students in segregated settings, but for co-ordinating provision for those students across the school as a whole.

In effect, as Dessent's definition implies, the whole school approach demanded a reorganisation and, in particular, a relocation of special needs education in mainstream schools. The entirely separate structures of special classes and remedial groups were to be dismantled, the resources which had sustained them (and, in particular, the specialist teachers who had staffed them) were to be redistributed into ordinary classrooms across the school and the somewhat isolated figure of the remedial teacher was to become an outward-looking co-ordinator, collaborating with and working alongside ordinary teachers in mainstream classrooms. It was, in Galletley's (1976) prescient phrase, an exercise for remedial education in 'how to do away with yourself'.

In many ways, the whole school approach moved rapidly from the status of a radical experiment to an educational orthodoxy. Its essential features were endorsed by Her Majesty's Inspectors of Schools (HMI) in England (DES, 1989; HMI, 1990). The advent of the National Curriculum in 1988 gave the approach a further boost; if all (or very nearly all) students were now to participate in a common curriculum, prescribed in detail, then there was clearly no room for entirely segregated provision focusing on 'basic skills' (NCC, 1989a and b). The adaptation of mainstream teaching was redescribed as 'differentiation' and became an essential underpinning of the delivery of the National Curriculum (Stradling, Saunders and Weston, 1991; Weston, 1992). And the role of the co-ordinator became formalised as that of the 'SENCO' in the Code of Practice (DfE, 1994), a document which, with its emphasis on provision in ordinary classrooms and on the centrality of the SENCO role, in many ways marks the apotheosis of the whole school approach.

These changes in the form of special needs provision in mainstream schools were paralleled by two other developments which were informed by similar liberal and participatory principles. The critiques which were formulated against segregatory forms of special education within mainstream schools could, of course, be applied even more forcibly to the placement of students with special needs in special schools (Galloway and Goodwin, 1979). The emergence of the integration movement in the 1970s, therefore, can be seen as part of the exploration in this period of ways of enabling students with special needs to have access, alongside their peers, to shared institutions, curricula and communities.

Similarly, during the 1960s and 1970s, the comprehensive school movement was beginning to break down the barriers between the separate forms of secondary schooling established by the 1944 Act. Just as segregated special needs provision was perceived as stigmatising and limiting, so separate schools for higher- and lower-attaining students and for students with a 'technical' aptitude came to be seen as restricting rather than creating opportunities and as leading to the reproduction of a divided and class-ridden society (Benn and Simon, 1972). In due course, the introduction of comprehensive schooling was supported and extended by a growth in 'mixed-ability' teaching, already relatively common in primary schools (Central Advisory Council for Education, 1967), by an increase in the number of schools which explicitly accepted a wider responsibility to the community as a whole (Jeffs, 1992; Vincent, 1993) and, ultimately, by the introduction of a common curriculum in the 1988 Education Reform Act. Since the aim (at least avowedly) of these developments was to create a school that would educate all members of the community and that would address questions of access, participation and equity, it is not surprising that some commentators (Booth, 1996; Sayer, 1994/1987; Thomas and Dwyfor Davies, 1999; Thomas, Walker and Webb, 1998) see 'inclusion' as no more nor less than a logical extension of the English tradition of comprehensive schooling – and, indeed, of much older traditions of social justice.

Inclusion and the transformation of schools

It is sometimes argued that a crucial difference between integration and inclusion is that the former implies finding ways of supporting students with special needs in essentially unchanged mainstream schools, while the latter implies a radical restructuring of schools so that they are inherently capable of educating all students in their communities (Corbett and Slee, 2000; Sebba and Sachdev, 1997). We suggest that, within the English tradition at least, this distinction is too simplistic. Given the long-standing expectation that mainstream schools would educate students with special needs, the emergence of 'whole-school' approaches and the linkages between inclusion and the older comprehensive school movement, it is at least arguable that English schools have been engaged in a long-term exploration of the ways in which the presence of students with special needs might require fundamental changes in practice and organisation. Tony Dessent, writing as an advocate of 'whole school approaches', some time before the term 'inclusion' became current, captures the essence of this exploration:

> It is in this area, the development of whole school approaches, that we can glimpse the potential which special education has to improve, and indeed revolutionize, our schools and our system of education. An 'ordinary' school aiming to develop a whole school approach will quickly perceive not only the enormity of the task and the obstacles to be confronted, but also the wide ranging implications for educational practice for all teachers and all children. The whole school response will essentially be a response to meeting the *individual needs* of children. As such it is not just about the size and shape of a school's special needs department – although the work of such a department will be vital. It is not just about meeting the needs of handicapped children or an ill-defined group who are 'below average' or who are slow to learn. *It is about all children regardless of age, family background, race and aptitude.*
>
> (Dessent, 1987, p. 121, emphases in original)

What Dessent saw was that, as the boundaries between special and mainstream education began to dissolve, so the categorical divisions between 'special' and 'ordinary' learners could also dissolve. Instead of thinking in terms of how schools might make provision for minorities of learners with special needs, it was now possible to think about how schools responded to the diverse characteristics of *all* their learners. The notion of 'individual differences' was, therefore, more useful than the notion of 'special needs'.

Once again, it is the introduction of the National Curriculum which appears to have given added impetus to this shift in focus. However complex the origins of that curriculum and the motivations which lay behind its formulation (Lawton and Chitty, 1988), it nonetheless required schools to develop ways of making the *same* curriculum accessible to *all* learners. In the years following its introduction, therefore, case studies began to appear of schools which were adopting approaches which seemed to take them beyond traditional assumptions about special needs, even as those assumptions had been modified in the whole school approach (Luscombe, 1993; Montacute, 1993; Pickup, 1995; Simpson, 1993; Wheal, 1995).

In the early 1990s, moreover, we undertook, with colleagues, a survey of schools which were moving 'beyond the whole school approach' in this sense towards what we chose to call 'innovatory practice' in schools' approaches to special needs (Clark *et al.*, 1995b; Dyson, Millward and Skidmore, 1994). We found a significant number of schools – particularly secondary schools – which were, to a greater or lesser extent, taking seriously Dessent's injunction to consider ways of educating all children, regardless of age, family background, race and aptitude, but which were now doing so within the context of a common curriculum. We found that these schools were 'transforming' themselves in a number of broadly similar ways:

- They conceptualised their approaches more in terms of a response to student diversity as a whole rather than simply as a response to special needs. In some cases, this might mean no more than including one or two 'new' groups – high-attainers, or students with significant difficulties – in the school's approach; in other cases, it meant a radical rejection of the language of special needs in favour of an approach based on individual differences.
- They attempted to merge, to a greater or lesser extent, their special needs infrastructure with the mainstream of the school. Again, in some cases this might mean no more than strengthening the links between the SENCO and class teachers; in other cases, however, it involved a wholesale dismantling of separate special needs education structures and the creation of structures for supporting the learning of all students.
- Whilst continuing to promote differentiation and support as a means of maintaining students with special needs in ordinary classrooms, they also focused on transforming the nature of curriculum and pedagogy in those classrooms so that they were inherently capable of responding to the individual differences between students.
- They redefined the role of the SENCO in line with these other developments, perhaps simply extending its responsibilities somewhat, but perhaps also replacing the special needs role with one concerned with co-ordinating responses to student diversity *per se.*

In many cases, the surface features of the school's approach remained essentially unchanged, but the boundaries of the whole school approach were gradually extended as strategies for supporting and enhancing learning became a feature of more classrooms and of more students' experiences in school. In a few cases, however, quite dramatic transformations were evident – schools which dismantled their special needs departments, abandoned all forms of segregated provision (even in the limited form of withdrawal groups), reinvented their SENCOs as 'Teaching and Learning Co-ordinators', embarked on intensive programmes of staff development, set up quality assurance programmes to enhance teaching and learning across the school and invested heavily in resource-based learning in order to create flexible learning environments across the school. In some cases, indeed, we found what amounted to a radical attempt to redefine the whole teaching and learning process in a way which would make it accessible to all students, regardless of their needs, difficulties or other characteristics (Dyson, Millward and Skidmore 1994).

Despite the many differences between the schools in our study, it seemed to us that what they shared was an attempt to 'embed' special needs provision. Continuing and extending the tradition of breaking down barriers between special and mainstream education which had been evident for many years, they were no longer content simply with maintaining students with special needs in ordinary classes through differentiation and support. Instead, they were trying to embed special needs provision in the daily practices of every teacher in every classroom. In this way, they hoped, the capacity to respond not just to special needs but to student diversity *per se* would become an integral part of the mainstream of the school, and the need both for segregated special needs provision and for those separate practices and provisions in ordinary schools and classrooms which had characterised the whole school approach would simply disappear.

Towards a definition of inclusive schooling in England

Many of the schools we studied in the early 1990s were seeking to extend the range of students for whom they were able to make provision. They were, therefore, inclusive in the sense that they educated students who elsewhere might have been placed in a special school. However, as Booth (1996) points out, in an education system which maintains a special school sector and where placement is a matter for LEAs rather than for individual institutions, few if any English schools can claim to be inclusive in the strict sense that they educate *all* children in their communities. The inclusiveness of English schools, therefore, has to be defined not simply in terms of *which* students they educate, but in terms of *how* they educate them.

The schools we studied, therefore, were inclusive in a way which emanates directly from the English tradition of special needs education. They accepted – indeed, welcomed – the long-standing expectation that, as mainstream schools, they would educate students with special needs. Where they could, therefore, they sought to break down the external barriers which resulted in some students being denied access to what they had to offer. However, they saw that the mere *presence* of students with special needs was not in itself enough. That presence, even if they could extend it, had to lead to *participation* and that participation had to be guided by notions of equity and of the development of a shared community. Moreover, they saw that the issues of presence and participation were not relevant to students with special needs alone. Rather, they were matters which impacted on *all* students in the school and which, if schooling were to be equitable, required that particular attention be given to all students at risk of marginalisation whether that risk related to their special needs or not. It was this realisation that led them to increase the presence of students with special educational needs where they could but, more importantly, to seek new and innovative ways of educating all of their students in line with principles of equity and participation. It is in this sense that these schools were 'inclusive'.

The aim of this book

This book is about inclusive schools defined in this way. At its heart lie case studies of four English comprehensive schools which had claims to being more inclusive than many and which were seeking to develop in a still more inclusive direction. At one level, our intention is to do no more than many other writers in this field – that is, to describe what these schools did to make themselves more inclusive so that other schools can learn from their successes and, indeed, from their mistakes.

At another level, however, we intend to do something more. Following our initial survey of schools moving 'beyond the whole school approach', we undertook a further, more detailed set of case studies of individual schools (Clark *et al.*, 1995a). Our expectation was that we would be able to find out a little more about the processes within these schools which enabled them to become more inclusive. In particular, we hoped that we might be able to test out Skrtic's (1991a, b and c) theoretical account (which we shall deal with in more detail in the next chapter) of the relationship between particular types of organisational configuration and greater or lesser degrees of inclusivity. In fact, what we found was a good deal more puzzling than we had anticipated. Certainly, we were able to identify some of the sorts of processes and configurations we were looking for. However, we also found that, as we 'scratched the surface' of our case-study schools, we found ever more layers of conflict, complexity and contradiction. It was not simply that school staffrooms were divided between pro- and anti-inclusionists (though this was certainly the case), but that pro-inclusionist staff often engaged in apparently anti-inclusionist practices, that school policy was often inclusive in one way and exclusive in another, that many practices were neither clearly inclusive nor exclusive, but could be read in either way, and that, in any case, schools seemed to be torn between their avowedly inclusive aims on the one hand and their need to obey the imperatives of somewhat differently-oriented government policy on the other.

Moreover, when we examined the literature on inclusion, we discovered little to help us understand what we were finding on the ground. That literature, even in the mid-1990s, was vast and since then has grown apace. However, it was and, to a lesser extent, still is characterised by separate traditions of analysis and opposed political and ethical standpoints. As we argued at the time (Clark, Dyson and Millward, 1995b), there was little sense of these separate contributions to the field interacting positively with each other to produce a more sophisticated and complex analysis. In particular, there were precious few case studies of schools which alluded to, much less helped to explain, the complexities of school processes. The conclusion we came to, therefore, was that we had to do this work ourselves.

Over a three-year period, from 1994 to 1997, therefore, we conducted detailed case studies of the attempts to maintain and extend inclusive practices in four comprehensive schools in the north of England. Learning from our previous studies, we focused particularly on the relationships between the schools' avowedly inclusive policies, the practices through which such policies were (or were not) realised and the understandings of special needs which different individuals and groups of staff held. By interviewing staff, analysing documents and observing lessons and meetings we hoped to be able to reach a little more deeply into these schools than we had been able to do in previous studies.

It is these case studies which are reported in the central chapters of this book and out of which the more ambitious aims of our work arise. Given the complexities with which we were engaging, this book cannot set out simply to describe and celebrate inclusive schools. It certainly does this, but it also seeks to identify the complexities, contradictions and conflicts within those schools. Most important, it aims to find ways of explaining how those complexities, contradictions and conflicts arise. In pursuit of this aim, it will be necessary to engage not only with the practicalities of inclusion but with the theoretical underpinnings of the inclusive school and with the sorts of theoretical accounts which might be brought to bear upon our understanding of such schools.

We begin this process in the next chapter, with an exploration of what we regard as the most comprehensive and thoughtful theoretical accounts of inclusive schools that are available – those produced by

Tom Skrtic in the USA and by Mel Ainscow in the UK. In the light of these accounts, Chapters 3 to 6 present the evidence we gathered in our four case-study schools. In Chapter 7, we trace the common themes that run across these studies and in Chapters 8 and 9, we attempt to develop a theoretical account of what we have found. Finally, in Chapter 10, we use this theoretical account to illuminate some of the developments in inclusion in England that have taken place since the election of the 'New' Labour government in 1997.

For the reasons that we set out earlier in this chapter, we regard it as important to retain a sense of the national and local context within which inclusive education is pursued. Despite the globalising impulse of the international inclusion movement, we remain convinced that the meaning of inclusion changes in important ways between these contexts. However, the theoretical accounts that we shall draw upon and the theoretical position that we shall ourselves attempt to develop recognise that schools across a range of contexts face similar challenges and are subject to similar processes. We shall set out, in Chapter 9, the proposition that inclusion is simply one resolution of fundamental dilemmas in education. If those dilemmas are not universal, they are at least endemic in all mass education systems. We therefore hope that our non-English readers will bear with the detailed accounts of the English context and of practices in English schools. Much in their own situation, we accept, will be different; something important, however, will, we suggest, be the same.

2

Inclusion, Special Education and Schools as Organisations

In recent years, we have become so accustomed to seeing the terms 'inclusion', 'inclusive education' and 'inclusive schools' used inter-changeably that it is tempting to see inclusion as being synonymous with the creation of inclusive schools. Certainly, the major national and international policy statements to which we have referred, such as the English Green Paper (DfEE, 1997a) and the Salamanca Statement (UNESCO, 1994), do little to dispel this impression. Moreover, many publications in the field give the clear impression that the realisation of inclusion is dependent on the creation of inclusive schools – *Effective Schools for All* (Ainscow, 1991), *Developing an Inclusive Policy for Your School* (CSIE, 1996), *Towards the Inclusive School* (Garner and Sandow, 1995), *Inclusion and School Reform* (Lipsky and Gartner, 1997), *The Making of the Inclusive School* (Thomas, Walker and Webb, 1998) and, of course, our own *Towards Inclusive Schools?* (Clark, Dyson and Millward, 1995a).

However, self-evident as it may seem, there is, in fact, a certain arbitrariness in this focus on the institutional level. Inclusion can, of course, be seen as involving one or more of a whole range of levels. For instance, it is possible to think in terms of:

- an inclusive national system, i.e. one in which all learners are offered a comparable education, albeit in different types of schools;
- an inclusive locality, in which a particular community (represented, for instance, by the LEA or by a cluster of schools in England) educates all its own children, though it may do so in different types of schools;
- an inclusive classroom, in which all learners are educated together, regardless of characteristics and 'needs';
- an inclusive curriculum, whereby all learners follow the same broad programme, though they may do so in different classrooms or schools;

inclusive learning experiences, in which learners with different characteristics work collaboratively and learn together; or

- inclusive outcomes, whereby all students achieve high outcome levels, or have enhanced life chances, or are enabled to participate in an inclusive society once their formal education is complete.

Moreover, not only can inclusion be defined other than in terms of inclusive schools, but there is some evidence that too narrow a focus on the institutional aspects of inclusion can actually produce non-inclusive outcomes. For instance, countries which are highly inclusive in the sense that almost all students attend mainstream schools can find themselves managing diversity simply by consigning large numbers of those students to special education programmes within those schools (Haug, 1998; Persson, 2000; Pijl, 1994a). Similarly, apparently inclusive schools can, in fact, create innumerable organisational sub-divisions which effectively separate students from each other and offer them quite different educational experiences (Booth, Ainscow and Dyson, 1997). Moreover, participation in inclusive schooling, however well-organised, is no guarantee of enhanced life-chances or subsequent participation in an inclusive society (Dyson and Millward, 1999).

The emphasis on the school as the key to inclusion, therefore, whilst understandable, is not entirely unproblematic. At the very least it begs the question as to why so much importance is attached to this level. The answer is probably complex. Historically, in England, as we have seen, and, quite probably in the USA as well (Lipsky and Gartner, 1997), the development of more inclusive forms of provision has involved a progressive refocusing from the 'needs' of individual students to more 'whole-school' approaches. There is a sense in which, by the late 1980s and early 1990s, we had reached the point where it was possible for some professionals and commentators at least to consider fully the organisational implications of inclusion in a way that had not been feasible earlier.

In terms of management of the system, the institutional level is not only the level where the bifurcation between special and mainstream education is most obvious, it is also the point where external intervention is most straightforward. Classroom practice is notoriously difficult to manage externally and schools' internal organisation, in England at least, has traditionally been viewed as a matter for managers *within* the school. However, the pattern of schooling and the allocation of students to different types of school is something which can be and has been managed through legislation, guidance and national and local administrative decisions. In this sense, creating inclusive schools is a much more straightforward matter for administrators and policy-makers than is the creation of inclusive classrooms or learning experiences.

Moreover, in terms of educational research, we have passed (and may still be passing) through a period where the institutional level is seen as the key to solving many of the problems that are endemic in the educational system. For a number of years now, the international school effectiveness movement has placed considerable emphasis on institutional-level factors as the key to improving the success of the education system as a whole (Reynolds *et al.*, 2000). Although this position has increasingly come to be regarded as too simplistic by school effectiveness researchers themselves (Reynolds, 1995), its continued influence on policy and practice remains considerable. In particular, it is but a short step from believing that the 'effective school' is the key to the effectiveness of the system to believing that the 'inclusive school' is the key to its equity. As we shall shortly see, some of the most important commentators on inclusive education have taken just such a step.

The influence of the school effectiveness movement may also explain, to some extent at least, the way in which the 'inclusive school' is sometimes characterised in the literature. Just as the school effectiveness movement has sought to define the key characteristics of effective schools, so there have been attempts within the inclusive schools movement to identify those factors which make some schools more inclusive than others. Lipsky and Gartner (1999) are typical in claiming that, 'While there is no single educational model or approach, inclusive schools tend to share similar characteristics and beliefs' (p. 17). They go on to produce an extensive list of such factors:

- school-wide approaches: 'The philosophy and practice of inclusive education is accepted by all stakeholders';
- all children can learn: 'Inclusive schools have a belief that all children can learn and that all benefit when that learning is done together';
- a sense of community;
- services based on need rather than category: 'Each student is recognized as an individual, with strengths and needs, not as a label or as a member of a category';
- natural proportions: students with special needs attending their neighbourhood school and being distributed across regular classrooms;
- supports are provided in general education;
- teacher collaboration;

- curriculum adaptation: 'Drawing from the school's general curriculum, inclusion provides adaptations to enable all students to benefit from the common curriculum';
- enhanced instructional strategies; and
- standards and outcomes: 'The learning outcome for students with disabilities is drawn from that expected of students in general'.

(Lipsky and Gartner, 1999, pp. 17–18)

This list is worth citing at length, partly for the help it offers and partly for the problems it raises. It is helpful in summarising the current state of knowledge about the characteristics of inclusive schools in a way which is accessible and immediately usable. However, it begs more questions than it answers. There are, for instance, questions about the face validity of some of the factors. The ideas that *'all* stakeholders' will accept a particular philosophy and set of practices, or that *schools* as institutions can 'have a belief' in something or other are attractive, but fly in the face of what we know about the complexity of school life. The unproblematic presentation of 'curriculum adaptation' as a characteristic of inclusive schools ignores what we know about the complexities and ambiguities of such adaptation and in particular about its tendency towards exclusion (Hart, 1992). The difficulties, complexities and ambiguities of teacher collaboration, too, are well known (Hargreaves, 1991).

There are also questions about the robustness of the knowledge base which is summarised here. Unlike equivalent lists in the school effectiveness literature (classically, Mortimore *et al.*, 1988; Rutter *et al.*, 1979), such lists tend to be based, it seems to us, more on *descriptions* of inclusive schools than on rigorous analysis. This in turn seems to relate to questions about the status of the factors identified. It is never entirely clear whether such factors *enable* schools to become inclusive, *cause* schools to become inclusive, are the *result* of the school's becoming inclusive, or are *defining characteristics* of inclusiveness. There is certainly a sense of circularity in such lists – a sense that schools which display these factors are inclusive because inclusive schools are defined by their presence – in a way which is not true to the same extent of factors in school effectiveness.

For practical purposes, such objections may seem rather trivial. Many practitioners and decision-makers may well find it helpful to have an indication of what inclusive schools should look like in order to guide their own development work. However, the difficulties with Lipsky and Gartner's list point to a more fundamental problem with large parts of the inclusive schools literature – that is, its atheoretical nature. The literature is strong in describing the features of inclusive schools and offering guidance as to how schools might become more inclusive (see, for instance, Booth and Ainscow, 1998; Clark, Dyson and Millward 1995a; Porter, 1997; Rouse and Florian, 1996; Sebba and Sachdev, 1997; Stainback and Stainback, 1990; Thomas, Walker and Webb., 1998; Thousand and Villa, 1995; Udvari-Solner and Thousand, 1995; Villa and Thousand, 1995; Villa *et al.*, 1992 amongst many others). It is less strong, however, in developing theoretical models which make it possible to understand how certain organisational structures and processes lead to greater inclusiveness on the one hand, while other structures and processes lead to exclusion on the other.

It may be that, for some commentators, such theoretical explanations are irrelevant because inclusion is essentially a matter of ideological commitment and political struggle (Ballard, 1997). For others, it may be that the answers to any questions that theory might address are entirely self-evident – that, in other words, it is obvious which schools are inclusive and why they are so. However, for us the theoretical questions lurk in lists such as that produced by Lipsky and Gartner. Why, for instance, is teacher collaboration so important? What is it about inclusion that requires teachers to work together in ways that are not required in less inclusive contexts? How do the shared principles and beliefs that allegedly characterise inclusive schools impact on practice? How do these shared beliefs arise? Would it be possible for schools to be inclusive in practice if teachers held different beliefs from each other (as, for instance, Skidmore, 1998, 1999, has recently suggested)? Which of the alleged factors are critical and why? Above all, perhaps, why is it that some schools develop these characteristics and become inclusive whilst other, apparently similar schools, do not?

These questions are theoretical in the sense that they take us beyond the observable surface features of schools towards accounts and models which seek to explain the emergence and nature of those features and to demonstrate their interactions. They lead us, moreover, in the direction of other bodies of theoretical knowledge – theories of inclusion, of schools as organisations, of educational change, of professional thinking, of policy formation and so on. As we have suggested, very few commentators have been willing to ground their accounts of the characteristics of inclusive schools in such theoretical concerns. However, there are at least two such commentators on whose work we can draw – Tom Skrtic in the USA and Mel Ainscow in England. Both have been concerned for a number of years, not simply with characterising the 'inclusive school', but also with trying to understand how those characteristics relate to inclusiveness, why some schools become inclusive when others do not and why it might be that

traditional forms of school organisation and process have tended towards exclusion. The consequence is that their work offers, in our
view, the most substantial theoretical basis from which to understand
the nature of inclusive schools. In the sections which follow, therefore,
we will present the work of each in turn.

Skrtic and the adhocratic school

The case for Skrtic's theoretical contribution is not difficult to make.
Alone amongst special education commentators, he has attempted to
ground the notion of the 'inclusive school' (though, as we shall see, he
distances himself for good reasons from that term) in much more
fundamental concerns in epistemology, sociology and political theory.
His major works (Skrtic, 1991a, 1991c, 1995a) thus constitute a *tour de
force* which can lay claim to being the single most important theoretical contribution to current debates in inclusive education. Indeed, it
may well be the surface difficulty of his work generated by these
theoretical concerns which means that it is much less well-known in
the UK than it deserves.

Skrtic's analysis of the current state of special education begins in
somewhat distant realms, with an analysis of what he describes as 'the
crisis in modern knowledge' (Skrtic, 1991a). This crisis is reflected
particularly in a loss of confidence in the professions as the guardians
of scientific knowledge and the means whereby that knowledge
would be used for the betterment of society. The professions, Skrtic
argues, have been subject to three critiques: sociological, philosophical
and political (Skrtic, 1991a, pp. 4ff). The sociological critique points
out that professionals do not, in fact, operate in some enlightened and
disinterested way, but rather work to realise the interests of their own
professional group and act within the context of organisations which
impose their own constraints and imperatives.

The philosophical critique stems from a much more wide-ranging
transformation in the way that knowledge and certainty have come to
be understood in recent years. First, it has become impossible to maintain that there is only one 'paradigm' through which knowledge can be
generated, particularly in the social sciences. Following Burrell and
Morgan (1979), Skrtic argues that the previously dominant functionalist
paradigm has been challenged since the 1960s by three other paradigms
– interpretivist, radical humanist and radical structuralist. It is no longer
possible to believe, therefore, that the social world can only be understood by observing, measuring and experimenting upon it – in other
words, by importing the traditional methods of the natural sciences.

However, Skrtic argues, the crisis is much deeper than this alone would imply. The fall from pre-eminence of the functionalist paradigm does not simply mean that one of its competitor paradigms must be installed in its place. Rather, the existence of competing paradigms suggests that no single paradigm can be regarded as the authoritative source of all knowledge. As Skrtic puts it:

> During the modern period, the general conceptualization of knowledge was *foundational* – the idea that there is a fixed set of foundational criteria against which all knowledge claims can be judged. This the modern perspective is *monological*; it regards knowledge or truth as a monologue spoken by the voice of a single paradigm or frame of reference. But the postmodern conceptualization of knowledge is *antifoundational* and *dialogical*; it is based on the idea that there are no independent foundational criteria for judging knowledge claims, and thus that the 'truth' about the social world is better understood as a conversation or dialogue amongst many voices
>
> (Skrtic, 1991a, p. 19)

The implication of this for the professions is that the professional knowledge to which they lay claim is itself literally without foundation. It is not that this knowledge is 'wrong' (since judgements as to what is right and wrong in this sense depend on a firm foundation of certainty from which the judgement can be made). Rather, it is that the claims to knowledge made by professionals are claims simply to one version of the truth – a version which has no greater claim to validity than many other, quite different versions. This in turn gives rise to the political critique of the professions. Historically, professionals have claimed the right to define and characterise other members of society and to make decisions as to what lay in their best interests on the grounds that they had access to a privileged form of knowledge about them. However, if the privileged position of professional knowledge is questioned, then so too must be the power that professionals exercise over other citizens.

It is from this basis that Skrtic launches his analysis of special education and his critique of its current practices and of the assumptions upon which they are based. Special education, he suggests, is grounded in four assumptions:

1. Disabilities are pathological conditions that students have.
2. Differential diagnosis is objective and useful.
3. Special education is a rationally conceived and co-ordinated system of services that benefits diagnosed students.

4. Progress results from incremental technological improvements
   in diagnosis and instructional interventions.

(Skrtic, 1991a, p. 54)

Not surprisingly, given the postmodern position which he adopts,
Skrtic argues that these assumptions cannot lay claim to being
grounded in foundational knowledge. It follows that professionals
working in the special education field cannot claim that their practices
arise from some privileged form of knowledge about disability or
diversity.

It is at this point where Skrtic's arguments connect most obviously
with developments in thinking about special education in the UK. In
this country, for instance, we are by now very familiar with claims that
the special education professionals act in their own rather than their
'clients" interest (Tomlinson, 1982, 1985), that special education is a
mechanism whereby some social groups exercise power over others
(Barton, 1988; Barton and Tomlinson, 1981, 1984), that 'special needs'
and 'disability' are not characteristics of individuals which can be observed but are the outcomes of processes of social construction and
creation (Abberley, 1987; Oliver, 1988, 1990, 1992b), that there is need to
set the 'voice' of disabled people in dialogical opposition to the mono-
logue of the professional voice (Abberley, 1992; Barton and Oliver, 1992;
Clough and Barton, 1995, 1998; Oliver, 1992a and b) and so on.

Similarly we are, as we saw in Chapter 1, familiar with the developments in practice and organisation which have accompanied these
shifts in thinking. Our whole school approach, integration movement
and, latterly, inclusion movement are paralleled by Skrtic's account of
the way in which the Regular Education Initiative in the USA has
sought to deconstruct practices based on the old certainties of special
education and replace them with differently grounded practices, in
which the sharp categorisations and segregatory structures of traditional special education disappear.

What makes Skrtic's work so significant is that his analysis does not
simply stop at this point with a rehearsal of the critiques of special
education which have emerged over the past two decades. Those
critiques, he suggests, have appropriately problematised the practices
and structures of special education. However, the proposals which
have emerged for *alternative* practices and structures have not themselves been subjected to adequate critical scrutiny. In particular, they
have failed to scrutinise the nature of schools as organisations within
which any such alternatives must be located and enacted.

Skrtic (1991a, pp. 161ff.) argues that, in industrial societies, schools
tend to 'configure' themselves as bureaucracies. Outwardly – in terms,

that is, of the way they are managed and governed within the education system as a whole – they are configured as 'machine bureaucracies' where the work is simple and routinised and where the activities of workers (teachers, in this case) can be governed by rules and procedures. However, this outward configuration is something of a myth which serves the purposes of public accountability but does not reflect the realities of teaching In fact, teaching is too complex an activity to be standardised in this way. Internally, therefore, schools are configured as 'professional bureaucracies' where individual professionals are allowed considerable discretion in carrying out their work so that they can manage complexity through the exercise of professional judgement.

Despite this contradiction, however, machine and professional bureaucracies share a common feature:

> Both are *performance organizations,* and therefore both require a *stable environment.* Thus, in principle, both are inherently non-adaptable structures at both the micro level of workers and at the macro level of the organization . . . professional practice is circumscribed because the standardization of skills produces professionals with a finite repertoire of standard programs that are applicable to a finite set of contingencies or perceived client needs. Although this pigeonholing process simplifies matters greatly for the professional, clients whose needs fall at the margins or outside the available standard programs tend to get forced artificially into the ones that are available, or forced out of the system altogether.
>
> (Skrtic, 1991a, p. 165)

At the same time, Skrtic argues, it is also possible to see schools as organisations in cultural terms. The knowledge which professionals deploy and the programmes which they develop and/or implement form part of their professional *culture* – the norms which govern the way they carry out their professional work. Inevitably, professionals have to respond to the challenges they face – the diversity, the complexity and the unexpected characteristics of the situations in which they work – in terms of their cultural norms. These cultural norms constitute a form of convergent thinking which unrandomises complexity by deploying standard responses. It is not surprising, therefore, that the pigeonholing which arises from the bureaucratic nature of the school as organisation also arises out of the culture of teachers and other education professionals.

The implications of this analysis for special education are not difficult to see. Students 'with special needs' are likely to constitute a challenge both to the bureaucratic configuration of the school and the convergent thinking inherent within the cultures of education professionals. The response of schools is to manage this challenge by creating separate structures and programmes, demanding different forms of specialisation but enabling the mainstream of the school to continue undisturbed. These separate structures and programmes are what we call special education. As Skrtic puts it:

> student disability is neither a human pathology nor an objective distinction; it is an organizational pathology, a matter of not fitting the standard programs of the prevailing paradigm of a professional culture, the legitimacy of which is maintained and reinforced by the objectification of school failure as student disability through the institutional practice of special education.
>
> (Skrtic, 1991a, pp. 178–179)

The problem of attempts to reform special education, however radical they may appear, Skrtic argues, is that they have not challenged either the bureaucratic configuration of schools or the convergent thinking of professional culture in a sufficiently fundamental way (Skrtic, 1991a, pp. 189ff.). As we saw with similar proposals in England, they tend to call for the dismantling of separate special education structures to a greater or lesser extent, for the placement of students 'with special needs' in mainstream education classrooms and for some form of collaboration between mainstream educators and special educators (perhaps with reconstructed roles) in order to maintain students in those classrooms. However, because they accept the necessity for the professional bureaucratic configuration of schools, it is inevitable that they will fall foul of the inability of such organisational forms and cultures to respond to diversity. They will, in other words, reproduce something that, in however restructured a form, remains a form of 'special' education.

Skrtic's alternative to these reforms is indeed radical. The bureaucratic configuration of schools is inherently incapable of responding to diversity. What is needed, therefore, is a quite different configuration – one which Skrtic, following Mintzberg (1979, 1983), designates an 'adhocracy'. He explains the difference between the two configurations in the following terms:

> The professional bureaucracy is nonadaptable because it is premised on the principle of *standardization*, which configures it as a *performance* organization for *perfecting standard programs*. The adhocracy is premised on the principle of *innovation* rather than standardization; as such, it is a *problem-solving* organization con-

figured to *invent new programs*. It is the organizational form that configures itself around work that is so ambiguous and uncertain that neither the programs *nor* the knowledge and skills for doing it are known.

(Skrtic, 1991a, p. 182, emphases in original)

Beyond this general commitment to innovation, the adhocracy has a series of characteristics (Skrtic, 1991a, pp. 183–184): 'collaboration' between professionals with different kinds of expertise, rather than the deployment of different kinds of expertise in different sub-units; 'mutual adjustment', whereby professionals co-ordinate their work through informal communication in the process of inventing novel solutions; 'discursive coupling' whereby professionals reflect on their practice and develop a team approach in which theory and practice are unified; and 'professional-political accountability' achieved through the 'community of interests' within which professionals share a common goal but where there is also a dialogue between professionals and client groups which acts as a control over professional work.

It is not difficult to see how the adhocracy overcomes the inherent contradictions in other attempts to 'reform' special education. A school configured in this way would see the diversity of its students not as a source of disruption to be minimised by 'pigeonholing' the students into existing or separate programmes, but as a problem to be solved through a collaborative commitment to innovation. Instead of pathologising those students, therefore, the adhocratic school would examine critically its own practices and structures to see how they could be modified or developed in order to accommodate that diversity. This means that the notion of professional expertise would be redefined. Instead of seeing such expertise as grounded in bodies of foundational knowledge, the adhocratic school would require a pooling of what were currently regarded as different types of expertise within a collaborative problem-solving process. Through a process of mutual adjustment in which different kinds of expertise would be transformed, shared solutions to common problems would then emerge.

Such a vision enables Skrtic to claim that adhocratic schools can resolve a fundamental paradox of education systems: they can be at one and the same time both excellent and equitable (Skrtic, 1991a, pp. 205ff.). Whereas bureaucratically-configured schools have to choose between accommodating diversity (equity) and developing programmes which drive up the attainments of those for whom such programmes are appropriate (excellence), adhocracies have to make no such choice. The very diversity of students which constitutes a source of disruption for bureaucracies is a motor for development in the adhocracy, so that equity actually becomes 'the way to excellence' (Skrtic, 1991a). As Skrtic explains:

> Regardless of its causes and extent, student diversity is not a liability in a problem-solving organization; it is an asset, an enduring uncertainty, and thus the driving force behind innovation, growth of knowledge, and progress.
>
> (Skrtic, 1991a, p. 177)

This in turn means that adhocratic schools have a further and wider contribution to make. Democracy, Skrtic argues, depends on the ability of the public to engage in critical thought. However, democracy in this sense is in crisis:

> Democracy continues to decline, not only because the bureaucratic form resists change but because the cultivated citizen continues to disappear. Moreover, as more of life comes under the control of the specialization and professionalization of the professional bureaucracy, the need to solve problems and engage in discourse diminishes even further. This reduces the capacity for critical thought and dialogical discourse in society *and* in the professions, which not only undercuts the ability of the public to govern itself democratically, but reduces even further the capacity of the professions to view themselves and their practices critically.
>
> (Skrtic, 1995a, p. 256)

Under such circumstances, the role of the adhocratic school is, of course, crucial:

> Given the historical conditions of a postmodern society and post-industrial economy, and the fact that democracy *is* collaborative problem solving through reflective discourse within a community of interests, progressive education and the adhocratic school provide us with the methods and conditions to resume the critical project of cultural transformation and social reconstruction. With adequate methods and conditions of discourse, we may yet be able to transform the American public and save democracy from bureaucracy.
>
> (Skrtic, 1995a, p. 259)

The adhocractic school: some questions and comments

This final quotation from Skrtic underlines an important aspect of his analysis. For him, the adhocratic school is about much more than inclusive education, at least insofar as that is narrowly defined as the education of students with disabilities in mainstream schools. As for some in the English tradition, the issue of 'special needs' is indistinguishable from the issue of how schools respond to diversity, which is itself related to the issue of the wider social function of education. Skrtic's concern with the future of democracy may be as stereotypically American as the concern with comprehensivisation and disadvantage is stereotypically English, but the location of inclusion within a broader framework on this occasion spans the Atlantic.

Having said that, there are two aspects of Skrtic's analysis which will become of increasing significance in our own analysis of 'inclusive' schools and to which, therefore, we should allude briefly at this point. The first is the relationship of that analysis to empirical investigations. Although Skrtic draws extensively on the research literature in special education and has, in the past, been an empirical researcher of some repute (Skrtic, 1985), his arguments ultimately are philosophical rather than empirical. In particular, they are grounded in the theory of knowledge rather than in studies of actual schools. There are, for instance, no empirical studies of bureaucratic schools in his work, much less of adhocratically-configured schools. Indeed, his principal example of an adhocracy is drawn not from education, but from the National Aeronautics and Space Administration (NASA) – and even that study is filtered through the theoretical lens supplied by Mintzberg (Skrtic, 1991a, pp. 183–184).

This in itself, of course, is no criticism of Skrtic's work. However, it is indicative of a certain syllogistic quality in his writing. A huge weight of philosophical argument is assembled in order to yield the notion of the adhocratic school as the best response to student diversity – then huge claims are made about the capacity of the adhocratic school to reconcile equity with excellence and, ultimately, to save democracy. Throughout all this process, the empirical realities of schools are not allowed to interrupt the flow of argument. Indeed, beyond the general characterisation outlined above and the solitary example of NASA, we are given little indication of what an adhocratic school actually looks like. It will, we are told, have no classrooms (Skrtic, 1991a, p. 199), but what it will have in their place – how teaching will be organised, what curriculum there will be, how students will be grouped (or if they will learn individually), what pedagogy will be deployed – all of this remains a mystery.

It is quite possible to advance good arguments for this absence of actual cases – empirical data is not the philosopher's concern; adhocratic schools comprise process rather than structures; elements of adhocracy are commonly observable in schools all around us; 'adhocracy' is an ideal type which is essentially unobservable, and so on.

Nonetheless, it does mean that Skrtic never requires himself to confront an actual school and declare the extent to which it is or is not
adhocratic, let alone to test out whether his predictions about the
adhocratic school's capacity to respond to diversity, ability to reconcile equity and excellence and capacity to save democracy are borne
out in practice. There is, therefore, a nagging doubt that Skrtic's arguments exist in a hermetically-sealed world – a doubt that is not eased
by the tendency of his major works to rehearse the same arguments
(sometimes word for word) rather than to develop them in new
directions.

This in turn relates to a second concern, which is to do with the role
of the social in Skrtic's analysis. Certainly, Skrtic's work is not lacking
in reference to the social – to the way professionals relate to each other
in organisations, for instance, or the relationship between schooling,
postmodern society and democracy. However, his view of the social
strikes us as somewhat thin. Indicative is the way he deals with a
central paradox in his work: if bureaucracies are held in place by
convergent thinking, professional cultures and 'pigeonholing' practices, how can they ever come to reconfigure themselves as adhocracies? Skrtic's account is as follows:

> Given the functionalist grounding of the professional culture of
> education and the bureaucratic work conditions and activities of
> school organizations, most often the value orientation of the or-
> ganization and its members is bureaucratic. On occasion,
> however, some group, or some event introduces or uncovers
> anomalies in the bureaucratic paradigm of practice that, because
> they violate the paradigm-induced expectations of the organiza-
> tion's members, increase the inherent ambiguity enough to cast
> doubt on the prevailing paradigm.
>
> Under this condition of heightened uncertainty, in which the
> prevailing paradigm loses some of its ability to maintain its alle-
> giances, someone or some group, acting on a different set of
> values, manages to convince itself and others to see things in a
> different way.
>
> (Skrtic, 1991a, p. 206)

Superficially convincing as this account is, it begs as many questions
as it answers: what sort of group or event uncovers anomalies? Why
does this happen in some schools and not others? Why does the organisation not deal with this event by pigeonholing? What 'different
set of values' does the dissident group adhere to? Where have these
values come from and how are they sustained in face of profession-
alisation? How does it manage to convince others to see things in a

different way? Why does the bureaucratic configuration of the organisation not reassert itself? Such questions, of course, demand more than an analysis in terms of a theory of knowledge. They also demand a theory of power – that is, an account which can explain why some ideas prevail whilst others succumb. However, it is difficult to trace such an account in Skrtic's work.

In the same way, Skrtic's account of the relationship between schools and society is somewhat sketchy. Certainly, there is a good deal about the bureaucratisation of democracy and the role of the professional. However, there is little about economics, politics and power beyond these areas. Indicative is Skrtic's commitment to 'critical pragmatism'. For Skrtic, pragmatism is the appropriate response to the abandonment of foundational knowledge. Given that knowledge can no longer be judged in terms of some absolute notion of 'truth', different criteria must be used. Skrtic therefore proposes:

> a radically open and participatory form of social discourse in which all forms of modern (and postmodern) knowledge are accepted or rejected, in whole or in part, on the basis of their contribution to the realization of democratic social ideals, rather than whether they are true in a foundational sense.
>
> (Skrtic, 1995a, p. 37)

In particular, Skrtic favours a form of pragmatism which moves beyond a simple concern with what 'works' here and now ('naive' pragmatism) to one which constantly deconstructs practices and the assumptions on which they are based and then reconstructs them in ways which serve the 'best interests of its clients and society' (Skrtic, 1995a, p. 38). It is this 'critical' pragmatism which is embodied in the fluid, problem-solving form of the adhocratic school and which enables Skrtic to claim that such a school constitutes a motor for change which is capable of saving democracy.

Again, Skrtic's solutions beg as many questions as they answer. Why should we assume that processes of deconstruction and reconstruction will always result in increasing congruence between practice and democratic social ideals? Why should those processes not be subverted by economic or political imperatives? Why should they not be seized by powerful groups less committed to democratic ideals? Indeed, what are those ideals? Given that self-styled democracies come in many forms, with different degrees and types of participation, given that they generate societies of very different kinds, where different social groups are more or less advantaged and where 'equity' arguably remains an illusory ideal, why should we assume that there is a single direction in which adhocracy will lead us?

Again, there is a sense that Skrtic's arguments subsist in a some-what hermetically-sealed world. His point is less that, *in fact* schools become adhocracies in particular ways and adhocracies promote democratic social ideals, rather that *logically speaking*, schools can only become adhocracies in particular ways and only adhocracies can promote democracy. Since schools where particular transformations do not take place or which fail to promote democratic values cannot be defined as adhocratic, Skrtic's arguments are essentially irrefutable. They are, therefore, at one and the same time both profoundly energising and profoundly trivial.

Ainscow and the 'moving school'

Ainscow's work is, perhaps, less obviously theoretical in its orientation. The reason for this becomes apparent in a story which he rather engagingly tells against himself:

> There is a story of a famous professor who, though he had written a number of significant papers about quality in education, had not visited a school for over twenty years. A new young colleague persuaded him to visit a local school that had acquired a reputation for the excellence of its work. On the journey back from the visit the young lecturer asked the professor to comment on what he had seen. After a moment's silence the professor replied, 'I'm just thinking, would it work in theory?'
>
> In many ways my own work addresses the same question. Perhaps the major difference between me and the famous professor, however, is that I continue to spend significant periods of my working hours in schools.
>
> (Ainscow, 1998, p. 7)

Unlike Skrtic, Ainscow's work does indeed draw heavily on his experiences in working with and in schools. In many ways, he is concerned simply to document 'good' (in his terms, 'inclusive') practice. However, this reporting of practice has formed for many years the basis of a sustained attempt to understand *why* that practice is 'good', *how* it comes to be the way that it is and *in what way* other schools can be enabled to develop similar practice. In order to answer these essentially theoretical questions, Ainscow has drawn upon a wide range of intellectual resources, ranging from the school effectiveness and improvement literatures through to Skrtic's own work. What emerges is a distinctive account of the inclusive school-as-organisation which is both persuasive and coherent and, which, moreover, is grounded in wider notions of institutional development, professional development and special education. It is this account, we suggest, on which Ainscow's claim to theoretical significance rests.

The trajectory of Ainscow's work could not be more different from that of Skrtic's. In his earliest incarnation (Ainscow and Tweddle, 1979), he drew upon behaviourist thinking in order to develop a pedagogy for special education that was, in practice, quite different from that of mainstream education. Within less than a decade, he had turned an apparently complete *volte face* and was advocating the development of mainstream education pedagogy as a means of responding to special needs (Ainscow and Tweddle, 1988). Shortly thereafter, he began to draw upon the effective schools literature to argue that it was possible to create schools that were 'effective for all' (Ainscow, 1991) and, from this springboard, began to explore school improvement literature and practice as a means of realising this ideal (Ainscow, 1995). In the final phase of his work, Ainscow has aligned his concerns with the international inclusion movement, leading UNESCO's Special Needs in the Classroom project (Ainscow, 1994). Increasingly, therefore, his later work draws upon his international experience of developing inclusive education in low-resource settings in order to understand what constitute the essential elements of inclusive practice (Ainscow, 1999).

For Ainscow, the notion of inclusion is defined as,

> a process of increasing the participation of pupils in, and reducing their exclusion from, the cultures, curricula and communities of their local schools, not forgetting, of course, that education involves many processes that occur outside of schools.
>
> (Ainscow, 1999, p. 218)

This, he argues, is a broad definition which is concerned with much more than the placement of students with disabilities or special needs:

> The agenda of inclusive education has to be concerned with overcoming barriers to participation that may be experienced by any pupils. As we have seen, however, the tendency is still to think of inclusion policy or 'inclusive education' as being concerned only with pupils with disabilities and others categorized as having 'special educational needs'. Furthermore, inclusion is often seen as simply involving the movement of pupils from special to mainstream contexts, with the implication that they are 'included' once they are there. In contrast, I see inclusion as a never ending process, rather than a simple change of state, and as dependent on continuous pedagogical and organizational development within the mainstream.
>
> (Ainscow, 1999, p. 218)

This broad notion of inclusion, of course, aligns Ainscow closely with the historical English concerns with comprehensive community education. Moreover, the arguments Ainscow deploys are very similar in outline to those developed by Skrtic. What is distinctive about Ainscow's work, however, is the way in which he links 'pedagogical development' to teacher professional development and links both to 'organizational development'.

Ainscow's position is perhaps set out most clearly in his work for UNESCO's Special Needs in the Classroom project (Ainscow, 1994) which required him to address the issue of how inclusive approaches might be developed in countries where levels of school resourcing and teacher training were low. In such countries, the option of responding to student diversity by adopting highly specialised approaches requiring high levels of teacher training and expensive classroom materials, even if desirable, would simply not be viable. Ainscow's starting point, like Skrtic's, is that, in any case, such approaches rely on a mistaken view of the meaning of educational difficulties. We have, he argues, traditionally relied on an 'individual pupil view', within which, 'educational difficulties are defined in terms of pupil characteristics' (Ainscow, 1994, p. 17). Such a view, he argues, deflects attention away from the factors in the learning environment which create difficulties for students and thus helps to maintain a *status quo* in which such students remain disadvantaged.

Instead, Ainscow suggests, we need to adopt a 'curriculum view' within which 'educational difficulties are defined in terms of tasks, activities and classroom conditions' (Ainscow, 1994, p. 21). From this perspective, it is the inadequacy of the learning environment which generates educational difficulties rather than the characteristics of students. Therefore the appropriate response to such difficulties is the review and development of that environment rather than individual interventions with students themselves. This, in turn, demands a particular approach from teachers – an approach which,

> involves teachers becoming more skilled in interpreting events and circumstances, and using the resources of other people around them as a source of support.
>
> (Ainscow, 1994, p. 21)

Echoing Skrtic, he argues that this perspective demands a focus on,

> the improvement of learning conditions as a result of a consideration of difficulties experienced by certain pupils in their classes. In this way, pupils who experience difficulties can be seen more' positively as a source of feedback on existing classroom condi-

tions, providing insights as to how these conditions can be improved. Furthermore, given the interconnections between individuals within a given context, it seems reasonable to assume that these improvements are likely to be to the advantage of others in the class. Thus a widening perspective with respect to educational difficulty can be seen as a way of improving schooling for all.

(Ainscow, 1994, pp. 21–22)

Clearly, teachers need to develop skills to maintain this 'curriculum view'. They need, in particular, to be able to interpret the feedback which their students' difficulties provide, to use it to review their current practice and to make changes in that practice to improve the quality of education they are able to offer. These are, of course, issues for professional development. However, such development is not something which is 'done' to teachers in isolation from their working context. On the contrary, it is inextricably linked to the development of the organisations within which teachers work:

staff development can facilitate improvements in schooling for all pupils but only when it begins to intrude into the deeper culture of a particular school . . . The proposals that we are making, therefore, are intended to create a culture within mainstream schools that will enable them to be more flexible in responding to all children in the community. Such a culture would encourage teachers to see pupils experiencing difficulties not as a problem, but as a source of understanding as to how their practice could be developed.

(Ainscow, 1994, p. 26)

For Ainscow, the 'culture' which is necessary to sustain the curriculum view is one which is predicated on co-operation:

In other words schools have to be organizations within which everybody is engaged co-operatively in the task of learning, both pupils and teachers.

(Ainscow, 1994, p. 27)

It is this co-operative approach which enables a school to bring all its resources to bear on the problems generated by student diversity and hence to reconstruct those problems as opportunities for learning:

Clearly the organizational approach we need to encourage is one that emphasizes co-operation. The aim should be to create a more tightly coupled system. In such a school staff strive for mutual benefit recognizing that they all share a common purpose and, indeed, a common fate . . . A school based upon a co-operative structure is likely to make good use of the expertise of all its personnel, provide sources of stimulation and enrichment that will foster their professional development, and encourage positive attitudes to the introduction of new ways of working. In short, it provides the culture necessary for helping teachers take responsibility for the learning of all their pupils.

                                                          (Ainscow, 1994, p. 29)

In his later work, Ainscow draws heavily on the school improvement knowledge-base in considering how such co-operative cultures can be engendered and sustained in schools. Characteristically, he sees school improvement not in terms of raising the attainments of the highest-attainers in a school but of 'improving the quality of education for all' (Ainscow *et al.*, 1994; Hopkins, Ainscow and West, 1994; Hopkins, West and Ainscow, 1996). Following Rosenholtz (1991), he argues that the key is to create a 'moving' school, defined as one 'that is continually seeking to refine and develop its responses to the challenges it meets' (Ainscow, 1999, p. 12). Moreover, he is, he claims, able to formulate 'a typology of six "conditions" that seem to be a feature of moving schools'. These are,

- **effective leadership**, not only by the headteacher but spread throughout the school;
- **involvement** of staff, students and community in school policies and decisions;
- a commitment to **collaborative planning**;
- attention to the potential benefits of **enquiry and reflection**; and
- a policy for **staff development** that focuses on classroom practice.
                              (Ainscow, 1999, p. 124, emphases in original)

It is at this point where Ainscow's work complements and extends most clearly Skrtic's more overtly theoretical approach. In many ways, Ainscow's 'moving school' and Skrtic's 'adhocratic school' are remarkably similar to one another. In particular, both are premised on notions of problem-solving and learning from the challenges posed by student diversity. However, Ainscow's greater commitment to empirical work and to collaborating with schools in development initiatives means that he is able both to articulate in greater detail the characteristics of a 'moving school' and that he has a much clearer grasp of the professional and organisational development implications of creating such schools. Not only, therefore, does he present us with the typology above, but he supports this with thick descriptions of such schools in action, with accounts of the process of 'moving' drawn from teachers in a variety of international contexts and with a range of school development activities which are intended to help schools to 'move'. It is this combination of a theoretically-persuasive account of the relationships between inclusion, professional development and organisational development with detailed presentations of the realities of actual schools which constitutes Ainscow's distinctive contribution to the inclusive schools movement.

The 'moving' school: some questions and concerns

Ainscow's work is undeniably powerful and persuasive. If his theoretical scope is less extensive than Skrtic's it is, nonetheless, more grounded in the realities of schools. Whereas, therefore, Skrtic can simply argue that adhocratic schools are theoretically possible, Ainscow is able to point to many actual examples of schools that he would regard as 'moving'. However, Ainscow's work remains theoretical insofar as it seeks to do more than simply describe such schools and to offer an account of how they come to be and to be maintained as they are. Moreover, we would argue that the notion of the 'moving school' raises some of the same questions as the notion of the 'adhocratic school'.

We argued in respect of Skrtic's work, for instance, that it was somewhat lacking in empirical evidence and that, as a result, it was never subject to the challenge of explaining particular cases. In one sense, Ainscow's work is as data-rich as Skrtic's is data-free. However, Ainscow's relationship to data is as singular as Skrtic's. He himself explains this relationship in the following terms:

> Over the last few years . . . I have been involved in a series of initiatives in schools, in this country and abroad, that have provided me with endless opportunities to reflect upon and engage with questions about how schools and classrooms can be developed in response to student diversity . . . How far these experiences represent what others regard as research in a formal sense is a matter of debate. What they have stimulated is a process of learning as I have sought to find meaning in and understand what I have experienced.
>
> (Ainscow, 1998, p. 7)

For Ainscow, research is not simply a process of the 'objective' and 'distanced' collection and analysis of data. Rather, it is a personal engagement with the realities of schools and classrooms as they emerge from encounters with them in the course of development initiatives. This engagement takes the form of reflection on the meaning of those realities, which in turn generates personal learning. It is for this reason, of course, that Ainscow acknowledges 'a strong autobiographical strand' (Ainscow, 1999, p. 218) within his work. Indeed, this process of engaging with and reflecting upon the realities of schools and classrooms as they present themselves in the course of one's normal working practice is precisely the process he advocates that teachers themselves should undertake.

The possibilities which this process opens up are obvious in Ainscow's work. However, it also begs the question as to how far such a stance is capable of posing real and fundamental challenges to the preconceptions with which the researcher enters the field. If schools are approached with a view to promoting their development, if only schools willing to 'be developed' are selected, if the overall direction of the development is determined in advance, if data are collected only in accordance with the imperatives of the development process, if the interpretations of data by practitioners – shaped by the researcher/developer – are dominant, if the researcher/developer's interpretations have to evolve in a way that is autobiographically coherent and sustainable, then the possibilities for such fundamental challenge seem somewhat reduced. These are not issues of which Ainscow is unaware (Ainscow, 1998) nor, although they are salient in Ainscow's work, are they peculiar to this type of research. Nonetheless, there is an important distinction to be drawn between the richness of the data which Ainscow presents and the extent to which those data are capable of problematising the account which he offers of the inclusive school. This is, of course, a problem which Ainscow's work shares with Skrtic's more overtly theoretical approach.

There are also striking similarities in the way in which Ainscow and Skrtic handle – or, rather, fail to handle – the issues of power and politics in schools. Ainscow is certainly not unaware either of the possibilities for dissidence within schools or of the impact of the (often hostile) external policy environment on would-be inclusive schools (see, for instance, Ainscow, 1999; Booth, Ainscow and Dyson, 1997, 1998). However, the analysis of conflicting interests is certainly not at the core of his endeavours. Moreover, it is as difficult in Ainscow's work as in Skrtic's to see why and how schools change from being 'stuck' to 'moving' or why a school which 'moves' must necessarily move in the direction of greater inclusivity. The intervention of external or internal facilitators seems to be the mechanism that Ainscow posits to explain why some schools begin to 'move' (see, for instance, Ainscow, 1999, p. 169). However, without an analysis of either the micro-political processes in schools or of the macro-social processes around schools the reasons for the impact or otherwise of such individuals remain essentially mysterious.

For similar reasons, the relationship between 'moving' and 'inclusivity' remains as syllogistic as Skrtic's account of adhocracy. Since a moving school is one with a collaborative problem-solving culture, in which teachers learn from the diversity of their students, movement and inclusion are synonymous. In other words, a school which was not becoming more inclusive could not be described as 'moving' and vice versa. In Ainscow's work, the elaboration of this syllogism constitutes a powerful heuristic which enables us to understand one way in which schools might change in order to become inclusive. However, it dismisses out of hand the possibility that schools might 'learn' how to become more exclusive, or that teachers might collaborate to set up segregated structures or, on the other hand, that a high degree of inclusivity might result from a somewhat managerialist and technicist approach which did not demand problem-solving, collaboration *or* teacher-learning – at least in the sense understood by Ainscow.

Ainscow and Skrtic: theories and heuristics

It is perhaps worth reminding ourselves at this point why we considered looking at Skrtic and Ainscow in such detail. Amidst all the advocacy of inclusive education and all the concern with promoting and developing the 'inclusive school', it is these two commentators who have, in our view, made the most sustained and thoroughgoing attempts to articulate a theoretical account of the relationship between inclusion and schools as organisations. For both, it is the fundamentally rigid and unresponsive nature of traditionally-organised schools which makes them incapable of responding to diversity and which gives rise to more-or-less segregated provision. For both, therefore, inclusive approaches depend on a restructuring of schools so that they are more flexible, more supportive of collaborative problem-solving amongst staff and more likely to see the problems posed by diversity as opportunities for learning and development.

Our critiques of Ainscow and Skrtic, therefore, are not based on flaws and weaknesses in their accounts so much as on what lies *outside* those accounts. There is, in particular, a world of power, interest and politics which scarcely impinges on their work. There is, moreover, a syllogistic quality in those accounts and a relationship to data which opens up the possibility of a multitude of other factors which might impact on 'inclusive schools' but which their accounts omit. As we suggested above, therefore, it makes sense to regard their accounts as heuristic devices – powerful and illuminating, to be sure, but not by any means comprehensive theoretical accounts of the 'inclusive school'.

How a more comprehensive account might be constructed is a question which we must now address. In order to do so, we will turn first to the evidence we gathered in our case studies of four English secondary schools which were seeking to develop more inclusive practices. Readers will recall that our focus in studying these schools was somewhat different from that adopted by Ainscow and Skrtic. Certainly, we wished to understand what they did that made them more inclusive and how they sustained inclusive practices. However, in the light of the issues thrown up by our previous studies of similar schools, we also wished to explore the complexities, contradictions and conflicts which we believed might lie hidden just beneath the surface of these schools. In particular, we wished to explore the relationships between the schools' espoused policy with regards to special needs and student diversity, the practices through which that policy was (or was not) realised and the understanding which different individuals and groups of staff had of special needs and student difference.

3

Lakeside Community College: Serving the Whole Community

We begin our case studies with Lakeside Community College. Of all the schools we studied, Lakeside was the one which most closely fitted a definition of inclusive schooling which would be recognised not only in England, but internationally. Located in a LEA which had itself pursued inclusive policies for a number of years, Lakeside served a relatively clearly-defined community and educated the full range of secondary-aged students from within that community. Its population, therefore, included students with intellectual and other disabilities who would have been placed in special schools almost anywhere else in the country.

The context

Lakeside Community College is an 11–18 comprehensive school, located on the fringes of a country town in an attractive rural area. Whilst many of its students come from the town itself, its total catchment area extends over approximately 420 square miles incorporating some 45 villages. At the time of our research, it had a roll of 1,250 for which it employed a teaching staff of 96. It was led by a 'Principal' who had previously been an LEA adviser and who had embarked on a programme of vigorous development in the school following his appointment at the start of the decade.

The College had originally been formed from the merger of two secondary modern schools and a key factor in shaping many of its policies was the continued presence in the same town of a selective grammar school. Historically, the grammar school had recruited students at the age of 13 and the College had complied in nominating its higher-attaining students for transfer. The new Principal had ceased this practice, with the result that there was now considerable competition between the two schools not simply for student numbers but also, in the College's case, for recruiting higher-attaining students. However, the College still did not have a fully 'comprehensive' intake. The grammar school, for instance, had some 84 per cent of students who gained 5 or more GCSE passes at Grade A*–C compared with only 33 per cent in Lakeside. According to the Principal there appeared to be a trend amongst parents of sending higher-attaining girls to the College whereas higher-attaining boys continued to be sent to the grammar school. However, the presence of a selective school did not appear to present any immediate threat to the overall level of recruitment to the College and, at the start of our fieldwork, there were over 230 applications from the 27 feeder primary schools for the 220 places available in the next academic year.

Vision and values

Spurred on, no doubt, by the existence of the grammar school, Lakeside's Principal had sought to establish a distinctive identity for the College. Central to this identity was the notion that it was not simply a school for secondary aged students but, rather, a resource for the whole community. The Principal believed that, despite surface appearances, this community experienced a diversity of needs which presented real challenges to the school:

> in amongst what appears to be, and is in many ways relative affluence, there is a great deal of hardship and difficulty for some families.

He characterised these difficulties in the following way:

> I'm concerned about lack of choice, lack of opportunities because of the deprivation in terms of transport infrastructure and very low pay which is common in our area. So we serve a community that has, as well as being a super place to live in many ways, has a number of problems to overcome when it comes to education and life choices. And we've set about trying to address that in a number of ways. One way is to say that we need to find ways of being responsible for all our community members. By that I mean that the community itself has to find ways of being able to cope with a very wide range of differences in terms of physical, intellectual and general talents that young and older people have.

This commitment to the community manifested itself in a number of ways. First, the College acted as a community resource, offering adult education in the evenings, but also opening its doors to community members in the daytime. Second, the College set out, not only to retain students who might otherwise have transferred to the grammar school, but also to offer a wide range of post-16 provision so that it could genuinely claim to offer post-compulsory education to all young people in the community. The aim was, one teacher told us, to

ensure that there is something for everyone, all students can take some form of public examination.

(Teacher A)

Above all, the Principal believed that commitment to the community meant commitment to *all* community members and therefore, included a commitment to children and young people with disabilities and special educational needs. Indeed, he described another town, a few miles away, as suffering from a sort of 'sickness' in its community because the local headteachers were fighting to retain its special school. The aim of the College, on the other hand, was

to give every student the opportunity to fulfil his or her own potential in as meaningful and challenging a way as possible,

(School brochure)

and this was reflected in the accommodation within the school of some 80 students with statements of special educational needs. Some of these were students categorised as having severe or profound and multiple learning difficulties who would have undoubtedly been educated in a special school in most other parts of the country. Indeed, as the Special Educational Needs Co-ordinator (SENCO) pointed out to us, their numbers were equivalent to the population of a small to medium-sized special school.

The presence of these students was the result of historical decisions taken beyond the school but vigorously supported and extended by the current Principal. In the mid-1980s, the local education authority had embarked on a policy of closing special schools and relocating students with special educational needs in resource bases within mainstream schools. Lakeside had been chosen as a base for students with moderate learning difficulties. However, a series of developments, including the introduction of local management of schools (LMS) and a financial crisis in the LEA, had resulted in the status of some of these bases changing. In the case of Lakeside, the number and range of students with statements had expanded. In particular, students with profound and multiple learning difficulties as well as those with physical, sensory and other learning difficulties were accepted by the school as part of its commitment to the local community. Its current admissions policy was that only those students with the most complex special needs requiring highly specialist provision would not be considered by the College. Lakeside was, therefore, a highly inclusive school in comparison with most other English secondary schools.

A change had also taken place in the extent to which these students participated in mainstream lessons. The original resource base had been a geographical location within the school and was staffed by its own specialist staff. This was still the case to some extent, but there had been a progressive erosion of the boundaries between the base and the mainstream of the school. Of the 80 students with statements, therefore, only four now spent no time at all in mainstream classes, despite the significant learning and other difficulties which many experienced. As the teacher responsible for the base explained:

> integration is the key but . . . we would look at everybody individually and make up special packages for them and hopefully that's what we've got, we've got the flexibility . . . so they can be integrated, any youngster can be included as they are able and be separate as they need to be.
>
>   (Teacher B)

This notion of flexibility and individual responsiveness was central to the College's approach, not only to its students with special educational needs, but to all its students. Our impression was that this was not an equivocating view of integration as no more than the acceptance of selected students on the very restricted terms offered by the mainstream. As the teacher responsible for the resource base put it:

> These kids are very much part of the school. They are not just a statement. The aims of the school are that the kids are here to achieve their potential.
>
>   (Teacher B)

Indeed, the College's commitment to students with special educational needs formed part of a much stronger commitment to a notion of individual difference and individual entitlement which transcended the traditional special–mainstream distinction. That commitment, in the words of the SENCO, was to

> the right of the individual to be seen as an individual. Everyone has the right to succeed and to achieve and have that opportunity to develop their talents. I'm saying everyone is special, in another way I'm saying, yeah, everybody's special but nobody's that special.

Systems and structures

The College's avowed commitment to its whole community was reflected in two major ways. First, as we have indicated, it offered a range of educational activities which extended well beyond those normally available in English comprehensive schools. For example, no clear boundaries existed between what might be regarded as the traditional school day and 'evening' activities: adults would join with the sixth-formers for A-level courses held during the school day and young people with learning difficulties and/or disabilities would attend leisure or vocational activities in the evening. Similarly the school remained open for seven days of the week and extended its role to include outreach work in the numerous villages which it regarded as part of its 'community'. The continuing education programme included parenthood classes, and a Rainbow Club for physically disabled and physically able members. As the SENCO proudly stated:

> We can offer provision for everybody from pre-school right through to 19 and we are now busy liaising with the colleges to get 19+ going. We are open from 9 am until 10 pm every day. I know which night classes are on for special needs people and when the special needs people are in during the day I come and see them.

Second, the College had set up an extensive system of provision for students with special educational needs which enabled them to participate as far as possible in mainstream activities. In addition to its statemented population, a further 180 students were recorded at stages 1–4 of the Code of Practice, so that about 20 per cent of the school population was regarded as having special educational needs. This population brought with it significant additional resources. Twelve Learning Support Assistants (LSAs) were employed to support the students with statements in mainstream classrooms, together with four full-time specialist support teachers and the equivalent of one full-time support teacher drawn from the mainstream teaching staff.

These resources were managed, not by a traditional 'Head of Special Needs' or 'Head of Unit', but by an 'Effective Learning Co-ordinator' who was a member of the College's senior management team. Although he acted as the College's SENCO, his responsibilities were for improving the quality of teaching and learning for *all* students, rather than just for those with a special needs label. He contrasted this with the more restricted role of his immediate predecessor:

I came to a different job than his. His was primarily learning support. Mine is effective learning across the curriculum and across the age range so that now [even] the most able children fall into my remit.

Although his own professional background was in special education, he was fully committed to Lakeside's inclusive approach. Indeed, he had previously been head of a special school which he had helped to close down five years previously as part of the LEA's move towards more inclusive provision. After our fieldwork was completed, he moved on to the headship of another special school – but one where his primary responsibility was for organising outreach to mainstream schools in another highly inclusive LEA.

The Effective Learning Co-ordinator's position as an Assistant Principal in the College gave him ample authority and control of resources to fulfil his extended role, particularly given the devolved style of management which the Principal favoured. However, his intention was not so much to create a special needs 'empire' as to give ordinary subject teachers the means to meet the needs of all students in their classes, including those with special educational needs. Indeed, he expressed the hope that, in the course of time, the role of Effective Learning Co-ordinator would become redundant as all of the staff took on a greater responsibility for the learning of all students. To this end, a substantial programme of professional development relating to special needs issues was planned for subject-teaching staff, focusing particularly on extending the role of form tutors. Moreover, subject staff were already involved in monthly review meetings with support staff regarding students with special needs and there were plans to form a more formal SEN link group with subject teachers.

The College also used its team of LSAs and specialist teachers in a distinctive way. They were organised into support teams which were intended to provide more than simply an 'extra pair of hands' in the classroom. Instead, the aim was that each team would develop expertise in a particular specialism – for instance, in literacy or behaviour. This meant that the College could provide 'in-house' the sort of expertise which elsewhere might only be available from LEA peripatetic services and, moreover, could make that expertise directly available to teachers in mainstream classrooms. As part of this strategy, the learning support assistants were undergoing training to equip them with expertise in particular areas of special educational needs. In order to recruit the most able staff, moreover, they were paid at a rate higher than was common elsewhere in schools in this LEA. Likewise, the support teaching staff (the equivalent of five FTEs) were encouraged to take up in-service opportunities to enhance their specialist expertise. The SENCO was therefore able to sum up the situation in the following terms:

> With the exception of visual [impairment] . . . I think we have somebody who has an interest or an expertise or a qualification in all the areas recognised by the [local education] authority, so that's making ourselves self-contained, as I firmly believe that in-house and ad hoc is far better than provision that has to be brought in from outside.

This emphasis on specialist expertise had implications for the way in which support was conceptualised. The SENCO headed not a 'Special Needs Department' but an 'Effective Learning Department' whose role was to add value to what subject teachers alone could provide. He wanted his staff, he said, to become

> people who are experts. I need my special needs teachers to be a teacher perhaps of a subject . . . and I need them to have the specific expertise or a portfolio of expertise in particular disciplines of special educational needs. So these staff are not just your teacher as a subject teacher might be . . . [but] have an added expertise.

'What we need,' he added,

> is the supportive expert and adviser and in that way we are moving towards that, reducing the teaching element and making it much more that advisory role that's important.

A final element in the College's approach was a recognition that its ambition to become an 'inclusive' provision would not be realised without a significant change of attitudes within the community it served. In its documentation there was a recognition that its vision could not be realised solely through its own endeavours or engineered as the result of short-term strategies. The College regarded itself as having a more general educative role which aimed, in the Principal's words, 'to shift attitudes and approaches' throughout the community. As a consequence there was an emphasis in the curriculum not just on the promotion of learning in traditional academic areas but also on preparing students for a role in the process of change that would help in the long-term realisation of the College's philosophy. There was, in particular, a strong emphasis on 'citizenship' in order to develop students both as individuals and as future members of the adult community. A fundamental aim of the College, therefore, was to ensure that all its students could come to terms with the fact that there are very wide differences between people and the contribution they can make to a community and what they will take from a community.

(School brochure)

Internal tensions

The extent of shared values

Although many staff supported the approaches and values outlined above, there was nonetheless a range of views both about the desirability of the course the College had taken and about its success. For example, the Principal acknowledged that there were different views amongst the staff about inclusion, but saw the extinction of non-inclusive views as being part of the cultural change which, as we have seen, was part of the 'mission' of the College:

> There will be different views from different perspectives. I think the notion of human beings accepting and having joy in the differences between people is something that will certainly take many generations. All of us are at an early stage.

These views were reflected by other senior staff. As the manager of the resource base noted:

> Obviously some staff are happier and more accepting of kids [with PMLD] . . . It's harder as you get up the school. There's not always that individual awareness amongst staff and there are still staff who don't want to teach kids who are PMLD.
>
> (Teacher B)

Despite this perhaps understandable caution, some staff felt that the Principal's hope for a cultural change was indeed being realised. As a literacy support teacher commented:

> I think at one time with the integration policy initially a lot of people were against having special needs students in class. That is changing and it has changed to a large extent. I think attitude is very positive now and I think a lot of staff who have taken on particularly difficult children have been rewarded if you like by what they have achieved.
>
> (Teacher C)

In support of this view, an LSA cited the example of a subject teacher who was over the moon when one 15 or 16 year old wrote the letter J. The teacher said it was the greatest achievement of his career.

(LSA 1)

Certainly, overt dissidence was difficult to find in the College. However, this was not to say that all staff were able and willing to translate their acquiescence in the move towards inclusion into changes in their own practice. The same LSA, for instance, felt that, in some lessons, students with special needs were accepted only in the sense that they were tolerated and ignored, rather than being faced with the high expectations that were placed on other students:

> I pass from class to class. In one, young Johnny is allowed to keep his jacket on and do nothing, in another he takes his jacket off and works, he doesn't chew gum and he doesn't look out of the window. To be fair the Maths Department is the department I admire most because they work in the old style.

Another LSA commented that some staff were not happy dealing with behaviour problems or even mild learning difficulties in their classrooms, and she felt that this might be linked to the personality and style of the teacher – 'some teachers are more formal than others' (LSA 2) Another LSA added that:

> Some of the mainstream staff don't actually appear to be that interested [in students with special needs]. Mainly it's lack of confidence but they don't have the time, the skills or the teaching experience to actually alter their teaching methods to cope with children who have SEN but because it's the policy of the school. It is being imposed on them.

(LSA 3)

Support and support teaching

One of the College's major strategies for including students with special needs in ordinary classrooms was the use of in-class support. Although, we were assured, this approach was now widely accepted, it had originally been somewhat contentious:

> You are very welcome into the classroom now. This has taken a lot of work because people like to hold on closely to their responsibilities and they found it to be a threat to start with. Now things are easing up over the last two years. It was like the blind leading the blind to start with, there was no relationship between the teacher and the learning support assistant. You will always come

across one teacher that resents the child that they cannot cope with. I think they feel threatened and they don't feel as professional as maybe they should because they can't cope with that child.

(LSA 1)

The successful implementation of support had depended, it seemed, on support staff's going out of their way to reassure subject teachers who might feel threatened by the presence of another adult in their classroom. This had, as one support teacher explained, required a delicate balancing act. On the one hand, it was important to

try to take away those feelings of inadequacy. I think it is import-ant to get the message across that whenever you are involved with a teacher and a particular child to make sure that you are saying to the teacher 'I'm not here because of you. I'm here be-cause of the child.' At the same time you have to be careful you don't locate the problem too much in the child either.

(Teacher D)

Preserving this balance involved a considerable investment of time in maintaining good communications with subject staff:

I think partnership is the word, I mean if you don't have part-nership you might as well forget it really. We meet with each teacher one to one during the lesson, before lunch or whatever.

(Teacher D)

Despite the positive light in which support work was presented, however, it was also surrounded by both ambivalence and ambiguity. Given that the College relied so heavily on support to maintain stu-dents with special needs in ordinary classrooms, there was a constant sense that its availability was never adequate to the level of demand:

As a subject teacher it is difficult to achieve the level of support I want at times. I'm aware of the constraints and of how thin that support has to be stretched.

(Teacher E)

Or again:

There is not enough money to provide learning support for every lesson.

(Teacher F)

One consequence was that support for students diminished as they progressed through the school, even though their 'needs' might re-main unchanged:

Support tends to have either been deemed unnecessary or have fallen away by the time they get to Year 10 or 11. It may be restrictions on finance.

(Teacher G)

Similarly, support could only be provided on a patchy basis, making it difficult to plan ahead:

It would be nice if you could plan to have a consistent programme going so that students who really needed help were helped or the behavioural problems were taken away so that you can get on with the job you were supposed to do.

(Teacher H)

Moreover, the inadequate level of support time meant that it was not always possible to maintain the high level of communication on which the system depended:

The biggest problem we have, it's very difficult to report back to the teacher because we move on timetables. It is difficult to find the time to write things up as well. And we are involved in all areas of the curriculum. Sometimes you're only involved in supporting one of three geography lessons and that can be a problem too.

(LSA 1)

In an attempt to increase the resources available for support, the College had begun recruiting adult volunteers from the local community and paying sixth-formers to offer help. Programmes of both literacy support and work experience for students with special needs depended on these additional helpers. However, there was an acknowledgement that this was a fragile basis on which to build inclusion:

The challenge is funding the group [of students with special needs] and keeping them going on placements and things. It's involving the public in [the town] and we have a sympathetic public . . . you can't expect an employer to take someone with special needs unless you can provide a helper. That's where we're so short of funds, I mean I pay sixth-formers to give up an afternoon and luckily it can go down on their pastimes for their university applications.

(Teacher A)

A separate set of concerns centred on the nature of relationships between support staff and 'their' students. A head of year explained:

Special needs teachers often form very close and I mean this in the most, best possible way, relationships with the children that they work with. Now whether this is why some of them, some of them lose the ability to maintain the detachment that all teachers ought to be able to keep with students that they work with. So an offspin of that is perhaps a tendency to a greater familiarity.

This in turn emphasised differences between staff with special educational needs responsibilities and subject teachers:

Some subject teachers raise an eyebrow at the cosiness which exists between special needs teachers and the children they work with.

(Teacher I)

The focus of this concern was over the management of behaviour. Whereas subject teachers were responsible for managing the behaviour of large groups of students in the relatively formal classroom situation, support staff seemed to be more concerned with developing a positive relationship with individual students. For instance, some LSAs encouraged students to refer to them by their first names – something which subject teachers felt overstepped the bounds of professionalism and posed a threat to their management of the other students. One of the LSAs was clearly aware of this concern, commenting:

I know teachers find it quite difficult. They see that as over stepping the mark. They are quite strict.

(LSA 1)

In effect, support staff – and LSAs in particular – occupied a mediating position between the formal demands of the mainstream classroom and what they saw as the needs of 'their' students. The positive aspect of this was that mainstream teachers would, as intended, come to them for advice. As one commented, it was

a really good self-esteem builder that heads of year are coming to me and saying what shall we do.

(LSA 2)

However, the corollary was that she was often placed in the difficult position of acting as a 'buffer' between teacher and student:

Being in the middle, they (the students) come to you before they go to the teacher and the teacher comes to you before he/she goes to the student.

Finally, despite the heavy investment in support, the College was unable to sustain totally inclusive provision in the sense of full-time mainstream class placement for all students. For instance, students at Key Stage 3 (ages 11–14) identified as having profound and multiple learning difficulties were routinely withdrawn from classes and taught as a discrete group in their base room. Certainly, this was not a simply case of 'hiving-off' a group of problematic students as they were taught by subject staff and not by members of the SEN team. However, these were not the only students who were withdrawn from ordinary classes. As the SENCO conceded:

> I do withdraw children for literacy if it is needed.

There was a sense that withdrawal was something of a last resort. Nonetheless, there was also a sense that this strategy would always be necessary, if not for the sake of the students who were withdrawn, then certainly for the sake of their classmates. As the Principal put it:

> There are from time to time individuals who for a variety of reasons need to be taken out of the National Curriculum . . . I'm trying to think of examples – one might be extraordinary be- haviour which is disruptive of their own education and other people's.

Student grouping

There were similar ambiguities in the College's use of grouping by attainment. Despite the many distinctive features of the College and, in particular, the emphasis placed on including students with special educational needs in the school 'community', its grouping system was one that many secondary schools would recognise. Students were placed in 'mixed ability' groups for their first year (year 7). Various forms of screening and assessment took place throughout this year so that, by the time they entered year 8, two parallel 'bands' could be created and subject departments were then free to create their own groupings by attainment within these bands.

There was some difference of opinion in the views of staff over the effectiveness or otherwise of this system. The Head of Maths, for example, favoured even greater setting as the most effective way of managing learning:

> We would very much rather have sets from 1–8 because we feel we can meet the needs of the students better that way. When you have students working at different levels you can't teach

efficiently. If you had basically a set that were working on the
foundation at the lowest level that would be more
straightforward.

(Teacher H)

Other staff favoured a 'mixed ability' system believing that it avoided
the labelling of children as being in the 'top' or 'bottom' sets. The
Special Needs Co-ordinator was of the view that, 'mixed ability worked
for year 7 but then it is better to set'. These differences of opinion did
not result in open conflict – not least because of the flexibility offered to
subject departments to group as they saw fit. Nonetheless, the grouping
system did mean that, after year 7, most students with special educational needs were taught for most of the time in 'bottom' sets.

Management of resources

Given the large numbers of students with statements, the College had
a substantial special needs budget of over £300,000. However, concerns were expressed at a number of levels about how equitably and
effectively this resource was being utilised. As we have already seen,
one set of concerns related to whether the available resources were
adequate to the task of sustaining inclusive provision. For instance,
one of the support staff, who was moving to a new post in a special
school, pointed out the apparent discrepancy between the resources
available in Lakeside and those in her new school:

> next term I have 7 children in my class and last Friday I visited
> (the special school) and was given £350 I was told for my class
> and was told if I wanted anything else at the beginning of term –
> 'you just get it', and I came back to my head of department and
> she had £110 for 25 children and it makes her feel put upon. Why
> do one group of children get more than another group of chil-
> dren? . . . In the last few years, everything . . . that we're always
> trying to achieve with less to spend and you've got to fight for
> every penny. It's very frustrating . . . It detracts from what you're
> trying to do all the time.

(LSA 3)

Within this sense of overall resource shortage, there were real dilemmas
over what constituted equitable resourcing. Some students consumed
disproportionate amounts of resource with little obvious return:

> I am a supporter but I can see that others would think too much
> time and effort has been put in. A lot of time and effort by two or

three staff in the last few years has been put into two extreme LD [learning difficulties] cases which has been worth it. Some would argue against this that time and money could be better spent.

(Teacher I)

On the other hand, the consequences of redeploying that resource to students who might make greater progress could be disastrous:

Even now I look at some of the older children and look at the standard of work they produce and I think how many hours this girl has had . . . but then how bad would it be without it.

Devolved management

We noted above that student grouping arrangements were relatively flexible, with a good deal of decision-making devolved to heads of subject departments. This reflected a more general devolved style of management in the College. In terms of provision for students with special needs, this meant that responsibilities were devolved progressively from the Principal to the SENCO, and from him to various co-ordinators – there was, for instance, a post-16 SEN Co-ordinator, a Behaviour Co-ordinator and so on – to support staff, to subject departments and to individual teachers. This had the advantage of encouraging all staff to take 'ownership' of students with special needs and enabling expertise to be developed 'on the ground' – for instance, through the work of the specialist LSAs. However, it also led to problems.

One problem was that this was neither a fully devolved management system nor a fully centralised one. Instead, there was a multiplication of centres of management for students with special needs, each one generating its own bureaucratic set of procedures. The Behaviour Co-ordinator, for instance, acknowledged that there was some confusion in terms of the systems he was trying to establish:

I would say that not everybody in the school yet is aware of the entire procedure we go through.

(Teacher D)

The SENCO likewise conceded that many aspects of the way special needs provision was managed were not fully understood by colleagues. The system worked, he guessed, 'for only 60 per cent of colleagues'.

A policy of devolving financial resources for non-statemented students to departmental level was also proving problematic, giving rise to misunderstandings about, for example, how in-class support should best be deployed and what teaching materials should be purchased. One subject teacher suggested that this was not a one-way problem. Devolved responsibility simply meant that staff were not kept fully informed as to the types of special needs students who were in their classes and the most appropriate means for responding to their needs. One teacher, for instance, said he was not always sure who was statemented, commenting

> You have to make up your own mind when you see which ones need special handling.
>
> (Teacher G)

The Principal was aware of these difficulties but saw them as part of the transition process that the College and its community were undergoing. He insisted that it was important that staff took responsibility for 'understanding their part of the jigsaw' and that bureaucracy was reduced so that 'meetings were kept to a minimum'. He was optimistic that routines to this end were gradually evolving, that his desire for the senior management to operate at a strategic level would eventually be realised and that staff would ultimately appreciate its benefits:

> there's a distinct working between areas and departments, with heads of year having overall cross departmental responsibility. Any problems which arise in this area or that area, academic or behaviour, we have an overall picture and can make suggestions.

However, the situation appeared differently to the staff who were 'part of the jigsaw'. Devolved responsibility, some felt, simply meant that senior managers became remote from the everyday realities of classroom life. In the words of one of the LSAs,

> There is a feeling that the senior management team pontificate and can be out of touch.
>
> (LSA 4)

The Special Needs Co-ordinator, she added, used to teach in the resource base but no longer did so. Other special needs staff likewise described the Principal as 'quite removed' from the day-to-day realities of special needs teaching.

Behaviour problems

In many ways, the issue of problematic student behaviour was a test-case for Lakeside's policy of inclusion. We have already noted how the support staff's attempts to include students by developing closer relationships with them raised anxieties amongst subject teachers who had to manage those students in formal classroom situations. Similar tensions surfaced over the issue of disciplinary exclusion. In the period of our fieldwork, the Principal unusually had permanently excluded a number of the College's youngest (year 7) students. When asked how he justified exclusion from an avowedly inclusive community school, he argued that 'the vision of equity requires some pragmatic decisions – doing the best for the most'.

For him, the issue of behaviour was gender related – a 'naughty boy thing'. He accordingly decided to offer a lead to staff by teaching an all-male year 9 (13–14 years old) group. His preferred strategy for dealing with this group was to 'disapply' them from the National Curriculum and provide them with an alternative consisting of large periods of work experience in the local community. Again, there were evident tensions around what might count as 'equity' in this situation. On the one hand, these problematic students were maintained in their local school and offered activities which they may well have found motivating. On the other hand, they were removed from the mixed gender groups which were the norm in the College, from the National Curriculum and from normal classroom activities.

Other staff suggested that the problem was not simply related to gender but to more general change in the characteristics of students entering the College:

> From my observations in the last three to four years there has been a big increase in children with behaviour problems as well as learning difficulties.
>
> (Teacher F)

The Behaviour Co-ordinator, on the other hand, saw the problem as emanating from the teachers themselves. The same sensitivities as beset in-class support, he suggested, had a negative effect on the ability of the College to establish a collaborative system for managing behaviour:

> The other big problem we have with behaviour is that it is bound up with this class management thing. I think a fair number of teachers are unwilling to admit that they are having problems because they think it's their problem and that nobody else has that problem with that group or child.
>
> (Teacher D)

Similarly, in some subject areas (notably Science), the content of curriculum was such that some students found it difficult and this in turn generated behaviour problems. The solution, she argued, was not to punish students, but 'to produce alternative curriculum packages especially for students in Key Stage 4'. Moreover, one of the LSAs, as we saw earlier, identified the inconsistency of teachers as another cause of behaviour difficulties – an inconsistency which allowed students to keep their coats on, chew gum, spend time off task and so on in some lessons, whilst these tendencies were strictly policed in other lessons.

The College was making a conscious effort to address the problems. The success of these strategies was, however, mixed. The behaviour support team offered specialist advice to other staff and had established a 'drop-in' centre for students – though the take-up of this facility had been low. The efforts of the behaviour team were widely applauded by their colleagues. However, one of the senior managers in the school was concerned that all the support provision was 'being captured' by the need to deal with behaviour problems (Teacher J).

As an additional strategy, the College had invested heavily in staff training. The aim was to encourage staff to use a praise and positive reinforcement approach across the whole school in order to achieve a greater degree of consistency in behaviour management. Training days had been held and outside experts invited to contribute to the programme. However, views on the take-up of this were mixed. The Behaviour Co-ordinator commented that 'some teachers were not wanting to get involved' (Teacher D) and preferred instead to rely on their own methods and approaches.

External tensions

Some of the difficulties which Lakeside experienced in its attempt to maintain inclusive provision and practice clearly had their origins outside the school. One such source of difficulties was the SEN Code of Practice. The College's aim, as we have seen, was to include students with special needs in mainstream classes, devolve responsibility for those students to subject teachers and to provide both teachers and students with high levels of support. Whatever the Code might have contributed to this process in principle, its actual effect was simply to bureaucratise the school's existing assessment and monitoring procedures. In particular, the LEA, following the financial crisis to which we referred earlier, was particularly keen to use the Code's procedures as a means of controlling requests for additional resources via statements. The consequence, as one LSA put it, was that,

Everything has to be written down now. I think the thing that's being emphasised is that everything has to be written down, you have to document it otherwise you don't get it. So that's why we're involved in encouraging people to get it down so that you've got a file.

(LSA 3)

Since this resulted in a good deal of time being expended on paperwork, the College introduced a computerised recording system. However, this still left the SENCO in particular with the problem of persuading staff that complying with bureaucratic procedures was important – not so much as a means of enhancing students' learning, but rather as a means of gaining access to LEA resources:

not everybody in the school is aware of the entire procedure that we go through with regard to taking it from concern to actual statement, but that's what our big push is for this year, is that we are talking as a team. We are talking to subject meetings, so we'll talk to the English Department, the History Department etc. about how we are operationalising the Code and what they can do and what their role is in it because they've got a big role to play.

The College experienced not dissimilar pressures arising from the delivery of the National Curriculum. As we saw in earlier chapters, the National Curriculum in principle ensured access for students with special needs to the same curricular experiences as their peers. In practice, however, Lakeside's staff felt that many aspects of it were inappropriate for such students. Some teachers, for instance, felt that there was insufficient time for 'basic skills' work in the crowded curriculum. Others felt that the inappropriate nature of the curriculum lay behind some, at least, of the behaviour difficulties manifesting themselves in the College. The response was partly to see what could be done by differentiating teaching materials and learning experiences, with the SENCO's extended role as Effective Learning Coordinator providing a stimulus for such developments. However, some responses also took the form of seeking ways of escaping the National Curriculum. As we have seen, the Principal was actively developing an 'alternative' curriculum for one problematic group, whilst students with the greatest learning difficulties followed their own programme. Similarly, the Science Department was actively exploring alternative forms of accreditation at 16+ for students identified as having special needs because, in the words of one member of the department, of, 'the nature of the National Curriculum and time constraints' (Teacher K).

Further tensions in the school related to the adoption of an inclusive policy by the LEA. Lakeside had responded to this in a very positive way, by trying to make itself largely self-sufficient in terms of special needs provision. It had become, in this sense, what the SENCO called a 'mini LEA'. However, there was a feeling that this policy of self-sufficiency had made it more difficult to liaise with the LEA and to access its services on the less frequent occasions when they were needed. Moreover, there were particular tensions over a suggestion that vacant rooms in a nearby junior school be used to establish a provision for students with emotional and behavioural difficulties. The medium-term implications of this were that, at age 11, these students would automatically transfer to the College. This would, of course, increase its intake of the very kind of student it was currently having difficulties in managing and might well threaten its ability to 'compete' in terms of exam success with the selective school in the town. To add to these concerns it was apparent that the LEA's financial crisis would eventually feed through to all the schools and result in cut-backs in the level of funding for students with special educational needs. There were, therefore some concerns that the College would not be able to maintain the level of support and expertise that it had built up as part of its response to the LEA's policy.

Finally, the context within which all of these pressures were emerging was one of open competition between Lakeside and its neighbouring grammar school. In terms of the education market-place established by the 1988 Education Reform Act, Lakeside was heavily disadvantaged. With its origins in secondary modern schools, its tradition of sending its highest-attaining students to what was now its competitor and its historical lack of sixth-form provision, it was likely to be no match for the grammar school in the eyes of parents who valued academic success. The direction it had taken since the appointment of the current Principal, therefore, was deeply ambiguous.

On the one hand, there could be no doubting the Principal's commitment to an extended, community-oriented view of the College's role and, in particular to inclusive education. On the other hand, the rebirth of Lakeside as a Community College, its avowed aim of providing for *all* the community's children and, in particular, its inclusion of students who could instantly be recognised as disabled were likely to be highly effective marketing strategies. Likewise, the exclusion of students whose behaviour proved disruptive and the resistance to accepting any more such students were unlikely to do the College's public image any harm. There is no suggestion that the College's policies were being driven exclusively by such considerations. What does seem likely, however, is that the all-pervasive pressure of competition both created a framework within which inclusive policies became viable and attractive and set limits to how fully inclusive those policies could be.

Emerging issues

In many ways, Lakeside is a model inclusive school. Not only did it educate a wide range of students, including some with quite significant special needs, but it was also avowedly working in the tradition of community comprehensive schooling which, as we saw in the previous chapters, has been so important in England. Moreover, its strategies for sustaining inclusion were those classically found in our own previous work and in the inclusive schooling literature: an assertive headteacher with a clear, inclusive vision; a shift from a narrow, categorical view of special needs to a much more flexible notion of individual differences; a sophisticated system of support aimed at giving all students access to mainstream classrooms; the encouragement of all staff to take responsibility for students with special needs; a SENCO operating in an extended role from a position of considerable authority – and so on.

However, some aspects of Lakeside's version of inclusive schooling were characterised by ambiguities. Students with special needs, for instance, were officially welcomed in the school – but that welcome does not seem to have been universal amongst the staff. Indeed, some sorts of students – those who disrupt the College community – seem not to have been welcomed by the Principal either. There is ambiguity, too, around the College's use of support as an inclusive strategy. Certainly, it gave many students access to much of the curriculum. However, because it was the main strategy for providing access, it seems never quite to have been adequate to the task in hand. Certainly, the persistence of grouping by attainment and of withdrawal work, together with the exploration of 'alternative' curricula, suggests that support was not entirely effective in securing access to common learning experiences in ordinary classrooms.

This, in turn, relates to the issue of staff responsibility for students with special needs. The aim of getting all staff to accept such responsibility was clear. However, there also seemed to be something of a cultural divide between subject teachers and support staff. Put crudely, the former were concerned with curriculum, attainment, the well-being of the majority and the maintenance of classroom order; the latter were concerned with specialist expertise, with the needs of the individual and, latterly, with the bureaucratic procedures of the Code of Practice. Whether simply placing them together in the same classroom – particularly with inadequate time for liaison – encouraged a transfer of expertise and culture is, to say the least, a moot point. Indeed, it is arguable that the College's attempt to turn itself into a 'mini LEA' had simply resulted in an internalised replication of the traditionally divided responsibilities between mainstream schools and the LEA's special needs services.

There were also externally-generated ambiguities felt within the College. The strait-jackets of the National Curriculum and the Code of Practice seemed not to be conducive to the development of inclusion. Moreover, the presence of the competitor grammar school made many of the College's policies deeply ambiguous.

The account offered by the Principal of all of this was that the school and its community were undergoing a transformation process which was not yet complete. The SENCO, too, seemed to feel that many of the current forms of provision represent a transitional phase in the College's development. It may indeed be the case that, as staff became more accepting of student diversity and more skilled in responding to special needs, many of the tensions in Lakeside would disappear. Certainly, this process would be aided by a more supportive external policy environment. However, it is notable that some of those tensions are not entirely attributable to the unreconstructed attitudes of teachers. Instead, they are to do with real dilemmas and difficulties about what constitutes equitable resourcing, about what an 'inclusive' curriculum might look like, about the real challenges of difficult be-haviour and about the purpose and practice of 'support'. It is, we suggest, the extent to which similar tensions are replicated in other schools which will tell us whether we are dealing with 'little local difficulties' or with something more fundamental.

4

St Joseph's RC Comprehensive School: Releasing the Students' Potential

The context

St Joseph's is a 1,200-strong Roman Catholic comprehensive school located in the suburbs of a northern city. In some respects, it was, at the time of our research, typical of many such schools: some 37 per cent of its students achieved five A*–C grades at GCSE (somewhat less than the national average), 20 per cent were in receipt of free school meals and a similar proportion were placed on the special educational needs register (of whom 12 had statements). In a city where a number of other comprehensive schools were experiencing difficulties, it remained popular with parents, had received a reasonably favourable Ofsted report and had a settled staff led by a headteacher with over 15 years' service to the school.

The school's voluntary-aided status gave it a degree of financial security and, more importantly, gave its staff a sense of mission over and above the achievement of good academic results. However, it also created some pressures. It meant, for instance, that the school recruited from a wider geographical area than its non-denominational neighbours, making a community role in the traditional sense problematic. More important, since the other Roman Catholic schools in the area were single-sex institutions with a history as grammar schools, there was a sense in which St Joseph's was at the bottom of the local hierarchy in terms of public perception. As a consequence, therefore, it accepted a greater proportion of students experiencing difficulties than these other schools.

What made St Joseph's interesting from our point of view was that the headteacher had led the school in adopting a 'thinking skills' approach for *all* its students, including those regarded as having special educational needs. In our initial encounters with the school, some claims were made that this approach opened up some radically new

and different ways of conceptualising and responding to 'special educational needs'. Moreover, since it was an approach which was based
firmly in a reconstruction of curriculum and pedagogy rather than a
reorganisation of systems and structures, it offered an important opportunity to explore a distinctive response to student diversity.

Vision and values

> All pupils have the potential to serve their communities as places
> of learning and faith and not as microcosms of the work place.

This statement from the school's brochure was one of many repeated
references to the notion of 'potential' and begins to give a flavour of
what was distinctive about St Joseph's approach. Partly, this dis-
tinctiveness was to do with an understanding of the aims of education
which was grounded in the Catholic faith and went beyond the
merely instrumental. It involved a belief that all children were of value
and that there was a Christian duty to care for those with the greatest
needs. In the head's words:

> In our aims and philosophy we say, 'care is by nature compensa-
> tory'. It's fundamental, it underpins it, it should be gospel values
> – those with the greatest need will [receive most].

Partly, however, it was to do with a very specific belief that all children had the ability to achieve to a higher level of intellectual development than was commonly supposed, regardless of any apparent
learning difficulties which they might experience. The headteacher
explained the origins of his thinking in the following terms:

> I'll go back to my own school days. Most of my friends failed at
> school and I realised that they were my intellectual equals . . .
> When I was in the Royal Navy, I enrolled as a divisional officer. I
> obviously was aware of all of my division's educational back-
> ground. I was aware that the Navy was able to take virtually total
> school failures and get them to a pretty high level – and that's as
> intellectuals – once they were motivated and in a disciplined en-
> vironment. That's contributed I think to my own philosophy. If
> there's a will, then human beings can very often find the way.
> And that's my belief – that all children have genetic potential to
> become higher level thinkers.

Asked whether he regarded this 'genetic potential' as unlimited, he
replied,

Well, unlimited in the sense that one cannot define it or set a limit to it – and we know in terms of studies of the brain, we actually use a relatively small percentage of its capacity.

Given this notion of more-or-less unlimited potential, the barriers which children experienced in their learning could not be understood simply in terms of a lack of intellectual capacity. Instead, the head argued:

> I would think of limitations more along the lines of attitudes and I would link it to a Jungian multiple personality pattern . . . There will be children who, in terms of their psychological development develop as their dominant function a sense of [feeling] and there-fore their inferior function would be intuition which would de-velop much later in life. Now a child whose inferior function is intuition is going to be in a great disadvantage in a culture that values the ability to recognise patterns, to see things as a whole. Likewise, a child who develops feeling and basic judgements on values as their dominant culture may develop that first then their inferior function would be thinking, so again the system that puts a high weight on analysis is going to be quite an alien environ-ment for that type of child.

Whether or not a child was able to learn in school, therefore, de-pended not on some fixed 'ability' but on a complex interaction be-tween personality type, attitude, cognitive style and the learning environment in which the child was placed. It was, therefore, the job of the school to do what he had seen the Navy do for those of his contemporaries who had apparently failed in their own schooling. On the one hand, the school had to create a 'climate of optimism' which would generate positive attitudes to learning and persuade both staff and students to recognise their 'potential'. On the other, the school had to find a way of creating learning environments which released that potential in students regardless of their individual styles and characteristics.

This position had radical implications for the way in which the head understood special educational needs. Certainly, he accepted that some students had what he called 'technical' difficulties in, say, read-ing and writing and that they needed a fairly traditional kind of assis-tance in overcoming those difficulties. However, since all children had considerable – and perhaps unlimited – potential, special educational needs also to him referred to the needs of those students whose poten-tial had not been adequately released by their learning experiences hitherto. He drew upon Piagetian developmental psychology to make this point:

in my mind our aim is to get all children all operating within formal operational thinking, because that's our belief . . . I'm not a specialist educational psychologist but I believe it's normal that children have potential to do things. Therefore all children who aren't formal thinkers to me fall into the category of S[pecial] N[eeds] because a child leaves school as a concrete thinker.

It follows that special needs provision for him had two components – a technical strand aimed at overcoming specific difficulties and a developmental strand aimed at releasing students' potential:

I see our school's distinctive vision on special needs as complementing the traditional view. One without the other is flawed. I think they complement each other in unique terms.

In addition to traditional special needs teaching, therefore, the head had introduced some eight years previously a series of 'interventions' aimed at releasing students' innate cognitive abilities. These comprised a set of 'thinking skills' approaches – some, like CASE and CAME (Cognitive Acceleration in Science/Mathematics Education) (Adey and Shayer, 1994) embedded in the mainstream curriculum and some, like Feurstein's (Feuerstein *et al.*, 1980) Instrumental Enrichment (IE) and Somerset Thinking Skills (Blagg, Ballinger and Gardner, 1991) delivered as stand-alone packages. These interventions, he argued, had produced tangible results. He produced data to the effect that 29 per cent of his current year 10 pupils who had followed the course for three years were currently at the 'formal operational stage' of thinking, compared with a national average of 21 per cent, and that some 70 per cent were at or above the level of 'concrete generalisation' compared to a national figure of 50 per cent. 'I know of no one,' he suggested, 'seeing any pupil or child who had limitations that they could define. Therefore we have to be optimistic.' However, that optimism was based, he believed, on tangible evidence that genuine transformations in students were possible.

Understandings amongst the staff

The head's views were clearly quite distinctive and it was apparent that, despite his disclaimer about not being 'a specialist educational psychologist', he was, in fact deeply influenced by an eclectic range of psychological theory. Some of his staff appeared to share these views. One teacher, for example, echoed his words almost exactly, commenting: 'all children have infinite potential, all children have special needs' and describing her approach as one of 'try[ing] to treat each child as special to meet their individual needs . . . they all have infinite potential' (Teacher A).

However, as we interviewed more staff it was clear that the notion of 'potential' was not really an organising principle in their understandings of special educational needs. On the contrary, there seemed to be an absence of any clearly-defined view around which such consensus could be built. As one teacher put it:

> I think if you've got 60 staff and say four special needs teachers you've got 60 different perceptions of special needs.
>
> (Teacher B)

Another commented:

> Individual teachers vary very much regarding SEN. Teachers at St Joseph's are left to develop their own response to special needs. Every department views special needs differently. My head of department would never take a special needs class.
>
> (Teacher C)

Even where teachers were committed to students with special educational needs, they tended to found that commitment on principles which were not clearly related to the head's views. Some, for instance, emphasised notions of equality of opportunity:

> all children are equals; all children should have access to the best teaching, to expertise, to the best resources. This includes those with low ability, behavioural problems and the able learners.
>
> (Teacher D)

Others simply accepted a somewhat loose definition of special educational needs as encompassing a wide range of 'atypical' students. It comprises, said one,

> a very wide sphere of children. A very wide group of children. Lots of different ways in which a child can have special needs. I would like to see in the future special needs extended to another area and that's children who are very clever who are not helped.
>
> (Teacher B)

Another suggested that the school's task was to

> identify the children with any kinds of learning difficulty and any kinds of special need, not just as far as their educational needs are concerned but if they have any medical problems as well.
>
> (Teacher E)

Another again suggested that the challenge was

to try to get the best out of kids and to make sure that those categorised as having special needs are getting the best possible from school.

(Teacher F)

Given these rather loose and conventional definitions, the introduction of the Special Educational Needs Code of Practice, with its formalisation of identification, assessment and recording procedures, was widely welcomed. One teacher commented that, until relatively recently, he hadn't been

particularly aware of which kids had been identified as special needs by whatever mechanism,

but that his increased awareness and understanding was a result of

all these new structures presented to us and our attention focused on them. I think the new structure has influenced at least the way we think and what we do in the classroom.

(Teacher G)

Another agreed that, as a result of the systematisation of special needs procedures, he would now

know which kids in my classes had special needs of any sort, be they medical or whatever, and would routinely mark that in a secret manner in my register and make some notes for myself.

(Teacher H)

There was little sense amongst the staff that the Code was undermining the distinctive nature of their school's approach. On the contrary, it seemed to bring an air of clarity to what had previously been a confused situation. One year head commented:

I think things are done much more on, how can I put it, a written down basis. Things are now set, and you have to do them, whereas in the past, before the Code of Practice etc. came in, yes, you had a Special Needs Department, but it was very much done on who was in charge of the department, how they saw things, etc., rather than perhaps doing them as a whole school policy. I think now it's a situation where everybody has to be involved and aware of what goes on. We have a lot more, as I said at the beginning, written things coming from the Special Needs Department as to what exactly has to be done.

(Teacher C)

What was clear, therefore, was that the radical redefinition of special educational needs proposed by the head had only minimal impact on the thinking of his staff. On the whole, their understandings of special needs were based around traditional notions of difficulty and atypicality which accorded well with the Code of Practice. This did not bode well for how the head's vision was likely to be implemented in practice.

Systems and structures

The school's use of thinking skills 'interventions' was focused on years 7 and 8 in the expectation that an 'acceleration' of thinking at this stage would produce tangible benefits when students took their end-of-key-stage assessments in year 9 and their public examinations in year 11. CASE and CAME were delivered in mixed-attainment groups as part of the Science and Mathematics curricula. However, students were setted for two further 'free-standing' interventions: Somerset Thinking Skills was delivered to higher sets and Instrumental Enrichment (IE) to lower sets.

St Joseph's SENCO was an experienced teacher who had worked in the school for some 19 years. A distinctive feature of her role was that she was trained in IE and was responsible for delivering this pro-gramme to 'bottom' sets. She told us that she had become a convert to the head's view about the possibility of releasing children's potential as a result of her own experiences in delivering this intervention. She had been, she said,

> very, very sceptical at first. I mean, it was something that – you know, the kiddies come in and they are slow learners, even with severe difficulties, some. But actually to see them make some kind of achievement is something that initially you wouldn't actually think it would happen . . . I think that, you know, certainly it was IE that forced me to put that in [to the SEN policy], you know, the fact that we don't write kids off.

Despite this conviction, however, there was little in the school's struc-tures to reflect a radical reconceptualisation of special educational needs. On entering the school, some students were immediately placed in a 'bottom' set on the basis of primary school information. Their peers remained in mixed-attainment groups for their first term until they too were placed in one of three pairs of sets across two half-year bands for most subjects. The original 'bottom' group remained as 'set 4' in one of these half-years. The SENCO managed a Special Needs Department which had traditionally operated a 'mixed economy' of in-class support, withdrawal and direct teaching of 'bottom' sets. The in-class support team had also been augmented by the use of subject teachers with unused time on their timetables. Some further support to individual pupils was provided by the peripatetic Learning Support teachers from the two LEAs which supplied the majority of pupils in the school.

The introduction of the Code of Practice had, as we have seen, formalised the school's previously rather loose systems of identification and assessment. The consequence of this had been that more students were now identified as having special educational needs and the demand for in-class support was correspondingly greater. The head's and SENCO's response was twofold. First, additional special needs staff were employed, including a full-time teacher to share the SENCO's workload and a part-time teacher charged with the task of improving literacy skills across the attainment range and working with pupils with specific learning difficulties.

Second, the SENCO and her new colleague had decided that, rather than attempting to meet the demand for in-class support, they would develop an 'Intensive Intervention Programme' which involved withdrawing students from their ordinary classes for individual and small-group work. The programme borrowed heavily from the notion, shared by the SENCO, that significant transformations could be brought about in children through targeted 'interventions' aimed at releasing their 'potential'. Something of its flavour can be gathered from an information sheet prepared for staff:

Aim. To intervene when a pupil has been identified as experiencing specific learning and/or behavioural difficulties within the classroom and as a result is having a detrimental effect upon the learning experiences for that class and/or the pupil is struggling to access the curriculum due to their own learning difficulty.

The Foundation years of 7 and 8 will be prioritised for this approach and there will be two distinctive levels of intervention. Level 1 will be children who have been identified as having learning/behaviour difficulties and level 2 will be other identified children where the main difficulty is learning.

Level 1 will receive up to 10 periods of support and level 2 will receive up to 5 periods of support each week . . . It is hoped that this specialist intervention will improve the literacy skills and social skills of the pupils so that they can re-integrate into their curriculum and thus be able to improve their learning potential.

Much of the drive to respond in this way to students whose behaviour presented difficulties came from the newly-appointed full-time member of the department. He had moved from a special school for children with emotional and behavioural difficulties and brought with him a commitment to a behaviourist approach. When we observed this intervention programme in action, therefore, it was not unusual to see the teacher handing out sweets as rewards for good behaviour.

Beyond these strategies, members of the Special Needs Department operated in an informal consultancy role with their colleagues and there were some plans to begin enlisting sixth-form students as providers of in-class support. There was also a redesignation of year heads as 'learning co-ordinators' to signal a refocusing of their role, though, we were assured, they continued to spend most of their time dealing with incidents of disruptive behaviour. Overall, therefore, the school's response to special educational needs issues rested on the twin tracks of the cognitive interventions and the targeted work of the Special Needs Department, with relatively little evidence of systematic approaches in other aspects of the school's structures and practices.

Internal tensions

Given the radical nature of the head's vision of children's unlimited potential, it is perhaps not surprising that there were tensions and even conflicts within the school. It is to these that we now turn.

The cognitive interventions

It was through the cognitive 'interventions' that the head believed his vision was to be realised. However, it appeared that there was something of a gap between the rhetoric of these interventions and their reality. A Science teacher explained:

> as a new teacher coming in, I took the stuff home over the summer and I read [the handbooks], you know, I watched the video. But when you get in front of the blackboard and the practice – I would like more support in terms of what is happening, you know. I watched the video and Damien and StJohn are happily engaged and Tabitha and Samantha are over there and the teacher's got his back to them and having a little chat. They don't have 'I'm not sitting next to him – he smells!' or 'Stop thumping each other!'
>
> (Teacher I)

This teacher's view, in fact, was that thinking skills interventions could not be used effectively until the students had had a 'communication skills' intervention by way of preparation.

Other teachers echoed these views. On one occasion, for instance, the Special Needs Department staff were invited to attend a Science Department meeting to see what help they could offer. The scientists put forward a shopping list of 'requirements and concerns':

More INSET time
More help for kids with SEN e.g. children not even reaching level 1 – how can they cope with [Key] Stage 3?
Help for specific learning difficulties children
How to manage children with behaviour problems
Inappropriate syllabus
Differentiating materials.

(Field notes)

Whatever the thinking skills approach may or may not have been doing in terms of releasing children's potential, therefore, it was clearly not enabling the Science Department to meet some of its basic classroom challenges.

Even when the SENCO herself was delivering an intervention, it was evident that, whatever benefits the cognitive approach brought with it were being offset by a constant battle against disruptive behaviour. Certainly, in the lessons we observed, both teacher and students were able to use the language and surface procedures of Instrumental Enrichment – 'focusing', 'eliminating', redesignating problems as 'temporary difficulties' and so on – but this was against a background of inattention and low-level disruption: erasers were thrown around the room, rulers were broken, some students spent their time making 'silly' noises, others were put on detention – and so on.

In other departments, the use of cognitive approaches was impeded by the lack of appropriate materials. One Geography teacher, for instance, commented that:

I go back to the time element that it's very difficult to create novel material 7 times a day, very difficult.

(Teacher J)

Similar concerns and anxieties were expressed by Maths teachers. For one very experienced teacher there were a series of issues:

I just wonder sometimes if I should be doing things differently. I certainly find it very difficult to cater in any class for individual needs. We try to resource things appropriately, I do strive to find appropriate material, but I find it quite difficult . . . I've just introduced new materials for Year 7 and 8 but the SEN material is on its way. I looked to introduce it because I felt there was a weakness in one area of what we're using at the moment – it didn't stretch or challenge the average child enough. So I'm looking for something with greater differentiation. I like something that's got a bit more challenge in it. So it's all right, it's got variety and it's well presented and well thought out, but it's death by a million worksheets.

(Teacher K)

In his view, the only solution to these problems was to expand the Special Needs Department still further. It should, he commented, 'be one of the biggest departments in the school'. For him, at least, cognitive interventions did not lead to a reconceptualisation of special educational needs so much as to their expansion.

Managing the curriculum, managing behaviour

The concerns of those teachers who were attempting to use cognitive approaches reflected wider concerns across the staff as a whole about how far they were able to manage the full range of student diversity. These concerns centred around two issues: responding to a wide range of learning needs in the classroom and managing disruptive behaviour.

Commonly, teachers saw these two issues as interrelated. As one of the learning co-ordinators commented:

Inevitably a lot of the ones who can't read and write very well are the ones who have disruptive behaviour.

(Teacher L)

The solution, they felt, was to find appropriate teaching materials which low-attaining students could manage. Without them, as one commented, such students

would just start messing around so that they would get thrown out or whatever.

(Teacher M)

The response to this need was mixed. Some departments had purchased commercial materials; some were attempting to produce their own. However, there was still a considerable dependency on the SENCO. As one teacher put it:

Although I'm getting better at producing my own materials and usually have a body of materials that I know will be suitable for special needs classes I go to the SENCO for material.

(Teacher N)

This dependency seemed to point to a failure in the school to develop any clear strategy for increasing the capacity of teachers to respond to diverse learning needs. It seemed to be a matter of every teacher for him or herself:

> obviously we do differentiation and things like that, each of us does our own, we don't really co-ordinate amongst the department what we are doing.
>
> (Teacher N)

As an experienced teacher acknowledged, staff were struggling to offer an appropriate curriculum to all students. 'We need,' he observed, 'some carefully planned in-service to bring everyone up to speed' (Teacher O).

It was because the issue of differentiation was seen as linked to that of disruptive behaviour that the SENCO and her colleague had introduced their 'intensive intervention programme'. The assumption, as we have seen, was that the intensity of this intervention would make it possible to keep it of short duration for each student involved. There was, of course, a price that had to be paid. Whatever else it achieved, it removed students from their ordinary classes and did nothing to support their teachers in making appropriate provision for them once they returned. Indeed, the commitment to behaviourist approaches meant that the intervention relied on a quite different style of behaviour management from that available to other staff in ordinary classrooms. The newly-appointed special needs teacher argued that students were 'not emotionally ready for task-intrinsic motivation and need external rewards', and therefore introduced the system of extrinsic rewards. The SENCO, too, concluded that the school's standard merit system was 'not concrete enough' for students in the 'bottom' sets, even if they were not part of the intervention programme. The Special Needs Department's own system of rewards she characterised as 'pure bribery – but if it works why not?'

Whatever the merits or otherwise of such behaviourist approaches, there seem to be some tensions within the school's approach to learning difficulties, behaviour difficulties and the link between them. Many teachers clearly found it difficult to respond effectively to the range of learning needs which presented themselves in their classrooms. The cognitive interventions on which the head pinned his hopes did little to help them and their own initial reaction – to find more and better teaching materials – turned out to be impracticable. However, there was no structured way in which the Special Needs Department could meet their apparent need for advice, support and training. Instead, it focused on intervening with problematic students in the hope of 'transforming' them in some way. In so doing, it offered them a quite different experience from that of the ordinary classroom and did nothing to prepare that classroom for their return.

Whilst it is easy to see the limitations of this approach from the outside, of course, in effect all the SENCO and her colleague were doing was replicating the model implicit in the head's reliance on cognitive interventions – and, in particular, on those which were not curriculum-based. They too did little to change teaching practices across the school as a whole, relying instead on the prospect of a significant transformation of students' attainments and learning characteristics as a result of a targeted programme.

Support for special educational needs

Given the problems which the teaching staff saw themselves facing, they not surprisingly looked towards in-class support to provide them with a way of managing their classrooms. Here, however, they encountered a number of problems. First, such support was at a premium, not least because the intensive intervention programme made two members of the Special Needs Department unavailable for this role. As a learning co-ordinator pointed out, the provision of support was very patchy:

> I think it gets implemented at the lower end of the school but not the upper, that's the weakness in it. I find the sort of help and support that people, that special needs kids get stops once they get past year 9 which I think is a bad thing. They've been protected all that time and then suddenly they're launched off on their own.
>
> (Teacher L)

Another teacher commented:

> Some people have requested it [in class support] . . . The availability of it is very limited, you might get one lesson here or there but it's not widespread practice.
>
> (Teacher J)

He added:

> If I've got a special needs class to a large extent I'm left on my own, or I feel as if I'm left on my own and I don't think that's just me, I think a lot of teachers are left on their own. What I would like to see and what happened in previous schools I've been in is support is available in the classroom. Now although I know some support does go on it doesn't seem to be widespread so I think there's little

a Special Needs Department can do for you unless they're there helping you on the ground, you know in the classroom. I would like to see them in classrooms with 7S, or whoever your special needs class is right through the school.

A further problem was that, even when support was available, it tended to be less productive than it might have been because it was not provided by teachers who were specialists in the appropriate subject area. A special needs teacher described his own experience in the following terms:

I did it last year and after three or four sessions I felt like a spare part.

(Teacher P)

From the other side of the situation, a Maths teacher described the dilemmas involved in finding an ideal support teacher:

I'll tell you what I'd really like, but I don't think it's achievable. What I'd really look for is a Maths specialist who has a genuine interest in this area. I don't know if that will ever happen but when I look and talk to people in the primary school and see how they cope, to me the secondary teacher is a different beast and we need something in between. So I'd look for something in-between – a Maths teacher who has a particular flair in this area . . . I feel in terms of support, I would like it to be an SEN person but I also find sometimes that an SEN person may not have the mathematical background that would help. I have sometimes been supported by people from different subject areas who are very willing to help out but don't have the confidence in the subject. Any help and support is a big help – it's remarkable what an extra pair of hands in the classroom can do; it means if one needs someone to sit down with them you can do that or having someone to float around you . . . Even sixth formers are a big help in that respect.

(Teacher K)

To all intents and purposes, what is set out here is a sliding scale of support teacher effectiveness. If the Maths teacher with a 'flair' for special needs is not available, then a special needs teacher will do; if a special needs teacher is not available, then a specialist in another subject will do; if a teacher is not available, then at least a sixth-former can be 'another pair of hands'. However, as we have seen, even this limited version of support was frequently not available, with the result that teachers felt themselves to be very much 'on their own'.

Setting

The second type of solution which some members of staff reached for in the face of their difficulties was setting by attainment. For some, setting was a taken-for-granted fact of school life, a purely pragmatic issue:

> you set because you've got to get 196 kids into seven sets.
>
> (Teacher K)

As the Head of English explained,

> The culture of the school is setting. There is no open debate about groupings – not that I'm aware of.
>
> (Teacher Q)

Some teachers, indeed, saw setting as a positive motivational force for students:

> [we] try to start with small [lower] sets so most of the movement is upward therefore, motivating.
>
> (Teacher R)

Even the SENCO shared this view:

> Success is about children with SEN moving between sets, getting a 'G' at GCSE and preventing a child with behaviour difficulties from being expelled.

However, there were some different views:

> There is still a discussion or argument going on in the school as to how best we set the kids. Do we have mixed ability teaching throughout the school or do we have them set in rigid abilities? So there is a range of things which need discussion. Nobody seems to be wanting to start the discussion, you know. It's as though some colleagues may have a vested interest in keeping it as it is.
>
> (Teacher P)

Those teachers who were unhappy with setting tended to criticise it for a range of different reasons. For some, mixed-attainment grouping was a means of maintaining a focus on the individual needs of students – a focus that related to the view, noted above, that special needs education was about responding to a wide range of essentially individual difficulties. As the Head of English explained:

> Mixed ability forces you to look at the individual therefore you are more likely to look at the whole range of needs including the

more able and if you change [to setting] after 6 weeks you lose all you know about the individual.

(Teacher Q)

The school's current commitment to setting simply clouded this individual focus and, she argued, had less to do with educational arguments than with a desire to please articulate parents:

Parents approve of setting . . . The voice of parents can influence whether a child goes up or down.

For others, unease about setting was more to do with the practicalities of managing the difficult 'bottom' sets that inevitably resulted from the current system:

In our bottom sets when I've looked around e.g. 8S4 with [teacher's name], he's tearing his hair trying to cope with them and they are a big problem . . . There is now so much stipulation with safety.

(Teacher I)

Or again:

I find the special need classes have a wide variety of ability ranges . . . and I suppose that is one of the major problems, is that at the top end you've got kids who can work on their own and do quite well and at the bottom end you've got kids that need constant help so you're forever facing the problem of the work that you . . . set for them.

(Teacher J)

In the face of these management difficulties, our own observations suggested that the main concern of staff teaching lower sets was to maintain a high level of direct control by using whole class approaches with little individualisation. It was not unknown, for instance, for the whole group to be engaged on the same task, using the same worksheet and having the same homework task set at the end of the lesson, with no check on who had completed the written task and no corrections of students' work during the course of the lesson. More individualised approaches only tended to emerge when support teachers were present. Moreover, we found little evidence outside the designated thinking skills lessons that cognitive approaches were used to address the problems created by the setting system.

Despite these anxieties and the diversity of opinion that was evident amongst the staff, no open debate about setting actually materialised. As our earlier informant suggested, it seemed that there was some reluctance to bring this debate into the open. The experience of one head of department suggests why this might have been the case:

> In 1986, just after I was head of department, I introduced a new Maths scheme which was highly individualised and it seemed to work very well for a long time until there was an organisational difficulty and the head directed that [students] should all go into sets. Once they were in sets it hit on the head [that approach] and for some reasons it just didn't work as well . . . So we moved away from the individualised approach and I'm aware that there has been some criticism of that approach anyway. I'd be grateful if somebody would just come clean and tell me which is the best way to do it.
>
> (Teacher K)

In some ways, the head's commitment to setting – and, indeed, the SENCO's support of the setting system – was surprising. Given their shared vision of the unlimited potential of all students, one might suppose that they would see grouping by current levels of attainment as either unnecessary or misleading or both. However, what is evident is that the notion of potential did not carry with it other notions of equity or participation such as characterised some of our other case-study schools. On the contrary, the 'twin-track' approach to overcoming 'technical difficulties' on the one hand and employing specific cognitive programmes to release 'potential' on the other seemed to imply separate grouping so that particular interventions could be targeted most appropriately. As the school's special educational needs policy put it:

> Everyone is intelligent in some way. The challenge is to find the way.

The equity of this approach, therefore, lay in the outcome of 'released' intelligence, not in the more or less participatory 'way' in which that intelligence is released.

The role of the Special Needs Department

Given the anxieties which emerged around setting, support, the 'interventions' and so on, it is not surprising that there were also uncertainties around the role of the Special Needs Department. The twin-track approach meant that in any case its work was divided between rather traditional remedial approaches and the delivery of cognitive interventions. However, there were other deep ambiguities in the

Department's approach. On the one hand, it sought to provide advice, assistance and in-class support which would enable students to be maintained in mainstream classes. On the other hand, it withdrew students from those classes in the expectation that it could transform them through the use of specialised teaching methods. At best, it was not able to resource both these strategies effectively; at worst, the use of quite differently oriented strategies gave mixed messages to the rest of the staff.

The ambiguities in the Department's role were encapsulated by the SENCO when she was asked what she felt was needed to develop the school's response to special educational needs further. Her answer embodied two different strands:

> I would like all staff to take the whole thing on board. I would like all staff to take note of the individual needs of the children. That's because so many, I suppose, it's a bit like the old grammar school ethos – you're teaching the kids that are either with you or they're not. I suppose really it's a child-centred, more child-centred than it is . . . What else? I think certainly if I was, if I had a bigger department which was able to trouble-shoot. I feel there's too few of us. I mean there's only [name] and myself and [name] on a part-time basis and I would love to have the opportunity to do trouble-shooting.

For the SENCO, there seemed to be no contradiction between her desire to see the whole staff become responsible for special educational needs on the one hand and a commitment to 'trouble-shooting' on the other. However, her newly-appointed colleague had a somewhat different perspective:

> I think the school has no clear-cut policy from the top. I don't think the senior management of the school fully understand or have fully looked at seriously enough how we, how special needs should be done within the school. They have in the sense that they have the intervention, they have the thinking skills, they have the IE, they have the CASE in Science, they have CAME in Maths so they are looking at that but there are other aspects in the Code of Practice and differentiation of work materials hasn't been addressed.
>
> (Teacher P)

Given these ambiguities and uncertainties, the Code of Practice came to be seen as a solid rock on which responses to special educational needs could be based. As we have seen, there was a widespread welcome for the formalisation of identification and procedures which the Code had brought. However, even here all was not well. The SENCO had responded to the Code by trying to set up formal channels of communication with subject departments and learning coordinators. However, there were problems at all points along these channels. Attendance at the meetings of 'link teachers' who were her departmental contacts had declined and heads of department had in any case tended to delegate that responsibility to relatively junior members of staff. They in turn had their problems persuading members of their department to keep them informed about students who might have special educational needs, while subject teachers themselves felt that the information and advice they received back from the Special Needs Department was inadequate. As one put it,

> I just find it a bit disconcerting when you get this quick kind of note saying, 'Give him a vocabulary book'. You don't get an overall picture of what's happening with an individual child.
>
> (Teacher L)

The situation was no better in terms of communications with learning co-ordinators. Some took the Special Needs Department's interventionist approach to mean that they themselves had no special needs responsibilities:

> I must admit that most of the special needs is taken care of by the Special Needs Department and I'm obviously kept informed as to what is going on. My direct input from that is, I would describe as very little at the moment. Other than that fact, they handle it all.
>
> (Teacher C)

However, as the SENCO explained, things were different when learning co-ordinators believed that she was trespassing on territory which they regarded as properly their own:

> it's a bit of a cleft stick and a bit of a nasty one at the moment because I think the learning co-ordinators were certainly very upset sometime last year . . . when we were actually saying the Code of Practice also includes behaviour problems because behaviour problems could very well be, leads to learning difficulties . . . We've actually been treading on eggs for the last few months over this. It's a difficult situation because, you know, year tutors . . . a lot of their time is taken up with the naughty ones and here they see us infiltrating their classes.

Clearly, whatever the Code might have achieved in terms of formalising procedures, it had done little to establish a common understanding of how the school should respond to students regarded as having special educational needs, of what role the Special Needs Department had within that response, or of what responsibilities other members of staff had in this respect.

Management style

A factor which underpinned many of the tensions which we have explored so far was the management style of senior staff in the school and, particularly, of the headteacher. He characterised his own style in the following terms:

> by nature I'm an intuitive person, so I tend to see a broad brush picture,

adding:

> I'm sure that my vision . . . is along the right lines.

Given this confidence in his 'vision', he saw one of his principal roles as being to appoint people who shared that vision:

> When I, with the governors, appoint new staff, I try to share the philosophy of the school with new staff . . . So I would try to make sure that people who joined the school were at least influenced, if not positive, towards the belief in all children's learning potential.

Indeed, his view was that teachers who did not share the vision would probably not apply for posts in the school.

However, the head also acknowledged some tensions in his position. First, the cognitive approaches had been running in the school for a number of years and a significant number of staff had now been appointed who had missed out both on the initial wave of enthusiasm and on the training which accompanied their introduction. Second, as we have seen, the interventions were confined to specific parts of the curriculum and did not appear to impact on teaching strategies in other subject areas. There was, therefore, a danger:

> it would obviously be a contradiction if the child is being taught in half their curriculum by people who are optimistic, good mediators, and then in other parts of their curriculum they are taught by people who have quite rigid ideas as to what's their entitlement. So that will be the head, senior staff role to help them uphold the culture of the school in terms of the values it transcends [sic].

Unfortunately, upholding the school culture and encouraging colleagues to be 'optimistic' are somewhat nebulous aims and it was not at all clear what specific steps the head was able to take in order to ensure that they were achieved. Indeed, his own emphasis on the need for 'technical' interventions in specific difficulties, his inclination towards setting and his willingness to countenance a clearly identified and separately-organised 'bottom' set seemed to contradict his own commitment to optimism and flexibility.

For some staff, therefore, the head's reliance on vision simply meant that there was 'no clear-cut policy from the top' (Teacher P). As one teacher put it,

> I think the school management find it difficult to do anything constructive. The school works as co-operative despite management. The current people who are in senior positions haven't adapted to change in schools and they don't know how to handle the requirements really.
>
> (Teacher S)

In particular, others pointed to the lack of any open discussion around the 'vision' and its operationalisation and to the lack of any properly structured in-service training activities to support it. As even one of the senior management team pointed out,

> I think the full integration of the school's policy right across every department hasn't yet been accomplished and part of that is down to the fact that we need to spend more time collectively or in small groups looking at particular aspects of it.
>
> (Teacher O)

Indeed, it appeared that there was no culture of professional development and little of reflective practice in the school. As the SENCO told us, 'INSET is a dirty word as far as some people are concerned', and even when development events were organised, she suggested, they tended to focus on a wide range of relatively low-level issues and were attended by teachers who claimed to be too exhausted by their teaching loads to participate fully.

If we add to this rather gloomy picture the difficulties which the SENCO and her department had in working developmentally with colleagues, some of the tensions and problems we have identified throughout this account of the school are hardly surprising. If staff did not both share the head's vision and understand how to operationalise it, there was little in the school to help them. Whilst, therefore, he continued to articulate that vision in impressive psychological terms, the reality for students was that they did indeed spend much of the curriculum with teachers who did not share or understand it.

External tensions

Not all of the issues which confronted St Joseph's emanated from within the school. As a voluntary-aided Catholic school with a distinctive sense of its own mission, it was partially insulated from some of the external pressures which other schools might have faced. Nonetheless, there was a sense throughout our time in the school that the staff were under constant, if not extreme, external pressure.

In some cases, this pressure came from the raised expectation of parents. Conflicts with parents were not acute, but heads of departments, learning co-ordinators and, above all, the SENCO, who worked most closely with them, had to be aware of their sensitivities. The SENCO, in particular, complained bitterly about the expectation of what she called 'some middle-class parents' that their child would receive substantial individual provision, even though the child's difficulties might be quite minor. However, as she also pointed out, for many teachers, pressure came less from direct interactions with parents than from the framework of accountability within which they had to operate:

> There is pressure from the National Curriculum and league tables and we are less prepared to take risks with kids who only attain a G. There has probably been a shift, society being the way it is.

Moreover, the National Curriculum imposed constraints on the style of teaching that was possible and made demands in terms of planning and recording. When we asked one head of department, for instance, if he would prefer to teach mixed-attainment groups, his answer was:

> If you can get rid of the National Curriculum, probably yes, but the National Curriculum put us under pressure, especially the record keeping side of it. It has improved, we no longer panic quite so much . . . [but] it really did drive us all at one time.
>
> (Teacher K)

This pressure in turn, however, was inextricably linked to the sense, which many teachers shared, that the school did not have the resources to meet all the demands that were now placed on it. There was a feeling, in particular, that the school was trying to develop a coherent response to special educational needs in the face of overwhelming odds. For some, the major problem was, as we have seen, the inability of the Special Needs Department to provide a comprehensive programme of in-class support and meet all the other demands made upon it. For others, the problem was the lack of time to undertake the development work that a more inclusive approach would involve. The staff needed, said one:

Time – time to sit down and consider . . . we've got a system whereby you've got kids who can barely read and write up to Oxbridge entrants and trying to bridge and be even handed and in many cases to positively discriminate demands imagination, demands a great deal of time and thought and discussion.

(Teacher T)

Under these circumstances, the Code of Practice, though useful in some respects, simply consumed more time in fulfilling bureaucratic rather than educational requirements:

You get wedges of things, you could spend all day you know just filling in forms and reading other people's.

(Teacher U)

The consequence was that the school's approach to students with special educational needs was always likely to be a compromise between the ideal and what was practicable given the constraints under which staff were operating:

My temptation would be to say that we're probably doing the best we can to get [the special educational needs policy] implemented from the bottom up, but at the end of the day we're not doing as much as we could . . . If it's because, for example, there's not enough money, you know, then you have to find some more money or say it's impossible, you know—No, it's not being implemented fully, but at least we do have a policy that we're trying to move towards.

(Teacher J)

Indeed, this highly experienced teacher, who had begun his career in secondary modern schools, perhaps gave the most honest and fullest appraisal of all as to how the pressures in current context was impacting on him and his colleagues:

I think a lot of us are frightened and that fear goes from what's this kid going to do when he can't do it? Is the chair going to go through the window? Am I going to hurt this kid by saying, 'Well, you've got a real problem' or whatever, or – let me explain – there's a danger of getting too close to kids. I think sometimes our physical limits are the problem. There never seem to be enough resources. Whether that's just a cop-out I don't know. I feel that sometimes it's bricks without straw. If you have an artificial system of governing the success of the place by saying how many 'As', 'Bs' and 'Cs' and sod the rest, then what are we doing? What message are we giving across to these youngsters when they know and we know that these artificial targets, they're just not going to hack it . . .?

Emerging issues

It is fitting that this final comment brings us back to the classroom realities which teachers in St Joseph's saw themselves facing. They clearly had a headteacher whose vision of how the school should respond to student diversity was distinctive and radical. Had that vision been realised, the 'technical' difficulties which some students experienced would have been overcome and the infinite learning potential of all students would have been released. However, that vision was patently not realised. Teachers found themselves dealing, not with young people who had suddenly become intellectually liberated, but with a familiar pattern of learning difficulties and problematic behaviour which had to be managed in a context of limited support and escalating external demands. If they did not, in most cases, openly reject the head's vision, neither was there much within it that could help them face these daily realities. It is not altogether surprising, then, if some of them felt, if not the 'fear' to which this teacher alludes, then at least some considerable anxiety.

The reasons for the apparent failure of the school's distinctive approach seem fairly clear. Undoubtedly, a major factor was the management style of the headteacher and, in particular, his failure to carry his staff with him in sharing and realising his vision. Indeed, some time after the ending of our fieldwork, the school received an Ofsted inspection which, while finding much to praise, also pointed to major weaknesses in the school's management – a failure to involve staff in decision-making, a lack of co-ordination of multiple initiatives, inadequate monitoring of student progress, poor communication with the staff, and so on. The head left the school shortly after this report was published.

However, inadequate management alone does not seem to tell the whole story. The deep ambiguities in the 'vision' itself seem also to have played a part. There was, for instance, the ambiguity of the 'twin track' approach. The thinking skills 'interventions' were going to liberate students' potential – but they nonetheless needed to be accompanied by some rather traditional remedial teaching for students experiencing 'technical difficulties'. They also, it seems, needed to be delivered in setted situations, with different interventions for different groups of students despite the claim that all students had *infinite* potential. Moreover, the emphasis on transformative interventions seems to have meant that little effort (compared, for instance, with our other case-study schools) was expended on developing other aspects of teaching and learning.

In many ways, therefore, the radical cognitive approach advocated by the head was simply superimposed on an otherwise unchanged and, in many ways, rather traditionally organised school. On the one hand, the interventions failed to bring about any fundamental trans-formation of students' learning; on the other, they apparently inhib-ited the development of more gradualist approaches which might have had a longer-term impact on students. This seems to have been a particularly significant factor in some of the tensions and ambiguities experienced by the Special Needs Department. The SENCO and her colleagues, above all, were caught in the ambiguity of the 'twin-track' approach, delivering a liberating intervention on the one hand and dealing with the learning and behavioural difficulties which it pat-ently failed to address on the other. Little wonder that there was so much uncertainty around their role.

The irony of St Joseph's is that it was, in many ways, the most radical of our four schools – at least in its espoused philosophical stance towards diversity and the potential within that stance for a reconstruction of understandings of 'special educational needs'. However, its outcomes were, in many ways, the most traditional of the four. Potentially, its approach could have led to the disappearance of special needs education; in fact, it simply led to growing demands for more special needs teachers.

5

Moorgate School: The Comprehensive Ideal

The context

Moorgate School is a large 11–18 comprehensive school with over 1,300 students on the roll. Situated in the suburbs of a small industrial city in the north of England, it is located on a private housing estate which constitutes its major catchment area. It is, in terms of many indicators, a highly successful school: well over 50 per cent of its students entered for GCSEs in the year prior to our fieldwork gained five or more passes at A*–C grade (the second highest figure for maintained schools in its LEA) and virtually all of those entered gained five or more passes at grades A*–G; it struck us as a calm and orderly place with relationships between staff and students seeming to be positive and relatively few incidents of disruption becoming apparent; it was also a stable community, with a large number of long-stay staff, including a number of members of the senior management team. The headteacher himself was relatively new to the school, having arrived some two years previously. However, he moved from the headship of a smaller school in the same LEA, had previously had experience as a deputy head, and had not introduced any major changes which might destabilise existing organisation and practice (although such changes were being planned).

Special needs provision in the school was managed by a Special Educational Needs Co-ordinator on a promoted post. She too was a long-stay teacher, having worked as SENCO in the school for some 17 years and having had some previous experience in SEN work. She was a graduate who had completed substantial parts of a master's degree and was in demand as a trainer of other SEN teachers by local higher education institutions. She managed teams of teachers operating mainly in an in-class support role, though with some withdrawal and consultancy work, and of classroom assistants who worked with students with statements. In addition, many subject teachers offered in-class support, within their own departments wherever possible, and some sixth formers had been trained by the SENCO to play a similar role. The school had some 150+ students on the SEN register without statements and a handful of students with statements – largely for moderate learning difficulties, physical difficulties and sensory impairments.

Moorgate had a number of competitor schools in its vicinity. In particular, one nearby school had students who achieved similar examination results and was perceived in the community as an 'academic' school. Moorgate's LEA pursued rather middle-of-the-road policies in respect of special needs education, maintaining a large special needs support service and a mixed economy of special schools and resource bases in mainstream schools.

Approaches and values

Views on how the school's approach to special educational needs and the values underpinning that approach might be characterised attracted a high level of consensus. As one member of the senior management team put it:

> generally at senior management level there's a total commitment to this provision – in class support and trying to improve the quality. There are some teachers who, the vast majority of our teachers I think generally see the importance of support – 80 per cent I would think. When it comes to it in, maybe 20 per cent who wouldn't say they didn't agree with it but they are not so keen to have anybody in there to see what's going on more often than not you know.
>
> (Teacher A)

Our interviews revealed this estimate to be, if anything, somewhat over-cautious, as teachers with varying levels of experience and responsibility, and from all areas of the school, described the school's approach in very similar terms and, with one or two exceptions, with high levels of approval.

As the senior manager's comments indicate, in-class support was seen as the central plank of the school's SEN work. One teacher, who had been in the school for 17 years, explained how this approach had developed over that time:

> It started very much with withdrawal. When I came to the school I was introduced to two special needs teachers who would take my

problems from me more or less and they would be dumped with them in some private room somewhere and their problems would be resolved and then the kids would be returned. Gradually, of course, we realised that that just doesn't work, it doesn't happen and reintegrating children is very difficult. They were taken out of lessons like Music, lessons like German or whatever, which meant that they were really losing out on areas on the curriculum that they should be able to cope with and I don't think they were getting anything else in compensation. Eventually, we did more and more focus in on in-classroom support so that the children were never, ever labelled and divided from the rest of the children, that they get the full curriculum, and I think that has been the main difference and I think just more communication between the staff, you know, we just don't have two people as special needs teachers, everybody is, and if there is a problem identified then all the teachers who share that problem will meet and try to resolve it rather than leaving it to somebody else. I think that's the major difference, the major shift, that the staff work as a team and the children are no longer divided.

(Teacher B)

This interviewee neatly encapsulates a number of themes which recurred throughout the interviews. The current approach, based on in-class support, was seen to have evolved gradually over time from a withdrawal-based approach. That evolution was not without pain, and a number of teachers found the change difficult to accept. In the words of one long-stay teacher:

There have been vast changes. Being old, and long in the tooth, it did take some getting used to. I don't think any of the staff, certainly the older staff we used to have [liked] teachers in their rooms, sixth formers in their rooms, and things of this nature

but, he concluded,

now of course I think all staff accept the fact that we have a policy that means that the special needs children are in with the rest of the school and have accepted that and they accept support, not just accept it but welcome it I think and in fact I'm sure they do.

(Teacher C)

Indeed, some teachers went so far as to see the move to in-class support as being a 'cultural thing' (Teacher A). This seemed to have two meanings. First, in-class support was seen as being in line with certain values about how students with special needs should be treated. They were to be 'in with the rest of the school' and 'no longer divided'. A number of interviewees referred to the core values of the school as being derived from the 'comprehensive ideal'. In the head's words:

> one of the things that the school does stand for is that it is a true comprehensive school, it's a school which aims to cater for every child regardless of their level of ability and regardless of their social background and many other factors which might impinge on their achievement, and do the best for them and ensure that by the time they leave that they have achieved everything that they can achieve academically and socially. That is our philosophy, that is our policy, that is what we are trying to achieve and therefore the way, the specific special needs policies that we have are very much set in that context.

This ideal implied non-segregation in a social sense, but also in a curricular sense – the participation in rather than exclusion from Music, German and the rest. In-class support, therefore, had a crucial role to play in securing this sort of participation. One of the support teachers, for instance, described successful support teaching in the following terms:

> the successes are when you get a child who started out nervous and anxious and unable to do anything and then is that confident little person who is prepared to put up their hand and join the rest of the class. That's when you can walk away and say 'that child is part of this group now and can operate within it', and that's lovely.

> (Teacher D)

The investment of so much effort in securing participation was seen as worthwhile because of the conviction, described by the headteacher, that even children with difficulties can achieve given the right level of support. This was not so much an untrammelled faith in the unlimited potential of all students as a values-driven belief that all children have a right to achieve that of which they are capable: 'our greatest pride is where children have overcome difficulties to get grades' (Teacher E).

This in turn was part of a deliberate attempt by the school to constitute itself as a caring community, reflected in a pastoral system built around cross-age 'houses' designed to create social stability in the school and to enable older students to support younger ones. The teacher just quoted captured the importance of the 'caring community' notion in describing the case of a girl with speech difficulties. Support in this case was not simply about giving students 'access' to the curriculum, but about sustaining the vulnerable individual within the school community as a matter of right:

> the girl who I have in year 10 at the moment, I supported in year 9 and the class was, it required an effort but in the end, the class became very supportive and when we were doing oral work you could hardly hear what she was saying. She gabbled her words, you couldn't understand what she was doing, but the class listened, the class had been brought to listen and to accept that they weren't going to hear or understand what she was saying but nevertheless she had a right to be heard and moments like that are wonderful.
>
> (Teacher E)

This extended notion of support aligned with the second aspect of the cultural change which interviewees reported. Not only were students now supported, but staff themselves were supported and offered support to each other. Much of this was attributed to the work of the Special Educational Needs team, who were seen as 'very supportive and very easy to communicate with' (Teacher F). However, there was an emphasis throughout the school on teachers working together to solve the problems presented by their students. For instance, there was a staff support group on the Hanko model (Hanko, 1995) which met regularly; there was a Special Needs Liaison Team which met to discuss students with difficulties and which comprised staff from across subject departments and the pastoral system; departments were encouraged to provide in-class support from within their own resources so that teachers within departments worked together on collaborative teaching; a multi-agency team met regularly to discuss individual cases; and throughout our time in the school we came across recurrent references to the ways in which teachers worked together in departmental teams to solve mutual problems.

This final point is indicative of a real attempt on the part of many subject departments to develop their own 'in-house' responses to special needs, particularly through differentiation. As one teacher put it, this was important 'whether there is a special needs support, whether they are in the classroom or not', particularly in years 7 and 8 where there is a good deal of mixed-ability grouping and, 'it's, you know, very broad, the range of abilities within the class, so always, you always have that in mind for your teaching' (Teacher G).

However, the SENCO and her team were central in supporting these initiatives too and it is perhaps worth emphasising just how highly regarded the SENCO in particular was amongst her colleagues. As a fellow head of department commented:

I think we are very fortunate in having [name] as our special needs co-ordinator in that she has demonstrated what can be done and what should be done and she has carried the staff along with her and she has made it into what it ought to be in a sense, one of the most important areas in the school.

(Teacher H)

Given all these positive factors, it is hardly surprising, therefore, that, in the words of a senior member of staff,

I think that there's general agreement that the system is working quite nicely.

(Teacher I)

Internal tensions

Despite the high level of consensus which had been achieved around the 'new' approach, many interviewees acknowledged the existence of dissident individuals and groups. In practice, we were not able to identify teachers who were simply opposed in principle to the school's approach *per se*. Instead we found individuals who, whilst they accepted the *principles* of the approach, voiced criticisms of the way that approach operated *in practice*.

Problems with support teaching

Typical of this was the concerns that were expressed about the efficiency and effectiveness of in-class support. One of the approach's strongest critics nonetheless articulated a balanced position:

At its best it [support] can be useful. Support is extremely expensive; there has to be a balance between the number of support to the individual and resources that can be given to the vast majority. It is difficult to know if you are giving the right balance; it often can be driven by what you can afford.

(Teacher J)

Even the advocates of in-class support, however, acknowledged that '[the SENCO's] team are spread very thinly and clearly it is perhaps very far from the kind of resourced area of education that we would wish' (Teacher H), whilst those involved in delivering support admitted that 'with an extra member of staff there's often nothing to do and that has to be . . . an unnecessary waste of resources' (Teacher D). These concerns were exacerbated by two factors. First, there was some difference of opinion amongst the staff as to whether non-subject-specialists made effective support teachers. One head of a practical-based subject, for instance, reported how he had fought to have some of his own teachers made available for support because:

> we originally had some staff coming in who were non-specialists and they weren't proving of any real use to us, because it's not the same as a teacher supporting somebody working with literacy and numeracy I think. Ours is a different environment.
>
> (Teacher K)

Second, some teachers (or, more accurately, pairs of teachers) appeared to work together less effectively than others. As one experienced support teacher put it:

> I think it's down to individuals because I've worked with two [senior colleagues] and they are totally different. One is the sort of person who can't, you can't really work with as a colleague. It's always very much a senior member of staff and a lesser member of staff . . . Even when asked in an informal way how he might change, there's that feeling that you cannot really tell him because he will perceive it as criticism even when it's not intended in that way.
>
> (Teacher D)

Although, therefore, there was a wide acceptance of in-class support in itself, its effectiveness remained prey to the personal styles and relationships of the individuals involved. Indeed, there were cases where the breakdown in relationships affected whole departments:

> The [name] department don't like the S[pecial] N[eeds] department. They see it as a 'them and us' scenario. They DON'T DIF-FERENTIATE . . . Younger staff are more aware of different needs and are open to advice. Older ones aren't ready for advice, they perceive it as 'criticism' about their teaching. Diplomacy is a big weapon – struggling still though with some – don't work very closely as a whole with all of the department.
>
> (Teacher L)

This last point about the lack of differentiation is one which is worth emphasising. The school in general, and the SENCO in particular, had invested a good deal of energy in promoting the notion of differentiation. However, our own evidence from lesson observation was that any systematic attempt to make teaching and resources appropriate to a diverse range of students was patchy, to say the least. Indeed, as one teacher explained, the availability of relatively high levels of support actually acted as a disincentive to differentiation:

It's very difficult. I mean, we're told, we try to differentiate as much as we possibly can, but you know, you've got the whole range of ability there, and it's very, very difficult. It's difficult to stretch those most able, as well as keeping hold of those who are least able, so if you have support in there, then that automatically takes some pressure off because you can say to yourself, 'oh well, there's so-and-so here to deal with, you know, whichever small group might need it'.

(Teacher M)

Understanding special needs

This departmental factor surfaced again in terms of how special needs were understood. The school's approach as a whole appeared to be premised on a rather broad and nebulous definition of special educational needs. The question 'what do you understand by the term special educational needs' therefore tended to elicit a very general response, such as,

those with special needs or learning difficulties or those who need learning support, because I don't see those, all of those with special needs as having learning difficulties because of course there are special needs at the other end of the scale. There are specific learning difficulties which are unrelated to intelligence and there are those who are gifted or very able who I think also have special needs.

(Teacher F)

Such definitions chime well with the school's attempt to enable every student to achieve his/her potential, but at the same time open the door to an enormous diversity of perceived needs. As we have seen some departments regarded themselves as constituting a 'different environment' in respect of special educational needs. A PE teacher, for instance, commented that:

our vision of what I would class as special needs kids would be somebody who was clumsy, awkward, overweight, because we do have quite a lot of children who basically suffer from obesity.

(Teacher N)

However, the school's SEN provision was not able to respond to this 'vision':

generally speaking if it comes to support and any sort of back up from the school, you know, in terms of what we offer in PE, physical co-ordination is bottom of the pile. It seems to be what matters least. I mean, fair enough, literally, literacy and numeracy are of paramount importance but you know it does tend to get ignored and again and again we have got children who, I can think of a couple of lads I teach, are unbelievably poor. They are not special needs because academically they are just average, but they have their own special problems that doesn't seem to get recognised by the school.

(Teacher N)

Given this situation, such departments inevitably saw themselves as having to 'fight our corner' (Teacher O) to get the school to make provision for these distinctive forms of special need.

Moreover, given the open-ended definition of special educational needs in the school, there was an almost inevitable multiplication of types of need to which the SENCO felt she must respond:

We have a few physical problems, we've got one child in a wheel-chair . . . we've got some, quite a number of specific learning difficulties and the range of physical problems, diabetic, and we got a child in September with bowel problems . . . I mean it's incredible, we have this bowel problem, we've got a hearing prob-lem, we've got learning difficulties, and you haven't got a state-ment . . . We've got another who's due to come in September, I mean there are terms that are just creeping in, you know dys-praxia is mushrooming, autism seems to be popular at the mo-ment, attention deficit disorder – parents are watching programmes now and they've decided to diagnose the condition, so I mean we've got the whole range of those, whether they are diagnosed or not, we've got symptoms. And we have a child coming with ME, and we already have a child with ME . . . We're getting a child in this year with a hearing loss.

Not surprisingly, the SENCO commented that 'I rarely stop at break-times, I work', and our own observations confirmed that she did indeed work intensively, troubleshooting with a large number of indi-vidual children, with parents and with staff.

Problems with behavioural difficulties

The school's broad definition of special needs led to particular prob-lems in respect of students who presented behavioural difficulties. There was, for instance, some uncertainty as to whether such students were the responsibility of the SENCO or of the strong pastoral system in the school. Despite normally good working relationships, therefore, the head acknowledged that 'there is a certain amount of conflict between the responsibilities of [pastoral and special needs] staff, or there's overlap'. However, the reality was that many such students effectively became the responsibility of the SENCO. Partly, this was because she was seen by such students as a supportive figure to whom they could turn as and when they needed. As she pointed out, despite an elaborate chain of communication and referral for such students, 'they've [the students] never gone to the designated people, they have always gone to the people they want to go to'.

Partly, however, it was because of the wider 'trouble-shooting' role she undertook within the school. As we tracked her work, it was not uncommon for us to see her with one or more students in tow who had been excluded from their lessons and who, therefore, spent the rest of the day following her round. Moreover, in allocating support, she found herself compelled to respond to behavioural crises as well as to students' learning difficulties. We observed one German lesson, for instance, where a group of disaffected boys were causing problems for the teacher. The SENCO's response was typical:

> I gave up my free time to go in and try to hold the whole thing together – 4 or 5 boys disrupting because they fail to see the relevance of learning German . . . I was asked to take out [two girls with statements for learning difficulties] but I picked off the disruptive boys and took them out.

Moreover, such problems were, in the view of many teachers, becoming more frequent and more acute and there were real doubts as to whether the school's support-based special needs approach was actually capable of meeting this new challenge. The SENCO herself described some of this behaviour as 'bizarre' and a member of the senior management team commented:

> I think we are getting some extreme cases now to deal with, in fact I know we are in the sense that special schools and things like this, they come in here now. You wonder sometimes, I wonder sometimes whether they should be in the school, but they are and we've got to get on with it.
>
> (Teacher C)

He continued:

> If they are backward readers or whatever, you can get round that I think, you can deal with it in various ways in the classroom, if they have got real emotional, desperate home problems and

things like that then it becomes far more difficult I think. You've got to be a psychologist haven't you really, rather than just, I mean rather than a teacher really. Some of the problems are so deep and it's difficult for us to deal with.

This sense that students presenting behaviour difficulties fell outside what the school could and should cope with contrasted sharply with an equally strong view amongst many staff that the school should do more for its 'more able' students. 'If we do have a weakness,' one teacher commented,

> it's that we focus mainly on the weak end of the scale. I think we've got a weakness, we are not really addressing problems with the brighter children who have got their own brand of special needs.
>
> (Teacher B)

In other words, there was, in effect, a distinction in the minds of some staff between the 'undeserving' needy – students with behaviour difficulties and students with learning difficulties in whom the school invested heavily – and the 'deserving' needy – more able students whom the school, they believed, tended to neglect.

External tensions

The tentative nature of this last teacher's criticism (*'If* we do have a weakness') should, however, remind us of the broad satisfaction with the school's approach amongst staff. However, interviewees' views of the external context of their work and of its impact on what they were trying to achieve were much more outspoken.

Balancing the population

A number of teachers commented on the way in which the very success of the school's approach threatened to make it 'top heavy with its special needs' (Teacher E) and thus destabilise the conditions which made that approach successful. A member of the senior management team explained the impact of open enrolment in this situation:

> in my view as a manager we have to look carefully at admission trends. [We] should be very careful as to what percentage it is. If you go to a middle class dormitory school, people in [name of suburb] if they have a bright child want to send them to [Moorgate's competitor school]. If not so bright they would like them

to come here and would blatantly manipulate the situation to get them here. This is all very well but if the numbers start to increase this can lead to an overall burden on support and facilities. It also mitigates [*sic*] against the school in the league tables which are printed without comment. I would like to see us develop more of our own way of things than have them imposed upon us.

(Teacher J)

Another senior manager highlighted the way in which the school's commitment to in-class support might soon become unsustainable:

we were starting to worry that we would start to take in these students, so you would have two or three in every mixed ability class and there does come a point where if you are trying to target support, then it just becomes a totally unrealistic proposition.

(Teacher A)

Parental demands

The strains imposed by attracting more 'difficult' students were exacerbated by a number factors. One was that the students' parents were sometimes proving to be as difficult as the students themselves. The SENCO, who had to bear the brunt of liaison work with parents, complained that 'the expectation of parents is phenomenal'. Despite the supposedly shared responsibility for this work, she added,

Most of it still ends up on my patch when it's, it has to be checked out or parents are getting difficult. I mean I do spend a lot of time with that, because we have that kind of catchment area, I mean since the first year parents' evening it's been very frustrating, they want a 'fix', they want a diagnosis, which we haven't got the resources for. And they go off to places like a private dyslexia clinic, and they come back with lists of what they've been told their children need, and if you put it onto the continuum, the kids are near the top.

Her frustrations with parents were taking her near breaking point:

I've suggested they get a switchboard in to take the complaints because trying to keep the parents who want to be informed, informed, means that you would be kind of held to ransom because you would be only reacting to phone calls instead of trying to work through all the existing priorities. I'm sick of parents!

Resource constraints

A second factor is hinted at in the SENCO's comments. It was not simply that the demands from students and their parents were high, but that the resources at the school's disposal are inadequate to meet those demands. Although the school's approach depended heavily on in-class support, the amount of support time that was available was decreasing. As one teacher put it:

> As I see it, our policy in very general terms is to help as many children as we can in as many subjects as we can, but unfortunately at the minute it seems to be diminishing, they seem to be being cut back.
>
> (Teacher P)

Or, in the words of another:

> this year it's basically, staff-wise, the [name] department is stretched to, in fact stretched beyond breaking point. There's been virtually no time given to any form of support.
>
> (Teacher N)

The consequence of this was that some students with special educational needs were left without support across many of their lessons, causing anxiety amongst their teachers:

> I'm sure there are problems in [that class] but they are going to have to be left in this class of 30 unless somebody gives them staff.
>
> (Teacher N)

At the same time, where support was provided, it was forced into a more hastily planned and *ad hoc* mode:

> There is never any time now to plan our support with the subject teachers . . . There isn't time to chase everyone up. Paperwork, space, time, and a lack of teachers are all problems. How to organise for next term with yet more needy children who can't read up to age 9 standard.
>
> (Teacher L)

Many teachers told us of the problems generated by the decline in support: collaborative arrangements that had worked well but were having to be terminated; support-teaching projects which worked well with one group but could not be replicated with other groups where students had equally pressing needs; teachers who had developed skills in support work but were now no longer deployed in that capacity. Certainly, we observed many examples of lessons where there was little or no evidence of joint planning between class teacher and support teacher and where, as a result, the latter was reduced to undertaking a series of *ad hoc* interventions to keep the lesson flowing smoothly and manage behaviour in the classroom rather than implementing any fully worked-out strategy for overcoming students' difficulties.

The irony of the decline in support was that it was occurring at a time when the school was highly successful in attracting new students, so that although the school was 'rich' financially, both the staffing and the physical capacity of the school were stretched. The head explained the economy of SEN provision which was partly responsible for this situation:

> there are staffing limitations if we were to significantly increase the number of children that we were taking in who had severe special needs, and they were special needs which were very demanding in time and resources because we are not resourced at that level and the resourcing which comes with children you know who have been through the statutory assessment procedures do not actually pay for the full cost. If you were to actually cost the amount of support that was given to some of the individual pupils, there's no way that it would be compensated for by the additional income that is generated through the local management formula. I think we are very close to that point. I think there is a point at which the structures that you've put in place, the people that you've got and the resources and accommodation that you've got are stretched to their limits and if you go beyond that limit then the quality of what we are providing starts to suffer.

National policy constraints

Although resourcing was an issue which many staff cited as a major problem for the school's SEN approach, there were further exacerbating factors. The head, for instance, explained the link between the shortage of resources and problems generated by the recently-introduced Code of Practice:

> at the moment like most schools, we've taken the documents produced by the Local Authority and taken the Code of Conduct [*sic*] and we've tried as best we can to implement it fully and do everything that it says we should. In practice we can't actually do all those things in the way that is promoted and survive. I think it's just expecting too much of schools with the resources they

have at their disposal to do it. I think our policy has got to develop in a way which is rooted in realism.

Similarly, the SENCO described the Code as 'more of an inhibitor than an activator; we've had to slightly change direction, and I didn't think it was for the good'. She explained how the volume of paperwork generated by the Code was threatening to overwhelm the school's approach, how difficult it was to keep track of IEPs if subject teachers were fully involved, and how there was a danger that she and her team would become side-tracked into perpetual IEP reviews. The Code in other words, was seen largely as a bureaucratic imposition which was simply unsustainable alongside the school's existing SEN approach.

Some of her colleagues similarly complained of the constraints imposed on their approach to students with special educational needs by the National Curriculum and its assessment. One teacher, for instance, described the implications of the rewriting of the examination syllabus in her subject:

> at the moment there is the problem of the new GCSE syllabus which is written – and this has been the way that syllabuses have been going – has been written so that the top 10 per cent if that, it would be challenging, stretching, rewarding for those kind of people to follow it. For much of the rest of the ability range it's just not really written with them in mind. I always get the impression of these crusty old blokes sitting round who've only ever known some kind of grand old public school . . . So there's trying to deliver that syllabus even to your middle ability range and learning a new syllabus, yet another new syllabus, I mean this is the third one I've had to teach in five years of teaching.
>
> (Teacher F)

A senior manager explained what the consequences of such demands were for the school's special educational needs approach:

> the pressure on individual class teachers constantly to adapt to change to cope with new demands is such that building on top of that planning time for the time you get support, when you might only have it in one of the five lessons, has to be questioned when you've got five lessons to prepare.
>
> (Teacher A)

The sense of pressure

Added to these major constraints were other minor, but nonetheless significant, exacerbating factors. As we have noted above, the school was successful in terms of attracting new students. However, this meant that physical space was at a premium, and the SENCO was not able to develop some of the facilities – such as a resource base – that she would have liked. Similarly, open enrolment within an urban area brought with it a multiplicity of feeder schools, so that liaison and the co-ordination of special educational needs record-keeping (let alone policy) posed enormous problems.

The consequence of all of these factors was that the staff of the school tended to see themselves as being under considerable pressure. We have already seen how the SENCO felt this pressure, and her account of her work is littered with comments about the 'unbeliev-able' demands on her, the sense of being 'in a terrible tangle', and the feeling that 'we're going to sink'. However, she was by no means alone. As the head of another department explained:

> Teachers are tired and frustrated and have constraints on them to get through a syllabus and you are juggling all kinds of extra problems over and above the specific needs of the children, but the knock-on effects on the classroom can be quite unruly at times.

There are, she continued, achievements in respect of students with special educational needs but,

> these achievements require tremendous investment and a lot of it is invisible investment that you don't even identify. If I was to sit down and write down the problems, I don't think I would think of all of them.
>
> (Teacher E)

Compromises and uncertainties

Given this account of both the internal and external problems encoun-tered by the school's SEN approach, and of the resultant pressures on teachers, it is hardly surprising that some compromises had to be made and that there were some uncertainties as to the viability of that approach.

Competing priorities

We have already seen, for instance, how the equation of increasing numbers of students with special needs, increasing severity of need and strictly limited resourcing led even senior members of staff to question the school's open-ended commitment to attracting and accepting such students. This was exacerbated by the pressure on the school to maintain its examination results. A member of the senior management team explained the dilemma which faced heads of department when they had to decide whether to resource support teaching or additional teaching groups:

> When they have to make a hard decision – do I keep this person off for 6 hours to provide support or to give them this class, which will affect their examination results and their profile – more often than not the pressure would be to deliver a key stage 4 class, and to some extent you've got a – it's not wrong, you see, do you . . . I think the answer is that whichever way you do it it's very, very difficult.
>
> (Teacher A)

There were similar compromises in respect of in-class support. Despite the widespread approval of support teaching in principle, some teachers were beginning to question the appropriateness of sustaining this approach. As one support teacher put it,

> Sometimes I'm getting to the point now with some [aspects of the subject] to feel that there would be times when I would like to take an individual child away from the class rather than try to keep them going in a classroom where the content is just too hard.
>
> (Teacher D)

Principles and practices

Indeed, despite the emphasis on the centrality of support, withdrawal in some modified form continued, in fact, to constitute a significant part of the school's approach. The headteacher explained:

> We also recognise that there are some children who do need certain types of help outside the classroom setting, particularly with the basic skills, literacy in particular, and the way we try and provide that is by organising certain things outside the normal lesson time, during family unit time, using paired reading schemes in particular and two of our special needs personnel who do not have family units and therefore are available at that time of day to provide that kind of service.

It is worth adding that the school also operated a 'time out' facility – which amounted to a *de facto* form of withdrawal – for students who were 'disruptive', and that at least one department had organised its own form of withdrawal from ordinary lessons.

Given this ambivalence about support and withdrawal, it is not surprising that there was a similar ambivalence about 'mixed-ability' teaching. If this was not a major bone of contention in the school (indeed, some teachers voiced their strong commitment to this form of grouping as part of the 'comprehensive ideal'), this may in part be because the school's commitment to mixed-ability was, in practice, rather limited. Even in the English Department, whose head strongly asserted her commitment to mixed-ability teaching, for instance, 'ability' grouping was used from year 9 upwards. The pattern throughout the school as a whole was the fairly standard 'mixed economy' with departments left to make their own decisions and a gradual increase in ability grouping as students got older. The consequence for students with special needs, of course, was that they spent much of their time in relatively small bottom sets – sets which, in practice, comprised a mixture of students with learning difficulties and students whose behaviour presented problems. Not surprisingly, we observed lessons with such groups in which students whose behaviour presented difficulties monopolised the attention of both class and support teacher whilst students with statements for learning difficulties were largely left to work unaided.

Moreover, teachers themselves were acutely aware of the challenges which 'mixed-ability' teaching posed for them. As one commented:

> It's very hard to properly teach mixed ability, you know, if that's what you do you'd have a lot more time to prepare for it but in reality you don't so everybody does as good a job as they can, but I don't think they do a very good job with it.
>
> (Teacher P)

This comment was, in fact, characteristic of an attitude which surfaced many times in our discussions with the staff. The school was premised on high ideals in respect of students with special educational needs, and the staff, by and large, shared a commitment to these ideals. However, there was a strong feeling that it was impossible in practice fully to realise those ideals, given the constraints and pressures under which the school was operating. Many teachers pointed out what they saw as the realities of their teaching situations:

> you get to the stage and you're working with groups of 32, you know, the weak kids who really need support, the really able ones, and you end up, you never quite get what you'd like with either group. You end up pitching in the middle and you just try and cater.
>
> (Teacher N)

Or again:

> My bottom set for next year has 24 in it which is kind of, I don't
> know how I'm going to teach it. There will be 24 pupils with some
> severe problems at the bottom, probably hardly any support so I
> really don't know how that's – I'm really, I'm not looking forward
> to that.
>
> (Teacher P)

The dilemmas which committed – and, to a certain extent, idealistic –
teachers faced in these situations were neatly summed up by a member of the senior management team:

> I happen to believe that we are going on the right way. I'd hate to
> see children withdrawn I think now, and made to feel as though
> they are something different. That side of me says that. The other
> side says, well, there are some children now that are almost im-
> possible to deal with in a classroom situation with 30 others. I'm
> not sure how to get round that really.

His solution was limited and pragmatic:

> I think that's out of our hands and we've – I think we are doing
> our best to keep the ship afloat.
>
> (Teacher C)

That pragmatic acceptance of what could and could not be achieved was
typical of many teachers. Asked whether the school's special educational
needs policy was fully implemented, one teacher commented:

> No, it is not fully implemented here. The ideals are there but we
> can't match the ideals but we strive to . . . You cannot ask for
> more commitment from the staff who are working at 100 per cent
> already . . . you can't keep asking for more and more of that,
> you'd just burn out.
>
> (Teacher Q)

Perhaps a statement by the headteacher most fittingly sums up much that
could be said about the school's approach to special educational needs:

> I think our policy has got to develop in a way which is rooted in
> realism. I think we've actually got to look at what we can actually
> achieve in order to do the best for those children concerned within
> the constraints of our budget and all the other things which im-
> pinge upon us, rather than having a policy statement which, if you
> like, is purely a set of aims and pure – something that is fine in
> theory but is actually impossible to achieve in practice.

Emerging issues

In reviewing these accounts of the school's SEN approach, it is easy to emphasise problems, difficulties and limitations at the expense of successes. However, there are good reasons for saying that the story of the school's attempt to develop a more inclusive approach was very much a *success* story. Here we have a school which had a history of innovation (at least in comparison with other local schools) and which had maintained a principled commitment to the 'comprehensive ideal' over many years. It is appropriate to talk of 'the school's' commitment because there was a very high level of consensus amongst the staff both about what the school was trying to achieve and about the appropriateness of the strategies it was using. Some, at least, of this consensus stems from the work of the SENCO, who was almost universally held in high regard and whose interventions with students and management of the support system were regarded very positively. It is also worth adding that in many other ways the school was successful: its examination results were well above the LEA average; it was a calm and orderly community; and it successfully included a number of students with statements who might elsewhere be placed in special schools.

Nonetheless, the school's approach was beset with problems. The consensus around aims and methods was widespread, but was not universal. Support teaching in particular, though much appreciated, raised considerable doubts, even amongst its supporters. There was an apparently ever-expanding population of students with special needs – partly because the school operated an open-ended definition of special need and partly because more and more 'extreme' students appeared to be attracted to the school. There were concerns about the adequacy of the school's approach to meeting this situation, particularly in respect of students whose behaviour caused problems. In addition, the staff of the school felt themselves to be under considerable external pressure and constraint – in respect of the Code of Practice, the National Curriculum and, above all, the limitations on resources that were available in respect of special educational needs. There were, therefore compromises: the school was a 'true comprehensive', but some students might not be welcome there; there was a commitment to mixed-ability teaching and in-class support, but ability grouping and withdrawal persisted; teachers sought to meet the perceived needs of all their students, but freely admitted that it might be impossible so to do. There was a sense, therefore, that the school's approach might be as much about 'keeping the ship afloat' as about the realisation of the high ideals of inclusion.

6

Seaview Comprehensive School: Change and Conflict

The context

Seaview Comprehensive is a medium-sized former grammar school, with 730 students on the roll, and is located in a village nestling between two large conurbations. For many years, it had been led by a headteacher who had effectively sought to maintain the grammar school traditions of high academic achievement and strong discipline. At the time of our fieldwork, the school had a successful academic record – over 50 per cent of students achieved A*–C grades as opposed to the LEA average of just over 35 per cent. It had appeared in a list of the 400 'best' state schools produced by a leading national newspaper and had recently undergone an Ofsted inspection which led to a broadly complimentary report. Not surprisingly, Seaview was popular with parents.

The school appeared to be under few pressures. Only 16 per cent of students received free school meals and only 58 students (8 per cent) were placed on its special needs register. A further eight students had statements of special educational needs, and seven of those were for specific learning difficulties. This in many ways reflected the special needs policy of Seaview's LEA, which had for a number of years pursued a rather traditional line, maintaining a significant infrastructure of special schools. The consequence was that relatively large numbers of students with statements continued to be placed in segregated settings.

However, this stable situation had begun to change by the time we began our investigation. Three years previously, the incumbent headteacher retired. Unusually for this LEA, his replacement was from outside the authority. The new head was, as we shall see, someone with clear views about education which would challenge many of the preconceptions and practices of the staff in Seaview. Within three months of arriving at the school, he had been able to appoint two new deputies and offers of early retirement were accepted by eight long-stay middle managers. Of the two new deputies, one was brought in from outside the LEA, the other was promoted from the existing staff. Moreover, both of the deputies were female, in contrast to the previously all-male management structure.

Central to the new head's agenda for change was a restructuring of special needs provision. Under his predecessor, the school had relied on a combination of rigid setting, small 'bottom' groups and selective withdrawal of students for the reinforcement of 'basic' skills. The system had been managed by a SENCO who spent her time working with the 'bottom' sets and teaching literacy skills in withdrawal situations; a second special needs teacher replicated her work in numeracy. However, the new head was profoundly unhappy with this system and the deputy he had brought into the school had come from a school where she had been responsible for running a much more inclusive approach.

By the time we began work in the school, therefore, some major changes to this system had already taken place and others were planned. The head had a 'vision' of how the school might change – and it is to that vision that we now turn.

Visions and values

The new head's views on special needs education were grounded in his previous extensive teaching experience and made him opposed to traditional, segregated provision with what he saw as its acceptance of low attainment. He had been instrumental at one point in his career in setting up a unit for disabled children in a mainstream school. At another school, he had worked successfully with challenging students, including those placed in an EBD (emotional and behavioural difficulties) unit. Here, he had undergone a formative experience working on a project aimed at integrating children with learning difficulties into the mainstream. The project had ultimately collapsed, but he took certain positive lessons from that collapse:

> They [the students in the project] were quite able . . . it was all in the way the curriculum was presented. So I didn't see any problems of curriculum presentation, or even pedagogy. The problems were all social. The thing eventually broke down because of social problems. Eventually we put them into one class and they were on a par. They were members of the same class with the same status. The children from the secondary school got very upset and

said that we were calling them 'mongies' [a term of abuse for people with learning difficulties], to use their word, that they were being brought down. We had lots of parental complaints to the head about us having these children in and about lowering the tone of the school, and the children smelled, and things like that.

In another school where he had been deputy head, he had built on these experiences by disbanding its special class and attempting to replace it with more differentiated approaches in ordinary classrooms – an attempt which had also provoked a negative reaction in the first place, though this time from teachers. He spoke nostalgically, therefore, of his 'romantic period' at the start of his career in an innovative school where such differentiated approaches were taken for granted.

Alongside these professional experiences, the head had a very personal reason for rejecting traditional forms of provision: his own son had significant special needs. As he commented:

I've seen him go through physically-handicapped schools and deaf schools and whatever, which were about 'strokes for different folks' rather than about education and to some extent that has coloured my view so that I'm not objective about special needs problems.

Given this experience, it is not surprising that he was not impressed by the special needs provision he found at Seaview. It was managed, he said, by someone who,

wasn't a strong teacher and she'd been put in a distant part of the building, away from everyone else, and basically left to fester with some of the more difficult children who just weren't making any progress. There was good social contact there, but the education was a bit like the kind of thing I've seen in special schools.

Instead of this segregatory approach, he wanted to create a much more inclusive school, one which would take,

everyone who applies here, every handicap, whether it's a 'mongie' [*sic – he is referring back to the 'mongies' episode in his previous school*] or not. I've always said to the parents, it's what *you* want. They can come here.

Putting this slightly differently (and somewhat more ambivalently), he told us that:

What I've proposed to the governors is that at the minute I would accept anyone, provided that we had the right funding for them, possibly not in wheelchairs because we haven't got the right physical dimensions in the corridors, but anyone else at all in the school.

However, this inclusive approach was not something which was confined to accepting students with special educational needs. Rather, it was part and parcel of an attempt to transform the school into,

a humanistic thing, a holistic thing of treating children as a whole.

This involved changing fundamentally the way that teaching and learning were understood, introducing

a constructivist approach, somewhere along the lines of Kelly's [*sic*] teaching and learning skills.

He outlined to us a set of proposed changes which were a mixture of what would be recognised as good practice in many secondary schools and quite radical proposals grounded in a psychology of learning which was current in his 'romantic period':

we're going to try to get a spiral curriculum, a Bruner spiral if you like . . . The Assessment Officer is looking at marking because we've moved in that marking and reporting aren't separate, but marking has moved to target-setting in the reports. The next move is what [a deputy head] calls 'curriculum mentoring' which is actually negotiated reports. We're doing progress monitoring which is picking up children every term, so that children don't slip through the rungs . . . We are really looking at learning, an Ausubel approach to marking where you are looking at misconceptions rather than just ticking things that are right. Now all of those things are whole school things but they are whole school things in the sense that they also reflect good practice that should be in the special needs, so the two are not divorced. And the Individual Education Plans were the first turning of that cycle.

Whilst this 'vision' was very much the head's, it was not his alone. The deputy head who had recently joined the school, for instance, described its former approach to special needs education in the following terms:

The school had a sort of deficit model of special needs and there had been a sort of a special co-ordinator and the school had been very rigidly streamed so most of the few special needs pupils that there were in the school were hived off into sort of little tiny old remedial groups and were with each other for most of the time and never really got to see the light of day.

She too saw the need to

> get away from a sort of remedial sink group and a special needs
> teacher. The philosophy was, and this is very much what the head
> came with (and myself, anyway) that it was everyone's – a whole
> school responsibility.

There were others outside the senior management team who held
similar views. For example, one middle manager described the
changes taking place in the school in the following positive terms:

> Well it's trying to level it out for them, trying to make them feel
> part of the larger community, not make them feel alienated by
> their special needs but it's setting out to make the way for the five
> years as easy as possible for them.
>
> (Teacher A)

Moreover, the 'vision' extended well beyond special needs. The head
had many other ideas – for the development of community education,
adopting the principles of high reliability schooling (Stringfield, 1995),
changing behaviour management, monitoring student progress, student tracking and so on. In other words, he envisaged a wide-ranging
transformation of teaching, learning and organisation in what had
been a rather traditional school. Underpinning all of this was the view
that the approach of teachers towards their own learning should and
could also be transformed. The school, he argued, should become a
'learning environment' in which there would be

> highly skilled staff who want to go on to develop their own skills
> and who are interested in what they do. For example, who are
> interested in children – the door is always open and there are
> always children in and out.

Reflective practice was, therefore, to be the order of the day, supported by powerful systems of appraisal, performance monitoring,
evidence-based teaching and close supervision by senior staff.

   The need for this breadth of 'vision' had, in fact, been signalled in
the Ofsted report to which we referred earlier. Whilst that report was
generally complimentary about the school, it did make a number of
critical comments about special needs provision and, more generally,
about teaching and learning, drawing attention to:

> significant variations in the quality of teaching and learning
> within year groups. Insufficient attention is given to matching the
> curriculum demands to the needs of the pupils especially the least
> able.

It suggested that many lessons were 'characterised by a lack of differentiation'. In particular, it pointed to the differential achievement of boys and girls leading to a relative underformance of the school in terms of examination results.

This report provided the head, as he told us, with a clear rationale for the changes he wished to introduce. However, that rationale was something of a double-edged sword. It was an opportunity to use the restructuing of special needs provision as the vehicle for a much more far-reaching transformation of teaching and learning in the school. It was also, of course, a clear indication to the headteacher that he had to address convincingly the issue of underachievement in examination performance. Potentially, these two agendas were one and the same. However, it was not difficult to imagine what might happen if the head allowed his personal ideology with regard to special needs to override the institutional imperative for 'improvement'.

Realising the new vision

The head, supported particularly by his deputies, took a series of actions to try to realise the new 'vision'.

Becoming inclusive

We have already seen how the head proposed to the governors that he should operate an 'open door' policy on the admission of students with special educational needs. In practice, his first step was to offer to act as the LEA base for students with specific learning difficulties. The next step, he suggested, would be to try to establish a 'sanctuary' provision for students with 'moderate' physical and learning difficulties. He had already forged links with the local Pupil Referral Unit and he believed he might be able to persuade governors, staff and parents to agree to this new provision if he could also suggest that it should cater for students already in the mainstream of the school. He was concerned, however, that

> this is more of a dream than a likelihood because I'm not sure how the authority is going to jump . . . My guess would be they're going to try and do as little as possible, if my other experience is anything to go by.

In the event, as we shall see, he was proved right.

Special needs provision in the classroom

Internally, the restructuring of special needs provision was more directly within the control of the head and his senior managers. The special classes and withdrawal groups which had characterised the previous system were disbanded. At the same time, the school's previously rigid setting system was loosened somewhat, a limited form of mixed-attainment teaching was introduced in year 7, and students from the old special needs groups found themselves placed in larger, more flexible sets containing a slightly wider range of attainment. To maintain them in these groups, a system of in-class support was introduced, staffed mainly by subject teachers.

In order to support teachers themselves, a programme of staff training and development was initiated, led by the LEA's Special Educational Needs Support Service. A major aim of this programme was achieving a greater level of differentiation in lessons thereby increasing access to the curriculum. In particular this programme focused on improving accessibility for those with limited literacy skills.

Alongside these changes in the 'technology' within the school there was a reframing of the various policy documents. As a focus for this, a new mission statement was developed. This closely reflected the 'vision' of the headteacher, having at its heart a commitment to develop a school which was

> caring, people centred, [with a] learning environment in which everyone pursues excellence.
>
> (School brochure)

The special needs policy document was similarly revised in line with the new position. It now articulated a series of key special needs objectives:

> to ensure that every pupil has equality of opportunity and access to a broad and balanced curriculum
> to provide help and support for individuals with SEN
> to develop pupils' self esteem
> to secure effective learning in a happy and safe environment
> to involve parents in a partnership to support the child's education
> to recognise and record the achievement of all learners
> to provide all pupils with a quality introduction to the world of work.

To support these objectives a SEN folder was provided for every member of staff which contained detailed guidance on teaching strategies, standard pro-formas, guidance on target setting, various checklists and other information thought appropriate for a staff who, in the opinion of one of the senior management team, 'hadn't yet developed the language to discuss special educational needs' (Deputy head/SENCO).

The management of SEN provision

The school also adopted a distinctive way of organising the management of special needs provision. Once the special classes and withdrawal system were disbanded, the teaching responsibilities of the school's existing SENCO were effectively at an end. She was, therefore, relieved of her duties and became Head of Religious Education.

In her place, one of the two deputy heads was given the responsibility of SENCO for the school and assumed particular responsibility for the small number of students at stage 4/5 of the Code of Practice, together with other statutory requirements associated with issues such as child protection and looked-after children. This deputy was also the senior manager with responsibility for finance and curriculum and was therefore, in principle at least, in a powerful position to support the implementation of the new approach to special needs education. However, the head and his deputy were both concerned that the SENCO should no longer be seen as the person with sole responsibility for special needs in the school. Accordingly, non-statutory special needs responsibilities were distributed across as many teachers as possible. For students placed at stage 2 or 3 responsibility was given to a Cross-Curriculum Co-ordinator (not a member of the senior management team). It was her task to co-ordinate IEPs, to allocate support and monitor the progress of students. For students at stage 1, responsibility was devolved to the other deputy head, who was also in charge of the guidance and counselling programme.

Within this structure, the formulation of IEPs was, as far as possible, devolved to heads of year. This reflected in part a desire to extend their role beyond a traditional concern with discipline. However, it may also have reflected the reality that many of the IEPs were in fact concerned with behaviour difficulties. In any case, once year heads had drawn them up, the implementation of IEPs was no longer to be the preserve of a SENCO working in isolation from mainstream classes and the mainstream curriculum. Instead, it was handed over to subject teachers who were to find ways of responding to special needs within their ordinary teaching. As the deputy head/SENCO put it,

I think the main thing is that it really flags up for every single teacher that it's *their* responsibility. You can't ignore this child.

However, the three managers did not entirely free themselves of the specialist role; although they might not be responsible for formulating IEPs, it was very much their job to co-ordinate the IEP process and maintain the records required by the Code of Practice; they also made specialist teaching and advisory inputs where the expertise of subject teachers was seen as inadequate and the new deputy head/SENCO had a particular role in respect of the traditional SEN concern of basic literacy; and it was their job to liaise with external agencies such as the Psychological Service and the Special Needs Support Service. Moreover, the new structure meant that the deputy head/SENCO, who was more experienced in special needs education than her colleagues, took greatest responsibility for those students who were seen as having the greatest special needs.

Management of behaviour

The management of behaviour was an area where particular changes were seen to be necessary. The previous headteacher, we were given to understand, had relied heavily on the positional authority of himself and a number of senior, male, staff. This was very much out of tune with the new head's more inclusive and participatory approach. The latter had, therefore, begun to replace this authoritarian stance with a style of behaviour management which relied much more on common understandings and clear expectations.

Accordingly, all of the staff in Seaview had collaborated in drawing-up a Classroom Behaviour Plan which was intended to inform the management of behaviour in the school. Parents were informed of this by letter and asked to endorse its principles. In his letter to parents, the headteacher stressed the role of the staff in 'emphasising clear and consistent expectations for classroom behaviour' and the importance of providing students with:

> positive recognition when they are doing what is asked of them, so that we improve self-esteem and increase the time spent on teaching and learning.

This emphasis on 'positive recognition' had initially caused some disquiet amongst staff, who felt that the very obvious support to their authority provided by the former head had suddenly been withdrawn. As one of the deputies put it to us,

> We had quite a lot of concerns about it last year, largely because management style within the school was different to what had gone before and we weren't going around berating and ranting

and so on at kids. The culture of dealing with kids with problems and difficulties and bad behaviour was different.

(Deputy head/SENCO)

In order to respond to these concerns, the senior management team felt it was necessary to replace the previous head's control with something different but equally powerful. Their chosen instrument was Assertive Discipline, a version of an American 'package' based on the principles of behaviour modification (Canter and Canter, 1976). The deputy head/SENCO explained its attractions in the following way:

It was very much a way of bringing coherence to the way things worked for children in school. It was also incredibly positive in that if it really works well, you create an incredibly positive reward-orientated ethos which is what we wanted rather than the negative disciplining ethos, so it supported the whole kind of special needs thing as well.

She added,

I think it helps the whole positive ethos of working with pupils with problems and it's working with them and it's not negative and that's what we've tried to develop on the special needs front – that everybody needs to work with these children, that they are not bad or wicked or thick, they've got a specific problem and we need to address it and that's everybody's role to do that.

Senior staff had attended a two-day training programme and an external trainer had been brought in to support the introduction of the programme throughout the school. This led to a further training initiative which extended over the course of a school year involving a series of 'twilight' sessions for all the staff. This, in conjunction with the programme of school-based training to encourage the use of more 'differentiated' approaches, represented a major investment of time on the part of the staff and was tangible evidence of the head's commitment to turning the school into a 'learning environment' for his teachers.

Responses and tensions

So far, we have tried to set out the head's 'vision' for the school and the practical steps that were taken to implement it. However, amongst the rest of the staff the responses to the new approach were mixed, to say the least. In this section, therefore, we will explore some of these responses and the reasons behind the doubts many staff were beginning to have.

Approaches and values

It will not have escaped readers' attention that it was the headteacher who was overwhelmingly responsible for setting out the new 'vision' of special needs education in Seaview. Whilst his deputy/SENCO was frequently to be found articulating elements of that vision, particularly in terms of their practical implications, there was very little evidence of other teachers doing the same.

To some extent, this could be accounted for in terms of a clear alternative view of special needs education which some staff appeared to hold. In some cases, for instance, there was evidence of values quite contrary to the inclusive and participatory stance of the head – such as the teacher who described a low-attaining teaching group in the following terms:

> Thursday is my worst day. I've got what I call the knackers.
>
> (Teacher B)

Another teacher similarly referred to 'scummy' students (Teacher C) whom he did not like teaching and who presented him with a number of behaviour problems.

Somewhat more elaborated was the view of the former SENCO. She had a series of concerns about the new approach:

> There is a lot of ill feeling; nobody really knows who is doing what. For example, the IEPs – nobody does them willingly. The paperwork is a bind to a lot of people. The school is just paying lip service to it. When it's [i.e. responsibility for meeting special educational needs] divided out to so many people, it's an impossible situation.
>
> (Teacher D)

She contrasted the apparent instability in the new arrangements with the certainty of the arrangements she had managed. For her, there were two key components in that approach. Firstly, there was what she described as, 'a lot of withdrawal by two key people for basic skills in English and Maths', and secondly, 'strict streaming which helped low ability learners'. This had resulted, she suggested, in a number of advantages, both academic and social:

> Pupils with SEN related to two key people and they were always entered for City and Guilds in English and Maths and it made the transition from primary to secondary easier.

She particularly felt that placing students with special needs into full-size sets worked to their disadvantage:

With the larger classes, and badly behaved pupils, the quieter ones with real learning difficulties don't stand a cat in hell's chance. That's always a bone of contention with me. The behaviour problems have worsened with a change of management.

She felt, moreover, that subject staff lacked expertise effectively to identify and meet the needs of all students in their classrooms:

A lot of staff who don't mark books are conned because children may be good orally but can't write effectively or read for information. More could be done for this type of child.

Such views were not confined to the former SENCO. A head of year, for instance, who, as such, was involved in formulating IEPs under the new system and who held a diploma in special needs education, spoke in glowing terms about the benefits of the now defunct withdrawal system:

[The former SENCO] came in and took out a group of people, well, a number of pupils and helped them and she had things like spelling workshops and helped them with their grammar and how to write things and they produced some wonderful work and the confidence given to those pupils was amazing . . . It really did help them and the pupils liked her and she only had them for a short while, perhaps a term, and they'd come up to me and say, 'Can we go back?' They didn't feel threatened for being withdrawn from classes because they feel different. They actually loved going because they were actually achieving something and they were special.

(Teacher E)

We also encountered a Maths teacher who expressed scepticism for current developments in terms of a commitment to what he saw as traditional values:

I suppose I'm more of the old school. You don't always have the time to sit down and explain. I'm here to teach Maths so this is how I want it to be. The modern trend – everybody's frightened of the word 'discipline'. There is a place for tolerance – you can't afford to confront – but you also need boundaries.

(Teacher F)

However, despite these dissident views, most staff at Seaview did not articulate elaborated ideologies of special educational needs, whether in line with or in opposition to that set out by the headteacher. Direct questions as to how they understood special needs or what they understood to be the purposes of the school's approach tended to elicit rather bland responses such as:

> Its aim is to recognise when particular pupils have particular problems
>
> (Teacher G)

or

> [the] special needs policy is structured to help the pupil to let them work on the strengths, recognise their weaknesses and perhaps do something about it.
>
> (Teacher H)

More important for the teachers seem to have been a set of pragmatic concerns. Even the teachers quoted above tend to have been concerned with pragmatic issues (how to manage classrooms, how to 'deliver' the curriculum, how to improve students' 'basic skills') first and foremost and to have been content for their ideological positions to remain implicit rather than explicit. The loosening of the setting system, for instance, tended not to be seen by Seaview teachers as an ideological matter (to do, say, with notions of participation and access) but as a practical issue: larger 'bottom' sets were more difficult to manage and made it more difficult to give students individual attention. Generally, there was a concern with managing a range of attainment in the same classroom and with the school's apparent lack of provision for 'more able' learners. There were (as we shall see) similar concerns with the practicalities of support teaching, IEPs and managing student behaviour. The consequence of this was that what we found was not resistance to the head's 'vision' based on a fully-articulated alternative ideology, so much as a concern with the practical implications of that vision and the way in which these impacted on the teachers' work.

Becoming inclusive

Likewise, the head's proposals for the school to include students with a wider range of special educational needs did not elicit any ideologically-based response from the staff. This seemed to be because, apart from the inclusion of one boy with visual impairment (who was in any case fully supported by an LSA), the head's proposals remained just that. As he himself acknowledged, he was forced to temper his 'vision' in the light of the practicalities of the school's situation. His proposal for a specific learning difficulties base, for instance, was not followed up by the LEA and he had to handle the more radical proposal for a sanctuary unit cautiously, because, he felt, it might provoke a backlash from parents and staff. He had contemplated a more thoroughgoing form of inclusion, he reported, but had come to the conclusion that:

> I wouldn't be able to do that here because of the background, middle class catchment area or whatever and their view of what education should be.

The head, however, fought the LEA's indifference to his proposals vigorously, saying:

> I have spoken against the authority's policies, both to the Director and to the Education Committee, because their policy is to take as many people and put them into special schools as possible and the reason for it is political, in the sense that there are factions based in [locality] and [locality] within the Council, each of whom have a special school on their patch. And they each like to see it there, 'for the bairns, the poor bairns'.

His view was that the LEA policies were fundamentally misguided:

> I think personally – and I have stated this to the Director of Education, if you like – they're wrong. They're wrong morally and they're wrong in educational terms, as far as I can see. But I do have to admit a prejudice, as I said before.

Despite this, however, he was not able to change those policies.

Support

A key feature of the new approach was the use of support teaching to ensure a greater inclusion of pupils in 'ordinary' classes. Views about its effectiveness were, however, mixed. For example, one head of department claimed that support

> is a big help, because if you have pupils with special needs, then it gives you extra help to target. When you haven't got the support teacher you can only do so much.
>
> (Teacher G)

For another head of department, however, there were a number of concerns which related to both the organisation and the actual mechanics of the process:

I don't think it's sorted out properly yet, I mean I was on French support last year and I was working with kids with special needs and they really, I was just handing out rulers and nagging at children for misbehaving which I don't think was a good use of anybody's time.

(Teacher I)

A number of factors seemed to be at work to explain these mixed responses. One was simply the personality – or perhaps, more accurately, the professional confidence – of the teacher in receipt of support. As one support teacher put it:

It's a very difficult thing to do really . . . Some teachers prefer just to be in a classroom by themselves and handle things the way they want but having somebody in your own room who is a colleague and a professional I think sometimes they find it a little bit daunting.

(Teacher J)

This in turn was compounded by the extent to which the students themselves reacted favourably to support:

You've got this double sided coin: do teachers want them there, do pupils want them there?

(Teacher J)

The consequence was that, as we ourselves observed, many support lessons took place where the relationship between the two teachers in the room was uncomfortable, if not downright hostile.

Another factor was the extent to which the role of the support teacher in the classroom was clearly defined. The teacher just quoted, for instance, characterised his role in the following way: 'I'll be there, yes, just around, sort of milling around helping the lower ones.'

However, for others, support was seen as something more targeted on individual students (such as the boy with visual impairment) whilst for others again, a somewhat wider role was possible. Support, said one teacher, offered opportunities for

observing and monitoring each other's lessons to expand the range of methods and strategies and then feed back to departmental meetings.

(Teacher K)

Such a view of the role clearly reflects the head's vision of reconstructing the school as a 'learning environment' for teachers. However, the extent to which support was able to serve this purpose seemed to be determined, in part at least, by whether the support teacher was a specialist in the subject being taught. If s/he were not, they became very much an 'extra pair of hands':

> I did find it helpful because it helps with the behaviour problems as well. I had a particularly big class, it was 28 which for a bottom set is not ideal really. They were able to go around and see to little things like having their pen, having their paper, having their book, things like that. So I did find that quite helpful but the people we had weren't French specialists at all so that's another thing as well. If you've got another French teacher in, that's even better you know. It certainly does help having another specialist in the room.
>
> (Teacher L)

Unfortunately, as the deputy head/SENCO explained, the matching of support teachers to subject areas was logistically difficult:

> It's not particularly brilliant – it doesn't work as effectively as it should do and I do think that's an issue we really need to look at. Learning support doesn't go first into the timetable if you see what I mean. Its unfortunately like in many places – it goes to the people who have time on their timetable. We do try to put it where it's needed – particular groups, not always the least able groups but where the challenging behaviour is.

Indeed, the extent to which the senior management team was willing to turn its avowed commitment to support into practical action remained in doubt. Not only did support not 'go first into the timetable', but it often seemed to be bottom of the list of priorities. During the course of our fieldwork, for instance, the deputy head/SENCO took the decision to give teachers an extra free period rather than increasing the level of support available. On another occasion, when she foresaw that one teacher was likely to need to take long-term sick leave, she loaded her timetable with support, 'to minimise disruption to the normal timetable'.

The lack of timetabling priority for support had consequences beyond the match with subject areas. One relatively inexperienced teacher, for instance, was puzzled that 'I don't have support in my classes but I'll support other teachers' (Teacher J). As he explained, 'That depends on timetabling and where things are going wrong'.

Indeed, the support teacher's role was often seen in these troubleshooting terms – as a means of helping individual students cope in ordinary classes, or of helping the class teacher cope with a difficult situation – particularly if those difficulties stemmed from behaviour problems in the class. Even though the 'bottom' sets were not large by the standards of most class sizes (15 students or so), we saw instances where the 'support' teacher was used, not even to help manage 'disruptive' students in the lesson, but to withdraw them when their behaviour became difficult. As the deputy head/SENCO implied, this view was to a significant extent officially sanctioned by the policy of allocating support not necessarily to students with learning difficulties and their classes, but to 'where the challenging behaviour is'. Under the circumstances, it is, perhaps, not too surprising that the 'milling around' notion of support teaching tended to dominate.

The SENCO role and IEPs

Other aspects of the new approach also generated difficulties. Individual education plans, for instance, were seen by the deputy head/SENCO as having a central function in the new approach to special educational needs:

> I think it has put issues of learning on everyone's agenda and I think that's very positive. People are talking about how I can access this kid, how I can do this, so I think that's part not just of the special needs, the whole change in the culture of the school in the last two years. The school is begining to talk about learning whereas it never did before.

However, even she expressed some ambivalence about their implementation:

> Not everyone operates an IEP as everyone else but I feel you get that anywhere in any institution. Most people are pretty good about filling them in; some are superb.

Other staff were much more critical. One head of department identified a number of very specific problems relating to IEPs:

> There is a limit to the time that HoDs can give to teachers to support the planning of individual work for pupils, therefore IEPs don't tend to be effective as a planning tool. The number of IEPs is increasing and they are a problem to distribute and collect – teachers tend to shelve them because they don't have time and they are difficult to implement in a classroom where there is no support – it's just not possible to support them without additional support given the size of the groups.
>
> (Teacher M)

This view was endorsed by other staff, who expressed concerns about what they regarded as the futility of the IEP system:

> sometimes it just seems you get these IEP forms and it's just a case of paper shuffling . . . I realise it's because of time and things, it's just that the feedback's not very good, you send stuff off to the senior management or whatever and you don't get a lot of feed-back about what's happening
>
> (Teacher C)

For others, there were concerns about which students were being given IEPs. One head of department referred to what he felt was an inconsistency in their use:

> I'm not happy with the range of children targeted – one girl has been identified and gets lots of help – many are missed. It's not worth identifying children in the [higher] sets as I know all those in the lower sets aren't receiving the additional support they need.
>
> (Teacher N)

To some extent, the difficulties with IEPs reflected a wider problem in the new approach to special needs. As we have seen, in order to avoid replicating a situation in which responsibility for special needs provi-sion was located in one individual, the head had established a some-what complex system of delegated responsibilities. He was satsified that this system was now working well:

> I think things are coming together reasonably well. Now I can sit back and leave it to [the deputy head/SENCO] as long as I know what's going on. And we're now trying to develop skills in the other middle managers by working together in small teams. We're offering support on a professional level and I say that be-cause we're a more professional school.

For others, however, the complex system did not lead to a greater sharing of responsibility – it simply led to greater complexity. The former SENCO characterised it as 'the blind leading the blind' and even teachers who were more favourably disposed to the new system confessed to some doubts. Asked if it was working well, for instance, one teacher commented:

> I sometimes think that some people need a bit of a reminder as to what exactly they should be doing and there are the odd prob-lems with information being passed on. That's really the main thing that I sometimes feel like I'm getting information a bit too

late. By the time I get any IEP sheets I'm about six weeks on and then I get this IEP sheet and I think, 'Well if I'd known about that I maybe could have been doing something different'.

(Teacher O)

The issue for such teachers was not, then, the ideology of the new system, but that it functioned inefficiently and made their tasks more difficult.

Managing behaviour

The ambiguities, differences and confusions amongst the staff were at their most marked in relation to the issue of behaviour management. Far from accepting greater responsibility for managing behaviour, as the head hoped, many staff shared the former SENCO's view that 'the behaviour problems have worsened with a change of management' and that, therefore, the problem was the head's rather than their own. In particular, they saw the move to larger 'bottom' sets as responsible for an increase in disruption. One teacher explained the interaction between set size, learning difficulties and behaviour problems in the following terms:

Of course when you get bottom sets as well you tend to usually get behaviour problems, stemming from the fact that it's because they are frustrated because they can't do the work and you can't give them the one to one attention.

(Teacher L)

Even the headteacher acknowledged this problem, though he tended to blame setting decisions made by subject departments themselves:

They're finding it very difficult in Science with the groups they've formed. One of the weaker teachers has had two riots over the last fortnight, with one of the all-boy classes and so we're going to have to look very carefully at that policy in the future.

The problem was compounded by the fact that girls tended to be heavily outnumbered by boys in 'bottom' sets and that 'most of the behaviour problems are boys' (Teacher G). The consequence of all this was that both special needs and behaviour difficulties tended to be conflated by teachers into a single issue to do with the manageability of these sets:

the biggest challenge I face is class sizes. When I first started I was doing work with [name]. There were nine in the class and that was lovely, whereas now it's a bit more hectic because the class sizes are bigger. It really is juggling so much you know, the behaviour as well as the special need, that's what I find.

(Teacher I)

The response of the school's management to this situation was to encourage staff to perceive behaviour difficulties as a *form* of special need, deserving the same sort of consideration and support. As the deputy head/SENCO put it:

They've just been considered naughty children, bad children, and we've done a lot of work linking in with the special needs side of things to support behaviour difficulties and emotional difficulties.

However, the consequence of this, as we saw above, was that a major element in the school's approach to special need – support teaching – became diverted into a means of behaviour management. As one teacher told us, when he was acting in a support role, he felt 'more of a policeman' than a teacher (Teacher B). Much the same fate befell the Assertive Discipline initiative. Although the deputy head/SENCO had high hopes that it would generate 'a whole positive ethos of working with the pupils with problems', we saw little evidence of this. Where Assertive Discipline was used (which, our observations suggested, was somewhat patchily), it appeared almost exclusively in its punitive aspect. Teachers were prepared to praise students, but tended not to use the structures of the behaviour management scheme to do this. The following sequence, from our observation notes, is typical. This was a French lesson with a 'bottom' year 8 set with 13 students – large by historical standards in Seaview – of whom eight were boys. The class teacher was valiantly trying to conduct the lesson in the target language:

9.40 a.m. At one point, [Student 1] asks for instructions in English, so that he can understand better. Instructions are repeated in French with more visual prompts, but at a very fast pace – constant commentary by Class Teacher, including an explanation of why she can't speak in English, which is lost on the group. [Student 1] and [Student 2] complain again that they don't understand. Concentration beginning to go at 9.45 a.m. Three warnings given when pupils begin to rumble and [Student 2] says again that he wants her to 'speak in English'.

10.02 [Student 2] given a 10 minute sanction.

Class teacher maintains continuous fast flow of instruction/ explanation with visual prompts.

10.00 – 10.15 a.m. Working in pairs – le visage – désume les yeux etc. Class more settled with the practical tasks of labelling and colouring worksheets

NB [observer's note] Assertive discipline – Classroom behaviour rules referred to at least 4 times during lesson. The need to warn/sanction appears to be induced by pupils' losing focus when they are attempting to interpret all instructions in French. (I find that my capacity to be an active listener has diminished considerably in the second half of the lesson!)

(Field notes)

Despite the efforts of the school to change the perception of and responses to behaviour difficulties and, indeed, despite the attempt to transform teaching and learning, in this case at least the unreconstructed cycle of inappropriate teaching, difficulties in learning, disruptive behaviour and punitive sanctions remains firmly in place.

The process of professional development

The various staff development initiatives also proved problematic, causing considerable resentment and provoking hostile reactions in many of the staff. As the headteacher explained:

> The staff development started off as a war of attrition involving unions and lots of other things, because change is difficult for people. Because we had a change of responsibilities where I appointed a third of the people on responsibility points. When I came there was a culture that said INSET was a laugh and pointless and certainly newly qualified teachers hadn't been on any courses even though they'd been in the school for five years.

The INSET programme, as we have seen, had a number of elements: firstly, training in the principles of Assertive Discipline; secondly, an introduction to the new systems and structures for managing special educational needs and, thirdly, sessions on developing alternative teaching strategies to enhance differentiation. The Assertive Discipline training was beginning to get under way whilst we were in the school, but received a mixed reception in its early stages. The issue was not that staff found the sessions irrelevant, but that they saw the system as having been imposed on them without discussion. This may well explain the rather patchy take-up which we observed earlier.

The differentiation training was delivered by the LEA support service and consisted, as the deputy head/SENCO described it, of:

A whole series of twilight sessions organised to look at the basics of literacy and how people could develop literacy skills in the context of the ordinary classroom. Everyone had a good sort of term's input on how you could work on basic literacy things in the context of the ordinary lesson. So that was a good grounding for everyone in the school at that time.

However, she was aware of certain weaknesses in this training and the consequences this was having for some of the staff:

Most of them found it interesting, it had more relevance for some than others, it was a bit problematic for the Languages department and Maths felt they needed some more specialist stuff.

A member of the Modern Languages Department put it somewhat more strongly:

We had a lot of in-service talks, you know, until 6 o'clock, 7 o'clock in the evening and that was the whole school and we found as I say that it was mainly geared towards English. Check the children's spelling and make sure they don't do such and such. But you can't do that in French because they haven't got the knowledge to be able to spell anyway, so it really was a waste of time. I think it ended up where the Maths people didn't have to attend as it was all English spelling, so it would have been far better in the English Department I think, but I felt, we felt, that for us it was a waste of time.

(Teacher L)

As the head of another department put it:

It's difficult when you have whole school INSET because sometimes if you are working with people who aren't in your department you feel as though you're doing it for the sake of it. I think when we're in our own departments it's quite useful to work on actual examples rather than just pontificating.

(Teacher I)

That these views reflect the somewhat bumpy road taken by this training initiative is clear. Whether, however, they constitute the headteacher's 'war of attrition' and whether they demonstrate that 'change is difficult for people' is another matter. The issue for the teachers we spoke to seemed to be not so much whether they were prepared to change as a result of training, but whether the training on offer related to what they understood to be the realities of their classrooms. Indeed, it was not uncommon for teachers to argue that they needed *more* training in order to cope with the changes introduced by the new head. Even the internally-promoted deputy admitted that she felt de-skilled by these changes and that 'maybe I need more expertise'. For some of them, therefore, training in the practicalities of literacy was very useful indeed and was gratefully received. For others, literacy skills in English were of limited relevance. Their reluctance to particip-ate is, therefore, scarcely surprising.

What is also evident from these comments is that the training pro-gramme on offer did not quite match the grand vision of school-as-learning-environment which the head articulated. The transformation of relationships within the school became reduced to training in a (poten-tially, at least) rather mechanistic behaviour management package. Similarly, the transformation of teaching and learning materialised as training in practical strategies for making worksheets accessible. More-over, the areas in which training was offered – behaviour management and literacy – were very much the historic territory of traditional special needs approaches. There seems, therefore, to have been little in this which was likely to turn teachers into reflective practitioners or transform their responses to the most problematic students.

Emerging issues

Trying to make sense of the changes at Seaview in the light of our concerns for 'embedded' and inclusive responses to special needs is deceptively simple. The mismatch between the head's 'vision' and what was actually happening in the school is so apparent and signifi-cant that it is tempting to look no further. However, it seems to us that Seaview may be more complex than it at first appears. In order to hold onto this complexity, therefore, we want to highlight at this stage some of the themes that emerge from our study of the school. In the following chapters, we will set these alongside the themes we identi-fied in our other schools and begin to explore the sorts of theoretical explanations which, together, they might call for.

The visionary head and the conservative context

We have seen throughout this chapter that the headteacher of Seaview was driven by a 'vision' of what his school should become and, in particular, of how it should respond to students with special needs. The problem for the head, of course, was that he was operating in a highly conservative (to say the least) context. He inherited a school which had seen little change since its grammar school days and where the external imperatives for change, given the apparent 'success' of the school, were minimal. Moreover, the school was part of a local education authority whose policies in special needs education were equally conservative.

Not surprisingly, therefore, there were conflicts between this 'visionary' head and the conservative elements on his own staff and in the LEA. The teachers who viewed students with special needs as 'the knackers' were unreceptive to the call for a transformation of teaching and learning, just as LEA decision-makers appear to have been unreceptive to his aim of becoming an inclusive school. The head himself was prone to seeing his situation as one of constant conflict, a 'war of attrition' with his staff over the professional development issue, for instance, together with a moral crusade which he was engaged in against the LEA over inclusion.

In fact, our own evidence suggests something less dramatic. We saw little open conflict, but we did identify the sorts of pressures and tensions just beneath the surface which we have described above. However, after we had left the school, these pressures began to erupt. The immediate trigger was a highly critical Ofsted report on the school which was published just over a year after our fieldwork was completed. It criticised the quality of teaching and learning, the progress made by students with special needs and, above all, the inadequacies of senior management, describing the school as having 'serious weaknesses'. Amidst growing discontent from the staff, the head took sick leave. When he returned, according to reports in the local press, the staff formally expressed their 'deep concern' about his ability to lead the school and supported a proposed plan of action drawn up by one of the deputy heads – the one who had been appointed from within the staff. The LEA became involved in disciplinary hearings against the head and ultimately he offered his resignation. He was replaced by a deputy head from another school in the same LEA.

The picture of a visionary head being undermined by more conservative forces is complete. If a combination of staff discontent and LEA intervention sealed the head's fate then the trigger was an inspection system which clearly placed less value on the head's capacity to hold onto a vision than on his more practical abilities to manage a complex institution and 'drive up' standards.

Mis-managed change

A second theme relates closely to the first. Many heads have grandiose 'visions' but manage to see them implemented in equally unpromising circumstances. There is, therefore, a clear sense in which the head mismanaged change in Seaview. Indeed, he himself admitted to weaknesses in his handling of change:

> We've tried to set up departments as quality circles and we tried, and failed initially . . . I should have done a 'Crazy Joe' really and been authoritarian, but I tried to be democratic as a leader and I tried to involve everybody and I didn't have the expertise to do it and it created a lot more problems, in hindsight, than if I had been more authoritarian.

Whether it was a more authoritarian approach that was needed, or a more diverse, subtle and all-embracing change strategy is a moot point. What is obvious is that neither the head, nor, come to that, his deputy/SENCO, seem to have had an effective means of sharing the 'vision' with their staff. Unlike some of our other schools – notably Moorgate – we did not find large numbers of staff able to articulate something that resembled the principles espoused by their senior managers. In many ways, the 'vision', like the head and the deputy, was 'parachuted' into the school and seems neither to have been 'sold' to them vigorously nor built up consensually from their own views and concerns. Instead, what the head seems to have preferred is to initiate change by manipulating the surface structures of the school – the organisation of special needs provision, for instance – and by subjecting (perhaps not too strong a word) his staff to training. It is no coincidence that Seaview is the only school where our own presence was not fully negotiated with the staff. Our invitation to participate was accepted by the head and his deputies and then other staff were simply informed that the school was taking part and, in some cases, that they would be required for interview. Needless to say, this caused us some difficulties in overcoming the resentment which this generated.

   In other, more favourable circumstances, such strategies may have been effective. In the unpromising situation which Seaview represented when he took over, they seemed to have little prospect of success.

A pragmatic staff

Tempting as it might be to explain the whole of what we found in Seaview in terms of these first two themes, that would be to overlook other themes that seemed to emerge. In particular, although the staff of the school may have been somewhat conservative in their approach they were not – at least while we were in the school – openly resistant. In particular, they were not resistant on explicitly *ideological* grounds. Certainly, we encountered embittered and embattled individuals – the former SENCO in particular. Certainly, too, the anxieties of some of the staff – over behaviour, for instance – increased while we were working in the school. For the most part, however, teachers were concerned with what they saw as the practicalities of their work. As we have seen, what mattered to them was not whether inclusion, or participation, or the transformation of teaching and learning were ideologically sound, but how their practical implications – restructuring 'bottom' sets, using in-class support, the IEP system, managing behaviour and so on – impacted on their work in classrooms.

This does not mean, of course, that the views of staff did not have implicit ideological underpinnings. However, ideological debate as such was absent from this school in a way that it was not in some others. Instead, there was, for much of the time, a *disengagement* between teachers' work and the headteacher's vision. Only when the vision impinged directly on their work and made it more (or, occasionally, less) difficult, were they concerned to address its implications. Even then, their pleas were not so much for an entirely different approach, but for practical help (support, training, behavioural strategies) in the implementation of that vision.

The ambiguity of the vision

Superficially, the head's vision constituted a clear and coherent view of how the school might become an inclusive institution, with the diversity of students responded to through flexible forms of teaching and learning and with, consequently, no necessity for segregated special needs systems and provisions. Beneath this surface, however, the vision was marked by deep ambiguities.

These seemed to be of two types. First, it was never entirely clear to us just how radical the head's vision actually was. We have seen how his notion of an inclusive school was reduced in practice to a modest proposal for a dyslexia unit which came to naught and an even more ambiguous idea for a 'sanctuary' which never even reached the proposal stage. Similarly, although there were radical restructurings of the management of special needs provision in the school, the restructuring of student grouping arrangements was far less ambitious. The school remained firmly committed to setting practices. Indeed, it is arguable that the head's only achievement in this respect was to increase the size of the 'bottom' set and thus make the provision more not less segregatory.

The restructuring of the special needs system is a further example. Students with special needs were still identified separately from their peers, still received distinct forms of provision – not exclusively in withdrawal situations, perhaps, but certainly in terms of in-class support and individual plans – and still remained the responsibility of specialist staff. There was no attempt, as we have occasionally encountered in other schools (Clark *et al.*, 1995b; Dyson, Millward and Skidmore, 1994), to abolish the special needs infrastructure entirely and to reconceptualise individual differences in a radically new language.

There is a second sort of ambiguity which seems evident in Seaview. Even where the head's vision was turned into (sometimes radical) action, it is noticeable how often its high intentions became translated into something much less far-reaching. The notion of changing teachers' approaches to teaching is a particularly salient example of this. In practice, the 'learning community' of the school became transmuted into a twilight course on literacy on the one hand and a rather bureaucratic system for managing IEPs on the other. A set of transformed relationships with and attitudes towards students with behaviour difficulties became the use of support and Assertive Discipline as mechanisms of control. In the same way, the attempt to get everyone to share responsibility for students with special needs manifested itself as a complex structure in which there were more managers of special needs provision than ever before. As one teacher put it, without a trace of irony, when asked if the school's special needs policy was working:

> Oh I think so, yes. We've always got bits of paper to fill in.
>
> (Teacher L)

Readers will not be unaware that some similar themes have surfaced before in our other schools. In the next chapter, therefore, we will examine these themes across the four schools and begin to consider what sort of account might fit our findings as a whole.

7

Common Themes

_____

Responding to diversity

In previous chapters we have described in some detail the evolving situation in four schools as they implemented more inclusive forms of provision. In each of the schools we identified both the positive steps which the schools were taking towards greater inclusion and a number of emerging issues which appeared to be threatening those developments. In this chapter, we will explore what the stories of the four schools have in common and in what ways they are different from each other.

A model of 'the inclusive school'?

Although the four schools were making different levels of progress towards more inclusive provision, it is possible to detect beneath those different developments a common model of what a more inclusive school might look like and how it might come into being. For instance, in each school there was a leadership which was committed to inclusive principles and which drove developments forward on the basis of those principles. In Lakeside, St Joseph's and Seaview, that leadership was provided by a headteacher with a clear 'vision' of the direction in which the school should move. In Moorgate, the head was moving cautiously following his relatively recent appointment – though he was beginning to articulate a clearer vision towards the end of our fieldwork. However, there was a much more consensual view of how the school should be than in the other cases and, moreover, the SENCO was a major driving force, respected by her colleagues even though she was located at the middle rather than the top of the school's hierarchy.

The schools also shared a real attempt to dismantle some of the structures and barriers which have traditionally typified special needs education and to replace them by a response to diversity which was more clearly located in the mainstream curriculum and classroom. The structural changes were most obvious in Seaview, where the SENCO role was distributed amongst a range of senior and middle managers, and in Lakeside, where a new senior role was carved out which extended well beyond the traditional boundaries of special needs education. In St Joseph's and Moorgate, traditional structures were retained, but here they were used for somewhat less traditional purposes – the delivery of a 'thinking skills' approach in one school and an attempt to develop collaborative approaches in the mainstream classroom in the other. In all of the schools, moreover, this restructuring meant that the traditionally low status of special needs provision was boosted – by a relocation of responsibility at senior management level, by the clear support of senior managers for the SENCO or by the involvement of the SENCO in management decision-making.

In all of the schools, too, these structural changes were accompanied by two further strategies. The first was a heavy reliance on in-class support as a means of maintaining students in the ordinary classroom. This was most obvious at Moorgate, where an army of sixth-form students supplemented the work of special needs staff, and at Lakeside, where LSAs performed a similar role. Such support was in turn linked to the second strategy – an emphasis on the professional development of staff as a means of embedding responses to diversity in the ordinary classroom. In some cases, this development took the form of fairly traditional training events, particularly centring on the theme of 'differentiation'. In other cases, however, it was seen as taking place through the establishment of collaborative relationships between staff with a specialism in special needs education and mainstream teaching staff, or indeed, amongst mainstream teaching staff themselves. Again, Moorgate was furthest advanced in this sense, with its developmental conception of in-class support, its SENCO with an overt orientation to the development of her mainstream teacher colleagues and the regular meetings of its peer support group.

Finally, three of the four schools were inclusive in the sense that they were deliberately trying to extend the range of students for whom they made provision. Lakeside, in particular, educated students who in most other parts of the country would have been placed in special school – and, moreover, it made every effort to include them not just in the building, but in ordinary lessons. At Seaview and Moorgate, working within less inclusive LEA contexts, inclusion had to be more a matter of intent and opportunism than of structural change (though there were plans for such a change in place at Seaview). Only St Joseph's was not inclusive in this sense, but even here the vision of students' potential was an essentially inclusive one and, we should remember, the school was already educating a wider range of students than its counterparts and competitors in the local Catholic schools hierarchy.

Despite the differences between these schools, then, there is an important sense in which they represent some common features of the 'inclusive school'. These features – visionary leadership, the dismantling of separate special needs structures, the development of mainstream teachers, the embedding of teaching practices and support mechanisms in the ordinary classroom – are, not surprisingly, close to those which we identified in our original study of 'innovatory' schools (Clark *et al.*, 1995b). Indeed, they have much in common with the characterisations of inclusive schools which, as we saw in Chapter 2, are beginning to emerge from a range of national contexts. To this extent, therefore, our work lends weight to the possibility that there may indeed be a model to which all would-be inclusive schools have to conform and which they can use to guide their development.

Inclusion and change

There is a further characteristic which all four of our schools share: in each case, inclusion is understood as a process. Unfortunately, this notion has recently become something of a cliché. However, we wish to use it in two quite specific senses.

First, in each of the four schools, the move to inclusion is seen as involving a process of structural change. In Seaview, for instance, that change coincided with the appointment of a new headteacher who set about the 'dismantling' process we described above. Even in Moorgate, however, where the current structures had been in place for many years, some staff were able to recall the time in the past where the current SENCO made her mark by shifting from a traditional out-of-class to what was then a radical in-class form of provision.

Second, and perhaps more important, there was a sense in each school that the change process was not a once-and-for-all structural reorganisation, but a continuing dynamic process in which practices had to be continually reoriented in a more inclusive direction. The heads of three of the schools, at least, and the SENCO at Moorgate clearly saw themselves as involved in what Vlachou (1997) calls 'struggles for inclusive education'. Indeed, for Seaview's head, the battle against his non-inclusive LEA was one which, it is arguable, contributed to his losing his job. Not surprisingly, therefore, the changes introduced in each school set in place dynamic mechanisms –

committed senior personnel, professional development processes, collaborative approaches, the progressive extension of the range of diversity in the student body – which would constantly problematise non-inclusive practices wherever they re-emerged and thus ensure the continuation of this struggle. It is in this respect, perhaps, that the schools come closest to Skrtic's (1991a) 'adhocracies' and Ainscow's (1999) 'moving schools', constantly exploring new ways of responding to an ever-greater range of student diversity.

The cohesiveness of the inclusive vision

It is at this point, however, where we have to begin to consider, not just the visionary direction plotted by heads, and not just the (relatively) straightforward structural changes which these managers were able to engineer, but some of the problems and ambiguities which characterised each of our schools. Our starting point in each of the four schools was an attempt to understand the 'vision' of the headteacher, to elicit their motivation and to establish the reason for their commitment to this principle. In pursuit of these aims we encouraged the headteachers to expand on their own biographies and to reflect on personal and professional experiences which might have influenced their thinking.

It was not therefore completely surprising to find that in each of the schools the origins of the commitments were somewhat different. For the headteacher in Seaview a crucial motivating force was his experience with his own son which convinced him of the moral 'rightness' of an inclusive approach. In Moorgate, on the other hand, it was an endorsement on the part of the headteacher of the concept of 'comprehensive' education which fuelled his commitment to the inclusive principle. As one of the 'first wave' of comprehensive schools the notion of a 'comprehensive intake' had become deeply ingrained in the culture of the school and was widely reflected in the way that the majority of staff spoke about student diversity.

For the Principal in Lakeside, inclusion had what we might call a political dimension, reflecting a commitment to and solidarity with the needs of the local community. His view of the school as needing to serve *all* the members of the local community was at the heart of the inclusive approach which the school sought to develop. In St Joseph's, the commitment to inclusion was shaped by two factors: the membership of a faith community with a particular view on the value of all individuals; and the headteacher's own commitment, strongly influenced by his studies in developmental psychology, to a notion of the innate potential of all students.

For these somewhat different reasons, then, the four headteachers sought to articulate their vision of an 'inclusive' school and to create the systems and structures through which it might be realised. For each of them, 'inclusion' was more part of their personal agenda than an externally-imposed requirement – though they were all acutely aware of the national policy context within which they had to operate. In effect, therefore, they were asking their staff to assimilate a heady mix of personal motivations and understandings combined with sometimes contradictory national policy imperatives. In this context it is hardly surprising that we began to identify some difficulties in establishing a whole school view of 'inclusion' for each of the individual schools let alone any common understanding between the schools.

Not surprisingly, therefore, the extent to which these visions were shared across the school was in some doubt. To a certain extent, this was simply a matter of 'resistance'. Given a radical vision, emerging out of a personal agenda and calling upon others to make significant and often uncomfortable changes in their practice, some overt or covert opposition is, perhaps, inevitable. In Seaview and St Joseph's particularly, the somewhat radical changes to rather conservative structures and cultures produced a backlash that might have been predicted. However, even Lakeside and Moorgate had their dissidents, despite the forceful leadership that characterised one and the long evolutionary process of development that characterised the other.

There was, however, more to the breakdown of consensus in these schools than simple resistance. Indeed, given the radical direction in which a literal interpretation of the heads' visions would have taken these schools, what is perhaps most surprising is the degree of consensus which they were able to command even in the more troubled settings. That apparent consensus, however, masked a process whereby the headteachers' idealistic visions became translated into something subtly different as they encountered the realities of classrooms, students and teachers' existing practices. We noted, for instance, how in Seaview the head's attempt to create a school which was 'a more humanistic thing, a holistic thing of treating children as a whole' became reduced to a series of operational initiatives – a rather bureaucratic system for producing IEPs, a somewhat narrowly-conceived programme of training, a largely punitive version of Assertive Discipline, and so on. In St Joseph's, likewise, the high rhetoric of the head's commitment to releasing the potential of all students translated itself into the practicalities of 'bottom' sets taught by special needs staff. The release of individual potential thus seemed to rely as much on conventional strategies to improve literacy as any 'breakthrough' from the thinking skills approach.

In Lakeside and Moorgate, the gap between rhetoric and reality was less overt, but it was, nonetheless, very real. The inclusive aims of both schools, for instance, were translated into an army of support personnel whose role was, to say the least, ambiguous. They may or may not, in some settings, have been bringing about a fundamental change of teaching practice in order to create inherently inclusive classrooms. However, they most certainly were also offering a means of managing troublesome students in classrooms which remained somewhat hostile to their learning needs.

Given this process of 'translation', overt resistance was, in effect, unnecessary, since the radical implications of the heads' visions were consistently deflected into more modest changes on the ground. Moreover, this process was assisted by inherent ambiguities in the visions themselves. The rhetoric of 'the comprehensive ideal', the 'community school', or whatever may well have acted to rally a diverse staff around an apparently consensual approach and to legitimate certain new practices. In this sense, they acted as what Edelman (1964) calls 'condensation symbols', enabling somewhat nebulous values and aspirations to 'condense' around a single notion. However, vital as this function might be in stimulating and legitimating change, it is evident that these rallying cries did not offer more precise guidelines as to what was and was not acceptable within the schools. Hence, each school retained a set of practices – setting by attainment, disciplinary exclusion, an intake restricted in terms of the range of special educational needs it contained, punitive approaches to behaviour management and so on – which stood in apparent contradiction to the rallying cry on the one hand, but seemed to cause no significant discomfort to the heads or other key players on the other.

There is, however, no need to impute bad faith to the heads and others. In attempting to chart a course for change amidst the complex realities of schools, they were able to indicate a broad direction in which they wished to move their colleagues. What they could not do, it would appear, is to plot the detail of the journey or to guarantee that at any given point they would not be living with significant contradictions between where they believed themselves to be heading and where they actually were. Whether this was a merely temporary state of affairs or something endemic in the inclusion project is an issue to which we will, in due course, return.

The technology of inclusion

The issue of what happens to the inclusive vision as it is translated into practice brings us inevitably to what we might call the 'technology' of inclusion. Extending the range of student diversity which can be accommodated in a regular school or classroom demands more than simply a commitment to particular values – essential though such a commitment might be. It also calls for a series of structures and practices through which the learning needs of a wider range of students can be met. In this sense, there is a 'technology' of inclusion – a technology which, in our case-study schools, took the form of in-class support, a restructured SENCO role, an emphasis on differentiation and so on.

What is striking as we look across the schools, however, is that the various aspects of this emerging technology were all seriously problematic. This was perhaps most evident in respect of in-class support. This was, as we have seen, delivered by a range of personnel – specialist teachers, subject teachers, specially-trained LSAs, relatively untrained LSAs and even sixth-formers – in a range of contexts: full-size classes, small 'bottom' sets, on a team basis with two subject-specialist teachers, as a form of general classroom assistance, as a form targeted support to a specified individual, with higher and lower levels of co-operation between the personnel, with higher and lower levels of pre-planning, and so on. It is hardly surprising, therefore, that the practice of in-class support was highly variable and offered no guarantees of minimum standards of provision.

Moreover, there was an evident gap between the demand for support and its availability. As the range of student diversity increased so the demands for support began to outstrip its supply. This led to a reliance on support personnel with very limited training (even sixth-formers in Moorgate) or with a specialism which the class teacher felt was inappropriate and detrimental to their effectiveness. It also meant that support for most students tended to be available only on a limited basis, frequently governed by timetabling logistics rather than any notion of 'need'.

This situation reflected a more fundamental tension in these schools' reliance on in-class support. Some of the heads and SENCOs clearly saw support teaching as a means of bringing about change in the practices of ordinary subject teachers. Certainly, there was an implicit assumption in all of the schools that in-class support was a means whereby students with special educational needs could 'access' the curriculum and be maintained in ordinary classrooms. In practice, however, where support was not allocated simply on the basis of logistical necessity, it tended to go where things were seen to be 'going wrong' – particularly where students' behaviour was becoming difficult for the class teacher to manage.

Under the circumstances, the evidence that support teaching was producing significant changes in ordinary classrooms and the practice of ordinary teachers was limited. Certainly, such evidence was occasionally forthcoming. Certainly, too, many – if not all – teachers welcomed the availability of support in their lessons. However, it was never entirely clear that the effect of support was to transform teaching, or even simply to help class teachers – or whether it was simply to maintain the *status quo* by offering teachers a trouble-shooter whenever things 'went wrong'.

Across the four schools, we noted similar ambiguities in respect of differentiation and the role of the SENCO. There were, without doubt, examples of imaginative teaching, successfully encouraging the participation of a wide range of students. There was also a real attempt in each of these schools to redefine the SENCO's role and instances where the 'reconstructed' SENCO operated as a major driving force in the move to greater inclusion. However, in both these areas, breakthroughs of this kind were sporadic and limited in scope rather than sustained and systemic. The limited observations of teaching we undertook suggested that, in all the schools, the principal mechanisms for responding to the individual characteristics of particular students were the widespread use of setting by attainment and the use of in-class support where available. Similarly, the SENCO was at least as likely to be found teaching students excluded from other classrooms, or trouble-shooting on behalf of colleagues, or managing bureaucratic systems as s/he was to be leading the development of significantly new and more inclusive practice.

What is evident from all of these aspects of the schools' approaches is that the technology through which their commitment to inclusion was to be realised was, indeed, deeply problematic. Not only was it often inadequate – in the sense that there simply was not enough of it to meet the demands that were made of it – and incomplete – in that it appeared patchily and spasmodically – but it was also ambiguous. Whatever the rhetoric, the structures and practices that were intended to support inclusion were just as likely to be used to maintain a rather non-inclusive *status quo*.

Moreover, given these inadequacies, it is perhaps not too surprising that some of the more overt forms of segregated special education were still maintained. We have already referred to the widespread use of setting by attainment. The appearance of small groups of low-attaining students – some of whom were well-motivated but found learning in other contexts difficult, some of whom were regularly disruptive – was a recurrent feature of our observations. Whatever the pros and cons of such an approach, it is, of course, one which would have been familiar to the pioneers of 'special classes' in the 1960s.

Similarly, the withdrawal of students from their classes for individual or small-group tuition was a standard practice in all of the schools. It was taken for granted that it was students 'with special educational needs' who should be withdrawn and, more often than not, the focus of the withdrawal sessions was on the teaching of 'basic' literacy and numeracy skills. Moreover, there was a suspicion – to put it no more strongly – that in some cases students were withdrawn as much to ease the burden on the class teacher as for their own benefit, particularly in situations where there were high levels of classroom disruption. Whatever the truth of this, just as 'bottom sets' looked like a hangover from the 1960s, so withdrawal would not have been out of place in the forms of special needs provision which predated the whole school approach. In these respects at least, the technology of inclusion looked uncannily like the technology of segregation.

Responding to behaviour problems

In all four of the schools, the ambiguities and tensions which surrounded the move towards greater inclusion became acute where students' behaviour presented difficulties to their teachers. The schools used a variety of strategies to manage these difficulties: diverting support teachers and LSAs to trouble spots, excluding problematic students from classrooms or the school as a whole, adopting punitively-oriented classroom-management techniques, and, of course, wittingly or unwittingly, concentrating students whose behaviour was difficult in low-attaining sets. All of these strategies raise questions about the realisation of greater inclusion.

In Seaview and Moorgate, the use of in-class support as a major strategy for responding to behaviour difficulties meant that significant amounts of human resource were tied up in, effectively, policing classrooms. The establishment of a behaviour support team at Lakeside and the reinforcement of the special needs team at St Joseph's by a teacher who established himself as an 'expert' in dealing with behaviour difficulties were superficially different strategies, but still involved directing additional resources at the apparent problem. In each case, these strategies diverted these resources from supporting the development of mainstream teaching practices into systems that seem to have been aimed primarily at maintaining the *status quo*.

The use of classroom and school exclusion was even more deeply ambiguous. In both Lakeside and Seaview, particularly, there were occasions when groups rather than individual students were excluded. In the course of our fieldwork a group of year 7 students were excluded from Seaview – albeit on a temporary basis – apparently as a signal to the whole of that year group as to where the boundaries of acceptable behaviour were in the school. Such actions were described by the headteacher of Lakeside, for example, as 'pragmatic decisions' a price that had to be paid to maintain 'the vision of equity'. It may be that this was indeed a 'price worth paying' for the stability of the school community as a whole. However, it is evident that reconciling an inclusive commitment with the exclusion of students means, at the very least, the translation of that commitment into something quite different from its original, rhetorical form.

The policy context

Although our attention was, as in much other inclusive schooling research, focused on the schools themselves, it is apparent that what was happening inside those schools could not be divorced from the policy context within which they were located. At the local level, the schools' moves towards inclusive approaches were set within the context of LEA policies which were themselves more or less inclusive. At the extremes, Lakeside had been specifically designated by its LEA as an area resource for students with learning difficulties, whilst the head at Seaview felt that he had to battle for his school to become more inclusive against the distinctly segregatory policies of his LEA.

Beyond these local variations, however, none of the schools could ignore the national policy context which was created by the establishment of an educational market-place, the introduction of the National Curriculum, the opening up of schools to publicly reported inspection and scrutiny through performance 'league tables', and the requirement that they 'have regard to' the Special Educational Needs Code of Practice. In Moorgate and Lakeside, the impact of this policy context was marked as each school was locked in competition with a neighbouring rival. It was this competition which, on the one hand, made senior managers at Moorgate somewhat cautious about becoming known as a school that was 'good at special needs' while on the other giving impetus to Lakeside's Principal's determination to market the College as a school for the whole community, in distinction to the selective policies of his neighbour.

At St Joseph's and Seaview, on the other hand, pressures of competition were, for differing reasons, less intense. However, they both fell foul of the Ofsted inspection regime in dramatic fashion. At the very least, the combination of public scrutiny and the need for all schools to maintain a positive public image meant that their headteachers were ultimately unable to push change through in the face of anxieties from staff within the school and parents and LEAs outside.

Moreover, all four schools had to contend with a National Curriculum which was widely seen as too rigid to accommodate the diverse range of students' learning needs and a Code of Practice which imposed significant bureaucratic burdens. Whatever their aspirations in terms of extending inclusive practices, therefore, parameters were defined for them externally. Given the imminence of inspection and the vigilance of at least some parents regarding their children's provision, they would have been foolhardy in the extreme to take innovation too far. It is necessary to look no further than the dim view that Ofsted took of the 'multiple innovations' at St Joseph's to see what the dangers might be.

The role of senior management

This reference to Ofsted inspections serves as a timely reminder that there were two important respects in which these schools differed from one another. Although they were all moving in a similar direction, their journeys had somewhat different starting points and they were currently being led by very different headteachers and senior managers. In terms of history, the sharpest contrast was between Moorgate, which had a long history of progressive development, and Seaview, where a new head and deputy had been 'parachuted in' to a somewhat conservative setting. In terms of management, the contrast was perhaps between the experienced, assertive and clear-sighted head of Lakeside and the idealistic but somewhat out-of-touch head of St Joseph's.

Under these circumstances, there were different change processes in each school being managed by individuals with different approaches and, perhaps, different levels of skill. The consequences were, perhaps, predictable. Moorgate and Lakeside had experienced headteachers working in a context where change had been ongoing for some time. They were assisted by SENCOs who were themselves experienced, skilled and held in high regard by their colleagues. Not surprisingly, these were the schools which appeared most stable, where levels of consensus seemed highest and where the move towards greater inclusion seemed most successful. In St Joseph's and Seaview, by contrast, various combinations of headteacher miscalculation, staff conservatism and a rapid attempt to radicalise practice generated tension, discord and, ultimately, public failure.

Given these differences, the task of disentangling the common features which the schools shared becomes complex. Even more so is the task of disentangling those features of the schools which are not only common to all of them, but which arise from their common move towards more inclusive practices. This is a task to which we shall turn fully in the next chapter.

An overview and a puzzle

For now, then, what can we say about these four schools? First, despite the surface differences of their approaches and despite the differences which arise from their varied contexts and the skilfulness or otherwise with which the process of change was managed, we can detect across the four sites a common model of how schools become more inclusive and what an 'inclusive school' might look like. Despite the problems which each school experienced, that model seems to confirm much of what has been learned from moves towards greater inclusion in other sites and seems to suggest that there is indeed a direction for development which can now be charted with some confidence.

However, it is equally evident that the move towards greater inclusion is not a serene journey to some unequivocally better place. Quite apart from the inherent difficulties of managing change and the perhaps inevitable doubts and resistances from some members of staff, other problems and difficulties begin to appear in these schools. As each school's distinctive but nonetheless apparently clear vision of inclusion encounters the daily realities of teachers, students and classrooms, something strange and troubling happens to it. It becomes translated into practices and structures which are less than, or even incompatible with itself. Its nebulous and ambiguous nature becomes exposed. The very practices and structures which are intended to realise the vision themselves become ambiguous, not only inadequate to the task but actually sustaining an approach which appears inimical to the vision itself. Moreover, all of this takes place within an external policy context which limits the freedom of action of managers and teachers in the schools and which demands the pursuit of goals which are, if not opposed to the original vision, at least significantly different from it.

It is, perhaps, the notion of ambiguity which most accurately captures what happens in these schools. What we have is neither unequivocally inclusive, nor unequivocally non-inclusive; instead, we have a complex interaction of more and less inclusive tendencies. This ambiguity and this complexity may be explicable in terms of what we already know about change in schools and, particularly, about the processes of creating inclusive schools. However, they do, we suggest, call for *some* sort of explanation and, in the next chapter, this is precisely what we shall attempt.

8

Explaining Ambiguity: Competing Theories

In the previous chapter, we explored the successes, but also the problems and difficulties which characterised our case-study schools. We made the claim that these schools were moving in a more inclusive direction; indeed, we suggested that they might imply a model of inclusive schooling that confirmed that which we had discovered in our earlier work and which seemed to offer a basis for the development of inclusive schooling elsewhere. Nonetheless, we also came to the conclusion that these schools were characterised by degrees of complexity and ambiguity which called for a different kind of explanation. The purpose of this chapter is to explore what sorts of explanations we might begin to offer.

Adhocratic and moving schools: the explanatory power of Skrtic and Ainscow

In Chapter 2, we argued that the work of Ainscow and Skrtic offered the best theoretical accounts currently available of the relationship between inclusion and schools as organisations. Both emphasise the importance of collaborative problem-solving facilitated through fluid organisational structures as a means of enabling schools and their teachers to respond to a diversity of student characteristics. Both also suggest that such problem-solving approaches obviate the need for rigidly-segregated special needs education structures. The obvious starting point for our exploration, therefore, is to consider how far Ainscow and Skrtic are capable of illuminating what we discovered in our case-study schools.

In terms of understanding the more positive aspects of what we found, it is clear that notions of problem-solving within a fluid structure – of 'adhocratic' or 'moving' schools – have much to offer. All

four of the schools were, for instance, in one way or another attempting to break down the rigid barriers between special needs education
and mainstream education – by, for instance, reconstructing the
SENCO as a supporter of and change agent for teachers, or distribut-
ing the SENCO role across a range of staff, or moving students with
significant difficulties into mainstream classrooms, or bringing all students under the aegis of a 'thinking skills' approach.

In each case, this meant, to a greater or lesser extent, casting ordinary teachers in the role of problem-solvers insofar as it became their
responsibility to find ways of educating a wider range of students. In
some of the schools, notably Moorgate, this expectation was conveyed
through the encouragement, advocacy and even cajolery of the
SENCO; in others, notably Seaview, it was formalised through the IEP
system and the symbolic removal of the former SENCO who had
offered a means of removing problematic students from ordinary
classrooms. However, the expectation of problem-solving also
brought with it opportunities for collaboration. In all of the schools, in-
class support was seen as a key component in enabling teachers to
respond to diversity and in at least three of them (Lakeside, Moorgate
and Seaview), there was an explicit expectation that there would be
some sort of pooling of skills between class teacher and support personnel. Together, therefore, they would be able to provide the sort of
differentiated access to the mainstream curriculum which neither of
them could provide separately.

In some of the schools, the impetus for collaboration was greater
still. Seaview's 'distributed' SENCO role, for instance, called for collaboration between class teachers, year heads and senior managers in
formulating responses to particular children's difficulties. Perhaps,
above all, in Moorgate, there was a long-established tradition of
shared decision-making; this was, for instance, the most difficult
school for us as researchers to gain access to, simply because the head
insisted on a multi-layered consultation process involving all of the
staff in some depth. Not surprisingly, therefore, not only did we find
Moorgate's SENCO operating in a determinedly collaborative mode,
but it was she who set up the peer support group which formalised a
notion of collaborative problem-solving as a major strategy for responding to student diversity.

Above all, perhaps, each of the four schools can be seen as a
'moving' school in the sense that it was examining critically its own
practices and making a serious attempt to reconstruct them in the
interests of greater equity. As we indicated in the previous chapter,
not only were changes currently under way in each of the schools, but
they tended to have established within themselves mechanisms which

ensured an ongoing process of critical review and development. None of these schools was 'coasting' in a state of complacent acceptance of its current practices. On the contrary, they were characterised by the discomfort and occasional conflicts which arguably are the inevitable consequence of a continuing process of development.

To this extent, Ainscow and Skrtic are useful in explaining how these schools were able to move in the direction of greater inclusion. However, they are also useful in explaining some of the difficulties encountered by the schools. In particular, many of the complexities and ambiguities we noted can be explained in terms of the schools' failure to go far enough along the route of adhocratic problem-solving. This is perhaps most noticeable in St Joseph's. Here, despite an apparently radical curriculum approach which promised to make traditional categories of and approaches to 'special educational needs' redundant, the structures of the school remained essentially unchanged. Setting by attainment, a separate team of special needs teachers led by a relatively low-status SENCO, separate groups of low-attaining students following a somewhat separate curriculum and withdrawal for literacy tuition all remained intact – as indeed, did the conventional decision-making structure of head and senior management team.

A similar conservatism can be observed in all of the schools. For instance, the role of the SENCO was extended, distributed and otherwise reconstructed in each school. However, in one form or another, the role remained in place and, to that extent at least, separate mainstream and special needs structures were left intact. Similarly, if there was collaboration between teachers and support personnel, that collaboration was, as we have seen, somewhat sporadic. Moreover, it often seemed to be a collaboration in which traditional hierarchical relationships remained intact; whatever LSAs, sixth-formers and non-subject-specialist teachers might bring to the mainstream classroom, there was no doubt that it was the subject teacher who remained firmly in charge.

Perhaps above all, it was in the schools' responses to behavioural problems that their innate conservatism was most apparent. It is at least arguable that the more students threatened the *status quo*, the less likely they were to generate a problem-solving response. Instead they were 'managed' in the classroom, or removed from it or, in the final analysis, excluded from the school altogether. The schools were indeed, as Ainscow and Skrtic suggest, prepared to use the difficulties presented by students as a means of reviewing and developing their own practices – but only up to a point. When those difficulties seemed to threaten rather than question, problems were less likely to be solved creatively than to be managed out of existence.

What is not explained

In these respects, Ainscow and Skrtic offer illuminating explanations of what we found in our schools. In return, our case studies lend empirical weight to the more theoretical aspects of their accounts. However, in reviewing Ainscow and Skrtic's work in Chapter 2, we also highlighted what we saw as some limitations in their approaches. It is at this point where those limitations become significant. We argued, in particular, that Ainscow and Skrtic offer powerful heuristics for understanding the nature of inclusive schools, but that neither is able fully to take account of the interplays of power, interest and politics in the development – or failure – of such schools. Moreover, neither engages with empirical data in a way which is capable of problematising their own theoretical accounts; such data is illustrative and suggestive at best, but is not used as a basis for the systematic generation of alternative explanations. Finally, we suggested that there was a syllogistic quality in both sets of accounts, partly because of this singular relation to data and partly because inclusivity on the one hand and 'moving' or 'adhocratic' schools on the other are effectively defined in terms of one another.

In reviewing our case studies, therefore, it is evident that there are some points where Ainscow and Skrtic have less to offer by way of illumination. The most obvious, perhaps, is in the complex interaction of schools which are seeking to become more inclusive and a national (or, in one case at least) local policy environment which is pushing those schools in a somewhat different direction. Such interactions cannot be understood simply in terms of the 'configuration' of schools as organisations nor in terms of the extent to which their staffs engage in collaborative problem-solving. At the very least, these characteristics of schools have to some extent to be understood in terms of the impact of the policy environment, the nature of which in turn calls for a different kind of explanation.

Perhaps more important, although Ainscow and Skrtic can illuminate how far a school is inclusive and the ways in which its 'adhocratic' configuration or 'moving' culture facilitate its inclusivity, they are less good at explaining *why* a school becomes – or fails to become – inclusive and adhocratic. The circularity of their explanations leaves them effectively in the position of saying that schools become inclusive by becoming adhocratic and they become adhocratic by becoming more inclusive. To be sure, there are, as we have seen, accounts of change in Ainscow and theoretical explanations of change in Skrtic. However, as we also saw, these beg as many questions as they answer. The sudden inner illumination of one or more professionals, or the intervention of internal or external change agents may tell us something about how the process of change might get started, but do little to explain why it takes one course in one situation and another in a different situation.

For this reason, although Ainscow nor Skrtic can help us to see that movement towards greater inclusivity in our case-study schools is promoted or inhibited by their different configurations or cultures, they are less helpful in explaining how those configurations and cultures came to be or how they change in some schools but not in others. Moreover, it is not clear that they explain in an entirely satisfactory way why it should be that, in all four schools, moves towards greater inclusion appear to be beset by endemic ambiguities. Given the range of responses to student diversity across the schools, the different histories, contexts, management styles, processes of change and personalities involved in each, can these ambiguities be explained solely in terms of the residual pathology of bureaucratic configuration or 'stuck' school culture? Do we not also need some explanation as to why these pathologies – if such they be – are so entrenched and why such different approaches to changing schools seem to produce such similar, and similarly disappointing outcomes?

As we suggested in Chapter 2, raising these questions is not to belittle the contribution that Ainscow and Skrtic make to our understanding of 'inclusive schools', nor is it to criticise them for failing to achieve what they in any case never set out to do. Rather, it is to indicate that we need to supplement the accounts they offer with explanations of different kinds and from different perspectives.

Inclusive schooling and the management of change

An important starting point in searching for these explanations is to elaborate on some concerns which are indeed touched on in some of Ainscow's work, particularly in his involvement with a school improvement project known as 'Improving the Quality of Education for All' (IQEA) (Ainscow *et al.*, 1994; Hopkins, Ainscow and West, 1994; Hopkins, West and Ainscow, 1996). The school improvement literature and the more general literature on the management of educational change have, in their recent incarnations, much in common with the sorts of accounts of 'adhocratic', 'moving', and hence 'inclusive' schools which we find in the work of Ainscow and Skrtic. Reynolds *et al.* (2000), for instance, describe two 'paradigms' which have successively dominated the school improvement field. The first paradigm was concerned with improvement as a top-down process, in which centrally-designed

innovations were transmitted to schools for more-or-less faithful implementation. The second paradigm, by contrast, has taken a much more
'bottom-up' approach, stressing the need to build on the professional
craft knowledge of teachers and to involve them fully in the change
process. Similarly, Fullan (Fullan and Stiegelbauer, 1991) points out the
limitations of externally imposed change and argues that those whose
task it is to make the change a reality have to share a common understanding of the 'meaning' of that change.

The implications of this 'second paradigm' are that change comes to
be seen as being about more than the quality of design and implementation of isolated innovations. Rather, it is about creating schools
which are capable of continuous self-improvement and developing
teachers who are capable of participating in such improvement. Con-
cluding his survey of the 'meaning of educational change', Fullan
concludes that:

> Taking on one innovation at a time is fire-fighting and faddism.
> Institutional development of schools and districts increases co-
> herence and capacity for sorting out and integrating the myriad of
> choices, acting on them, assessing progress, and (re)directing
> energies.

However, he adds:

> We cannot develop institutions without developing the people in
> them. That is why teacher development and professionalism,
> along with student engagement and active involvement of each of
> the constituencies, have figured so prominently in the earlier
> chapters. Combining individual and institutional development
> has its tensions, but the message of this book should be clear. You
> cannot have one without the other.
>   (Fullan and Stiegelbauer, 1991, p. 349)

It is, of course, a small step from this model of change led by 'individual and institutional development' to the concerns of Ainscow and
Skrtic with schools which are structured in such a way as to enhance
the capacity of their teachers to respond to diversity. However, there
is a difference. The change literature is concerned not (or, at least, not
to the same extent) with the impact of what Ainscow calls 'organisational conditions' (Ainscow, 1999) on the inclusive practices of
teachers, so much as with how such conditions can be generated in the
first place – or, indeed, with how other forms of change can be initiated and sustained. There seems to be consensus that these processes
are complex and multi-dimensional. Writing about school improve-

ment initiatives, for instance, Scheerens (1992, p. 104) is typical in
arguing that successful projects

are directed to the principle of synergy in two ways:

- to work simultaneously at the levels of the classroom, the
  school organization and the relevant school environment;
- to try to use several levers for introducing change at the same
  time: achievement stimulating incentives, training, recruitment
  and development activities, technological innovation, and more
  pronounced evaluation activities and facilities at the various
  levels of the school organization.

The key concept here, from our point of view, is that of 'levers'.
Change is not merely something which emerges from and within
appropriately-structured institutions; it is something which can be
consciously planned and managed. It is for this reason that Reynolds
et al. (2000) posit a 'third wave' of improvement projects, drawing
heavily on knowledge, support and a 'technology' from outside the
school, but carefully adapted to particular schools' situations. It is for
this reason, too, that Harris (2000), surveying the current state of the
school improvement field, is able to point to a series of strategies –
establishing a whole-school vision, involving teachers in leadership
and decision-making, focusing on change at school, teacher and classroom levels, and so on – which are likely to lead to more successful
improvement efforts.

In seeking to understand our schools through the work of Ainscow
and Skrtic, we focused on whether the tensions and ambiguities in
those schools could be explained in terms of 'organisational conditions'. Through the change and improvement literature, however, we
can ask a related but different question. How far can our findings in
the case-study schools be explained in terms of an inadequately-
managed process of change? In particular, did the leaders of change –
the heads, senior managers and SENCOs – fail to ensure that they
generated a shared 'meaning' for those changes? Did they fail to initiate change at all the necessary levels and/or fail to use all the 'levers'
of change that were available to them? Is it the case, therefore, that,
given a differently-managed change process, or a longer period for the
change to be embedded, many if not all of the problems would have
disappeared?

The attractions of such explanations are immediately obvious. Undoubtedly, in some of those schools – indeed, in perhaps all of them at
various points – the complexity of change appears to have been seriously underestimated and, in particular, the extent to which teachers

who were to implement the new inclusive approaches needed to share the 'meaning' of those approaches seems to have been completely misunderstood. The clearest examples of this are, perhaps, in St Joseph's and Seaview. In both schools, the changes in approach to special needs education had meaning for the headteacher as part of a more-or-less clearly articulated 'vision' of education which itself emanated from the head's personal and professional biography. However, in neither case was there much evidence that this vision was shared beyond, perhaps, a small group of the head's close associates and therefore, not surprisingly, the changes had quite different meanings for other teachers who were required to implement them. For these teachers, the changes were, if anything, about disrupting well-established systems, creating new and unmanageable demands, and glossing over the real challenges which they faced in the classroom on a daily basis.

Moreover, it is not too difficult to see that neither headteacher had found particularly successful ways either for enabling his teachers to share his vision or, at the very least, for offering them incentives to implement the changes he was pursuing. At Seaview in particular, the 'parachuting in' of a new senior management team, the sidelining of long-established members of staff (such as the previous SENCO) and the imposition without real discussion of changes which were, in some cases, not even technically efficient seemed guaranteed simply to deepen the hostility and suspicion felt by the bulk of the staff towards the head and the new approach to special needs education.

It is also clear that, in some schools, the multi-level nature of the change process was not well understood. Again, Seaview and St Joseph's are the most obvious examples. In the former, a good deal of managerial reorganisation took place (the 'distributed' SENCO role, the new IEP system and so on) together with a certain amount of rather narrowly-focused training. There was a clear *expectation* that this would change classroom practice, but there were no very obvious *strategies* for impacting either on classrooms as such or on the understandings, skills and practices of individual teachers. Similarly, at St Joseph's the thinking skills approach was, as we have seen, superimposed on a set of structures and practices that remained fundamentally unchanged. However successful it might have been in its own right, it is difficult to see how it could have any wider impact across the school as a whole.

More generally, despite whatever surface changes in structure there might have been in our case-study schools, their underlying structure remained that of the hierarchically- and departmentally-organised secondary school. Insofar as teacher collaboration happened, it happened within – and almost in spite of – a structure which was essentially based on the model of individual professionals accountable to their superiors through a line-management system, rather than groups of professionals working together in problem-solving teams. It is indicative, for instance, that in at least three of the schools, the introduction of more inclusive approaches was an initiative taken by the head and senior management team rather than a solution to a problem felt, defined and responded to by class teachers.

On the other hand, there were also clear examples of the effective management of change. Through somewhat different processes, a relatively high level of consensus had been built up in both Lakeside and Moorgate around a common 'vision'. In the former, this was attributable largely to the efforts of a charismatic and dynamic headteacher. In the latter, the process was much more evolutionary and much less localised in the head – which may well be why this was probably the school with least overt dissent. Similarly, in Moorgate it is possible to see how the sustained and substantial impact of in-class support, combined with the mixture of pressure and support from a well-respected SENCO and the collaborative orientation of the peer-support group, constituted at least the beginnings of multi-level strategies which had some prospect of impacting on practice and understandings.

What is not explained

There is no doubt that many of the problems and tensions – and, indeed, the successes – experienced by the case-study schools are explicable in terms of the failure of their leaders adequately to manage the process of change. However, what remains puzzling is the way in which somewhat *different* change processes generated remarkably *similar* problems in each of the schools.

There is little doubt, for instance, that the management of change at Moorgate and Lakeside was significantly more effective than at Seaview and St Joseph's. To a certain extent, this is reflected in the outcomes of change – higher levels of consensus, more firmly established systems for responding to diversity and, perhaps, more genuinely collaborative cultures. However, the problems and tensions around managing behaviour, around the 'technology' of inclusion, around the impact of the external policy environment and so on are present in the well-managed schools as much as in those which are less well managed.

The same is true if one looks at the duration of the change process. The turmoil at Seaview is perhaps an inevitable consequence of the relatively recent collision of a 'radical' headteacher with a conservative institution. It has its parallel in the early history of Moorgate, where there were vivid memories of how the shift from withdrawal to in-class support had caused similar acrimony. The passage of time at Moorgate and the sustained pressure for change had overcome many of these difficulties. However, although Moorgate's current difficulties were less acute than those at Seaview, they were nonetheless real. Even here, there was not total consensus around the school's approach to diversity and neither had the school been able to find a way through all of the more practical problems associated with that approach.

Explanations based on the management of change, therefore, seem to be illuminating, but nonetheless incomplete. It would appear that the effective management of change ameliorates the sorts of problems encountered by our schools, but does not make them disappear. It may just be that there is some still better way of managing change, or some even longer period of time that is needed for change to become embedded. Just possibly, under these circumstances, the move towards more inclusive practices would ultimately become problem-free. However, given the differences which already exist between the change processes in these schools, it seems more likely that we need different kinds of explanations.

Power, interest and micro-politics

At this point a somewhat different analytical tradition is able to add to our understanding. As we noted in Chapter 2, Skrtic and, particularly, Ainscow focus heavily on institutional-level factors in the establishment of more inclusive approaches and are somewhat less concerned with a detailed exploration of the interactions between schools and the wider social and political contexts within which they are located. Similarly, the more general change literature tends to concentrate on what managers of change can actually *do*, and therefore pays somewhat less attention to the contextual constraints which might limit or thwart their actions. Even where these constraints do appear, they tend to be presented as obstacles to overcome through better change strategies and are rarely analysed in their own right.

However, there is a well-established body of literature which is explicitly concerned with the social and political contexts within

which schools are located and which is particularly concerned to analyse the ways in which social and political processes might act to
thwart or subvert efforts at change. Its starting premise is that the
social world is characterised by groups whose interests conflict and
whose capacity to realise those interests – whose 'power' in other
words – varies. In its earlier incarnations, it focused on the distribution
of power between interest groups at the macro level, the unevenness
of which, it was argued, inevitably led to the reproduction of a social
status quo favouring those groups which were already powerful. The
education system, therefore, necessarily served those powerful interests who were able to shape it to their own ends and consequently
functioned as a mechanism for social reproduction rather than social
change (Bowles and Gintis, 1976). Under these circumstances, even
apparently 'progressive' changes might be subverted in such a way
that they served the interests of those who were already in privileged
positions (Sharp and Green, 1976). In terms of special needs education,
similarly critical analyses suggested that what appeared to be an attempt on the part of the education system to 'help' students with
disabilities and other disadvantages was actually a mechanism for
removing troublesome students from the mainstream system and ex-
panding the control exercised by professionals over deviant groups
(Barton, 1988; Barton and Tomlinson, 1981, 1984; Golby and Gulliver,
1979; Lewis and Vulliamy, 1980; Tomlinson, 1982, 1985).

More recent work has somewhat modified this rather uni-
dimensional and determinist model of the education system as a vehicle for social reproduction. Instead, attention has shifted to the way in
which power and interest play out in the 'micro-politics' of the school
(Altrichter and Salzgeber, 2000; Ball, 1987; Blase, 1991; Hoyle, 1986) or,
particularly, in the processes of education policy 'formation' (Ball,
1997; Ozga, 2000). The underlying assumption remains that vested
interests are at work within the education system and that the operation of these interests produces outcomes which, however they may
be presented rhetorically, remain essentially inequitable. However,
power and interest are now more likely to be seen as operating at
every level of the education system, rather than simply at the 'centre'
or in underlying social structures and processes. It follows, therefore,
that a whole range of individuals and groups seek to exercise power
across a whole range of contexts, producing a complex interplay of
interest with outcomes that are difficult to predict and are not repro-
ductive in any simple sense.

This has implications for the way in which schools are seen. If it is
not adequate to see schools simply as vehicles of social reproduction,
neither is it adequate to see them as 'machines' within which 'levers'

can be pulled to bring about change, nor as homogeneous 'cultures', nor as adhocratic or bureaucratic 'configurations'. Rather, schools are to be understood as 'sites' in which 'contests' between different interests take place (Fulcher, 1993). Similarly, education policy cannot simply be seen as a technical-rational process of formulation and implementation. What may seem like a rational process of 'formulation' is actually one of contest, conflict and compromise out of which may come policy positions that are far from coherent. Moreover, these processes continue in the arena of 'implementation', where 'official' policy is reinterpreted and reshaped. It thus makes less sense to see policy-making as a top-down process than as an endemically contested process which takes place at every level of the education system (Bowe, Ball and Gold, 1992; Ozga, 2000).

The emergence of these understandings has been particularly helpful in making sense of the constant 'struggles' (Vlachou, 1997) which seem to beset attempts to develop more inclusive forms of provision. It has made it possible to understand why apparently well-intentioned policies of 'inclusion' or 'integration' or 'whole school approaches' so often seem to deliver less than they promise. In particular, it has illuminated the way in which such policies, both in formation and in practice, are shaped by, *inter alia*, ambiguous and contradictory national imperatives, interacting with the competing interests of headteachers, class teachers, parents and others with a vested interest in the nature of that provision (see, amongst many others, Bines, 1995; Booth, Ainscow and Dyson, 1998; Gold, Bowe and Ball, 1993; Gross, 1996; Persson, 1996; Riddell, Brown and Duffield, 1994a and b; Rouse and Florian, 1997; Vincent *et al.*, 1994; Vincent *et al.*, 1995; Vislie, 1995; Vislie and Langfeldt, 1996).

Perspectives which foreground power, interest and conflict also seem to explain much that we found in our case-study schools. Perhaps most obviously, they explain the contradictions between the espoused policies of the schools and the national education policy environment within which they were operating. We should expect that the liberal approaches emerging in these schools would be particularly vulnerable to the operation of the much more powerful vested interests represented in national policy. We should be prepared, therefore, to find that they, like other comprehensive schools in the same period, would experience a 'values drift' away from inclusive and comprehensive principles and towards the values of the market environment in which they were inescapably located (Gewirtz, Ball and Bowe, 1995). Likewise, we should expect the internal conflict which we found to some extent in each of the schools and to a marked extent in some of them. From a micro-political perspective, conflict is normal and is by no means an indication that some change process or other has been mis-handled. Indeed, some commentators have argued that conflict, far from being pathological, opens up spaces in which new ideas can emerge and be tested (Rizvi and Kemmis, 1987; Skidmore, 1998, 1999).

At the very least, what we see in the case-study schools is a process of 'contestation' around the school's espoused policy. The attempts to develop more inclusive approaches in these schools are attempts which are articulated at and driven from senior positions. However, they have to be put into practice by teachers throughout the schools. It is not surprising, therefore, that the different interests and understandings of different groups and individuals cause the policies to be reshaped in practice. In some cases, this process can be detected in the overt opposition of teachers to the school's espoused policy. More often, however, an apparent acceptance of the policy conceals what we called its 'translation' into practices with quite different meanings.

It is also possible to explain some of the contradictions that we have noted even *within* the schools' espoused policies. If such policies are seen as unambiguous articulations of an unequivocal commitment to inclusive approaches, then it is indeed puzzling that, as we saw, they apparently permit the policy-makers themselves – particularly, the headteachers of the schools – to condone practices which seem decidedly anti-inclusive. The persistence of 'ability' grouping and the disciplinary exclusion of students are two such practices that we particularly noted. However, if we accept the view of policy 'formation' as itself contested, then it is not difficult to see how apparently contradictory policies might be pursued simultaneously as heads and senior staff respond to conflicting imperatives. Moreover, if we see the articulation of policy as an idealised *representation* (Bowe, Ball and Gold, 1992), rather than a comprehensive description of the reality of policy-in-practice then it is not difficult to see why the grand rhetorical claims of espoused policy depart at so many points from what actually happens in the schools. Not only are the 'visions' which seem to drive these schools contested as they are turned into practice; not only are they themselves compromises between competing tendencies; but they are also to be understood as an attempt by heads and senior staff to articulate some necessarily generalised intent rather than a detailed prescription for action.

What is not explained

These conflict perspectives inevitably make accounts in terms purely of the management of change or of the development of particular types of problem-solving schools seem somewhat thin. More charitably, they inject explanatory dimensions – in terms of interest and power – which those other accounts tend to overlook. In particular, they help us to understand why, even in schools such as Moorgate, where change is relatively well managed and where problem-solving processes are evident, conflict, compromise and contradiction still emerge.

However, we are not convinced that such accounts explain *everything* that we found in our case-study schools. Much of the analysis which typically emerges from these perspectives focuses on the *form* of conflict, contest and struggle. In other words, it is concerned with who is struggling with whom, what interests are at work, what forms of power and resistance shape the contest and so on. However, in our schools at least, such contests are underlain by very real *questions of substance*. In other words, there is a *what* of contest as well as a *how* and a *why*. To take some of the examples above, the issues of how the school should respond to behaviour problems and to learning difficulties are indeed contested. Nonetheless, these are also substantive issues which permit no easy solutions. Given that these schools are pursuing more inclusive approaches, then these approaches should embrace even those students whose behaviour is problematic and whose levels of attainment and facility of learning are some way behind those of their peers. However, it is far from clear that there are effective means of achieving this. Moreover, the absence of such means generates real dilemmas in terms of the rights of other students to learn at their own rates in a conducive environment.

It is certainly true that, on this basis, many conflicts can arise. In particular, the way forward proposed by espoused school policy may be one that is rejected or resisted by particular members of staff. However, such contests arise not simply out of the conflicting interests of different groups but also out of the substantive nature of the issues around which the contests take place. If managing behaviour or learner diversity were a simple and straightforward matter, in other words, it is difficult to see how or why these contests would arise. Moreover, it is, we suggest, precisely because these problems and dilemmas are substantive that they generate, in some of the schools at least, rather less conflict than might be supposed and why the tone of teachers in commenting on them is often 'more in sorrow than in anger'.

As with the change perspective, therefore, we believe that the conflict perspective explains much about our schools – but not quite everything. If we are to understand the substantive issues to which we have alluded and the role they play in explaining the difficulties which those schools encountered, then we need a different perspective again. It is to this which we now turn.

9

Dilemmas, Contradictions and Dialectics in Responding to Diversity

Reviewing the issue of the disproportionate representation of ethnic minority students in US special education, Alfredo Artiles (1998) introduces a key concept for understanding how education systems in general and schools in particular respond to student diversity. That concept he refers to as the 'dilemma of difference':

> the ways in which we treat difference are problematic. For example, we deal with difference by treating certain groups of students differently (e.g. educational programs for limited English proficient students) or the same (e.g. recent university admissions criteria for ethnic minority groups). Interestingly, both approaches to dealing with difference achieve exactly the same thing: they affirm difference. Thus, it appears that to acknowledge difference in any way creates a dilemma that poses seemingly insurmountable choices between similar or preferential treatment, between neutrality or accommodation, or between integration or separation.
>
> (p. 32)

What Artiles' comments point to, we suggest, is a fundamental contradiction within mass education systems. Those systems are established to deliver to all students something called an 'education'. However the notion of education is understood, it has to have some basic common features in all cases for it to count as education. In most national systems, these features will be quite extensive; there will, for instance, at the very least be a common core of skills and knowledge which will be offered to all students and there may well, as in England, be a national curriculum which defines what counts as an education in some detail. Moreover, this education will be delivered in broadly common circumstances – in schools which have many similarities, by teachers with similar levels of training, through a pedagogy which does not vary greatly from site to site and so on. These common features of mass education are no accident. If a society (or, more accurately, state) is to continue to fund and otherwise sustain its education system, it will expect it to fulfil certain functions, even if it is not able to articulate these with any clarity. They might include, for instance, preparing a skilled workforce, or transmitting key social values, or promoting social cohesion, or promoting the personal development and quality of life of its citizens (see, for instance, Carroll, 1992, for an account of the changing functions of the US school system).

However, if education is to fulfil these functions, it can only do so by acting at the level of *individual* students and those students are inevitably different from each other in ways which are pertinent to their engagement with education: they learn at different rates; they have different interests and aptitudes; they experience different sorts of difficulties; they come with different expectations and cultural values, and so on. Alongside, therefore, the requirement for the education system to do something recognisably *similar* for all students, there is an equal and opposite requirement for it to do something *different* for every student. Education systems, it follows, are necessarily pulled in different directions by these different requirements.

As Artiles points out, for those who work in education systems – policy-makers, administrators, headteachers, teachers – this contradiction manifests itself as a series of *dilemmas* which centre on the issue of difference. They are expected to find ways of, on the one hand, delivering a common education to all and on the other of responding to the different characteristics and needs of each individual. To a certain extent, the dilemmas which arise are technical in nature – how to find ways of teaching particular skills or areas of knowledge to students with different attainments and aptitudes; how to organise the grouping of students so that they all learn to their maximum potential; how to deploy resources in ways that are equitable, that promote learning, but that are responsive to individual differences and needs.

However, since the business of education is necessarily shot through with social, political and ethical questions, the technical dilemmas inevitably interact with other kinds of dilemma: some ways of teaching, grouping or resourcing may be technically effective but carry with them overtones of discrimination, stigmatisation or marginalisation; particular forms of practice may disadvantage some students *vis-à-vis* others; culturally-valued forms of knowledge may conflict with students' own cultural values, and so on. These dilemmas take many forms, but they all arise from the fundamental contradiction of an education system which is at one and the same time based on what students have – or are expected to have – in common and on the differences between each individual. At heart, as Brahm Norwich (1994), in a thoughtful analysis of the complex issues around 'differentiation', points out, there is,

> a dilemma in education over how difference is taken into account – whether to recognise differences as relevant to individual needs by offering different provision, but that doing so could reinforce unjustified inequalities and is associated with devaluation; or, whether to offer a common and valued provision for all but with the risk of not providing what is relevant to individual needs.
>
> (p. 293)

If we look at the structures and practices which education systems have developed over time, we can trace the different ways in which they have attempted to resolve this basic dilemma (Clark *et al.*, 1997). In England, for instance, the 1944 Act formalised a system both within and beyond the field of special needs education which was premised on including children in a common education *system* (very nearly all children were in a school of some sort), but responding to their differences by placing different 'types' of children in different types of schools – grammar schools, secondary modern schools, technical schools and, of course, special schools. From the 1970s onwards, however, as we have seen, there has been a growing exploration of how far it might be possible to include all children not only in the same *system* but also in the same *school*. Moreover, this exploration has also, at various times, included experiments with educating children in the same *curriculum* (following the introduction of the National Curriculum) and in the same *classroom* (in so-called 'mixed-ability classes'). Within this more inclusive approach, student differences have not disappeared; they have simply been accommodated at the level of the school (for instance, by setting or streaming) or of the classroom (by 'differentiation') rather than at the systemic level.

Franklin (1994) traces a very similar process in the history of American schools. Children with learning difficulties, he argues, have been successively labelled as 'backward', 'learning disabled' and 'at-risk' as the nature of student difference and the relationship between what makes students different and what they all have in common have been conceptualised and reconceptualised. At the same time, the managers of schools in different parts of the country evolved an array of special classes, special schools, remedial programmes, alternative curricula and school reform efforts in an attempt to respond to student difference within a system of common schooling. At the heart of all of these efforts, Franklin identifies a 'contradiction':

From the first, the efforts of American school managers to provide for students with learning difficulties have pulled them in contradictory directions. Not certain as to whether they wanted to provide for the individual needs of these children or to assure the uninterrupted progress of the regular classroom, these educators embraced a recalibrated common school ideal that resolved the dilemma through curriculum differentiation. The result has been the creation of an array of special programs to remove these children from regular classrooms.

(Franklin, 1994, p. 153)

It is not difficult to see how a similar analysis might be applied to the emergence of the inclusion agenda in England (see, for instance, Croll and Moses, 2000a) or, more particularly, to our own case-study schools. Here, too, we have a commitment to the same inclusive notions as Franklin's 'ideal of common schooling' (1994, p. 154). The language is, of course, different; it is the language of the 'comprehensive ideal' or the 'community school', or the 'unlimited potential of all students'. However, underpinning it is the notion that there should be one school – and, we might add, curriculum and classroom – for all. This leads the schools to take the somewhat radical steps we have described in earlier chapters to ensure that all students can be maintained, valued and educated within this 'common' context – the restructuring of special needs systems, the emphasis on in-class support, the moves towards greater differentiation, the welcoming of a wider range of student diversity and so on.

However, these inclusive moves also generate dilemmas in the schools. As the schools include all students more fully within a common framework, so they encounter the substantive differences between students. Somehow, they have to respond to those differences at the same time as they sustain their common framework. In some cases, managing this contradictory requirement is problematic: students fail to learn effectively within their ordinary classrooms; attempts at differentiation fail to meet individual needs, or become impracticable in the context of large and diverse teaching groups; above all, the presence of some students disrupts the education that can be offered to others or consumes inordinate amounts of the resources available to educate all.

In response to these difficulties, or in order to forestall them, schools set up systems for addressing particular sorts of difference whilst attempting to maintain a somewhat modified common framework. Hence, they have in place support personnel for some students but not others; they have special needs teachers, teams and

SENCOs; they mix grouping by attainment with mixed-attainment grouping; they withdraw, segregate or exclude students. These systems, in Franklin's terms, 'recalibrate' their espoused inclusive ideal. On the one hand, they make it possible for the school and its teachers to accommodate a wider range of student diversity than might otherwise be the case. On the other hand, they introduce elements of segregation and exclusion. Not surprisingly, therefore, they frequently appear to be ambiguous in their operation and effect, sustaining inclusion under one set of circumstances and something more like exclusion under another.

Not surprisingly either, the dilemmas to which teachers and managers have to respond generate considerable tension within the schools. Just occasionally, these tensions are voiced in dilemmatic form – senior managers musing about the tension between the comprehensive ideal to which they are committed and the real problems that are being generated by accepting growing numbers of students with special needs; teachers avowing a commitment to mixed-attainment grouping on the one hand, but acknowledging the impossibility of doing it well on the other; other teachers valuing support but wondering whether the time and effort put into some students was really worthwhile. More commonly, tensions manifest themselves through blame, contest and, sometimes, open conflict. The problem, we are told, is the result of too little support teaching, or too few resources, or insensitive government policy. The head, teachers tell us, is out of touch with classroom reality; the teachers, the head assures us, lack the skills to respond effectively to diversity.

Under these circumstances, the interplay of power and interest becomes significant. Preferred ways of responding to the dilemmas which present themselves in the school are inevitably mediated by personal biography and professional role. For senior managers and SENCOs, there is an incentive to push forward with a more inclusive model which may well not only be in line with personal commitment, but is an attractive way of making their professional mark. For class teachers on the other hand, such a model involves them in facing considerable practical difficulties and making significant changes in their practice. Some have personal and professional identities which lead them nonetheless to pursue more inclusive practice; others, however, can see little that they have to gain by further increasing the challenges that are always inherent in teaching. Moreover, all the staff of the schools – heads, SENCOs, teachers and LSAs – have to respond to these dilemmas within an environment that is not of their making. The external policy imperatives that they must obey, the constraints of the curriculum, the necessity for competition with other schools, the increasing demands of parents – all impact on their freedom to act and their appraisal of the choices which face them.

It is little wonder that these schools are complex places, filled with tensions and ambiguities. It is little wonder, either, that they fall some way short of meeting the high standards of 'adhocracy' or 'inclusiveness'. Indeed, it is difficult to characterise them in any way as stable entities with fixed characteristics. Rather, they are sites in which a fundamental contradiction of mass education erupts, where it generates a series of powerful dilemmas, and where tensions, contests and conflicts arise as the individuals within the school seek, in different ways, to come to terms with those dilemmas.

Towards a theory of schools, diversity and inclusion

So far in this chapter and the last, we have set out a series of theoretical approaches to explaining the tensions and problems we found in our case-study schools. The temptation is to try to identify one or other of those accounts as 'true' and to reject the others as 'false'. However, there is an alternative position. As Morgan (1997) points out, we can view organisations such as schools in terms of a number of 'images'. By trying to understand organisations through these images – as though, for instance, they were machines, or brains, or organisms or, even, as though they were prisons – it becomes possible to illuminate different aspects of the complex set of phenomena which we label 'the organisation'.

In many ways, the positions we have outlined are images of this kind. As such, it is possible to value each one for what it illuminates rather than to discard it for what it fails to explain. In line with much post-modern thinking, it then becomes possible to see each as what Skrtic (1995a) calls an 'optional' theory, or to see them as part of what Ball (1994), following Foucault, characterises as a 'tool-box of theories. However, we do not believe it is necessary to adopt an entirely relativist position in which one 'image' is as good as any other. On the contrary, it seems to us possible to develop a position which respects the differences between these theoretical accounts but nonetheless is able to relate them one to another in order to offer a more coherent perspective not only on our case-study schools, but more generally on the relationship between schools as organisations and student diversity.

That position is grounded in the notion of contradiction. In England, as in other western countries, education systems have been developed which seek to offer something recognisably common by way of education to individual students who are recognisably different one from another. Although the precise nature of what counts as 'education' and the detail of the structures and practices through which it is offered change from place to place and time to time, the contradiction remains.

This contradiction in the way we have just seen generates in turn dilemmas for decision-makers at every level in the education system – national policy-makers, local administrators, senior managers in schools, teachers in classrooms. Sometimes these dilemmas are explicit, but more often they remain implicit, hidden even from the decision-makers themselves. Essentially, however, they have to find ways of responding simultaneously both to the commonalities which students share and to the differences between them.

It follows that the structures and practices which constitute both education systems and their component parts, such as schools, are founded on contradictions and arise out of the decisions that are made (conscious or otherwise) in an attempt to resolve the 'dilemma of difference'. Moreover, since dilemmas, by definition, cannot be solved and since the contradictions which underpin them remain, this process is dynamic. Whatever decision is made, whatever resolution of a particular dilemma is arrived at, the underlying contradiction makes it inevitable that the dilemma will re-surface in some alternative form. If segregated systems are set up to respond to the differences between students, the inadequacy of those systems to respond to the common humanity and needs of students will become apparent. If all students are included in the same schools, curriculum and classrooms, their differences will pose the most direct challenges to the teachers and school managers who have to make such an inclusive system work.

In other words, the structures and practices of education systems are the outcome of a constant 'dialectic' (Benson, 1977, 1983). However stable they may appear to be at a particular time, they are fraught with tension and will inevitably change as their inherent contradictions pull them apart. It is at this point where conflict theories become especially illuminating. The dialectical process does not take place in a social vacuum. On the contrary, the decision-making out of which education systems and their component parts arise are firmly set in a social context. Indeed, the fundamental contradiction itself arises in the context of particular social values, practices, cultures and histories.

Inextricably woven into this social context are the interests of groups and individuals and their power to pursue those interests. As we have seen, the level at which power and interest operate and the manner in which they operate are complex. However, their presence means that the ways in which dilemmas come to be resolved inevitably reflect their operation. Indeed, it is precisely because there are dilemmas which open up the possibility of different resolutions that contest and conflict have some substantive issues around which to focus. If the creation of special schools, for instance, reflects a particular resolution of the dilemma of difference, it is a resolution which will also reflect the interests of some groups more than others and which will inevitably be intensely contested.

An account based on contradictions, dilemmas and power contains powerful elements of pessimism and scepticism – elements which stand in sharp distinction to the overwhelmingly optimistic tone of much current literature and advocacy in the field of inclusive education. In particular, such an account is sceptical about the possibility and meaning of 'progress'. Attempts to bring about 'change for the better', however defined, will always be contested and may well be thwarted if the power of resistance is too great. More importantly, the very notion of 'progress' has to be treated as problematic if every form of provision, however new, simply embodies the old contradiction and generates the old dilemmas.

On the other hand, this is far from a simple determinist position. Although change cannot remove either dilemmas or the contradiction which underpins them, it does constitute a particular 'resolution' of dilemmas and a particular way of managing the underlying contradiction. Moreover, not all resolutions are the same. Different resolutions embody different values, produce different outcomes, favour different groups. At any time and place, therefore, one such resolution may indeed seem better to some group of decision-makers than the available alternatives. Under these circumstances, the issue changes from one of which resolution is preferred to one of how to implement that resolution. How effectively this is done will depend, in part at least, on what those decision-makers understand about the management of change and what they understand about the technical realisation of their preferred resolution.

Where change is managed badly, as we saw in our case-study schools, conflicts will be exacerbated, dilemmas will be sharpened and the preferred resolution will not be realised. Where, on the other hand, change is managed skilfully, although neither the specific dilemmas nor the underlying contradiction will disappear, some new resolution may well emerge and be realised with a relatively high degree of stability. Likewise, the new resolution will carry with it technical requirements for its realisation. If, for instance, it is inclusive schooling which is seen as the way to resolve the commonality–difference dilemma, then it will be necessary for decision-makers to understand the sorts of technical knowledge which they can glean from researchers and others who have tried to analyse what enables schools to function in more inclusive ways.

It is not, therefore, that accounts of inclusive schooling or the management of change, any more than accounts of the interplay of power and interest, are superseded by a perspective which emphasises dilemma and contradiction. Rather, each type of account illuminates schools – and, in our case, inclusive schools – in different ways. Moreover, each type of account illuminates each other type of account. If we – whether we are decision-makers, advocates or other citizens with a stake in how the education system responds to diversity – wish to understand what makes a school inclusive, we go to Ainscow, Skrtic or other scholars who have addressed this issue. However, we need to do so in the knowledge that creating schools of this kind demands a change process and that we know something of what this process might look like and how it might best be managed. At the same time, we also need to know how power and interest will impact on our endeavours, how they might thwart us and how they might subvert our idealistic intentions until our 'inclusive school' comes to serve inherently *exclusive* interests.

Beyond this, if we are not to be trapped into a particular resolution, we have to have some understanding of the contradiction which confronts us and the dilemmas to which we must respond. We must be able to evaluate the choices we make in the light of the alternatives that are available and the possibilities we reject. We must be aware of the current resolution and our own preferred course as products of a particular time, place and set of circumstances. We must know that different choices have been made in the past and assuredly will be made in the future. Only in this way is it possible to know that our own choice is the best that we can make.

Theorising inclusive schools

It is our contention that the theoretical framework we have just outlined, drawing as it does on multiple perspectives, offers a powerful means of understanding the ways in which education systems respond to diversity and informing the decisions that we ourselves might take about how to formulate such responses. In particular, it allows us to interrogate the notion of the 'inclusive school' which is currently so dominant in educational thinking and which informed, in different ways, the work of our case-study schools.

What it tells us first of all is that there is no reason to suppose that inclusive schooling is in any way above or beyond the fundamental contradiction we have outlined or the dilemmas which this contradiction generates. Inclusion does not offer an escape from this contradiction but rather arises out of it. In particular, inclusion is one attempted resolution of the dilemma of difference amongst many and, like all such resolutions, has emerged at a particular point in time and will, our theoretical framework suggests, disappear at some future point in time. Insofar, therefore, as its advocates posit the emergence of the 'inclusive school' as some sort of final answer to the problems which education systems face when confronted by diversity, we have to reject their position.

In particular, we should expect the move towards more inclusive forms of provision to be fraught with technical difficulties. To a certain extent, these difficulties will arise from the inherent inadequacies of resources, professional expertise and systems and structures which were designed to sustain one form of response to diversity and are now required to support another, quite different one. The head and senior management at Seaview, for instance, are quite right, up to a point, in blaming their difficulties on the failure of their staff to understand the changes in practice demanded by more inclusive approaches. However, these technical difficulties will also arise because the substantive differences between students will not disappear and because the more inclusive provision becomes, the more challenging it will be to construct an educationally effective response to those differences. Better differentiation, better behaviour management, better social relations, less discriminatory teacher attitudes will all help – but they will not remove the inherently problematical nature of a system which seeks to educate diverse students within a common framework.

Similarly, we have to conclude that any attempt to create inclusive schools inevitably takes place in an arena characterised by contests between different interests and the exercise of power on behalf of those interests. Since inclusion appears to challenge some powerful vested interests – many regular school teachers, some parents, many special educators and allied professionals – it seems likely that it will be resisted vigorously. Moreover, where, as in England, it attracts the support of policy-makers at school, local and, particularly, national level, we would do well to interrogate their motives, to see how far their support constitutes a commitment to the liberal (or even radical) principles of inclusion and how far it stems from somewhat different policy aims which may ultimately require inclusion to be jettisoned. This is an issue to which we shall return in the next chapter.

Beyond this, our theoretical framework has something important to tell us about the concept of the inclusive school on the one hand, and its likely future on the other. It has, as we have noted earlier, currently become something of a cliché to characterise inclusion as a process rather than a state. However, there is a sense in which this accords with the view of the 'inclusive school' which emerges from our own work. The so-called 'inclusive school' is actually a site which is shot through with contradictions, dilemmas, conflicts and ambiguities. Within this site, there will be processes at work which are more inclusive in their effect; equally, as Booth (1995; Booth, Ainscow and Dyson, 1997, 1998) consistently points out, there will be other processes which tend towards exclusion. It makes little sense, therefore, to talk of an 'inclusive school', other than as a rather crude and arbitrary label to attach to some of the school's more superficial characteristics. Indeed, as a dialectical analysis of organisations suggests, it makes less sense to talk of any organisation as a fixed entity than of a continuing process of 'organising' (Heydebrand, 1977; Zeitz, 1980).

On this basis, it is more helpful to think of inclusion as an *outcome* of actions within a school rather than as an inherent *characteristic* of the school. It is, we should expect, an outcome which will be limited and provisional. It will be an outcome for some students at some times and in some circumstances rather than some sort of stable 'good' which all students can enjoy. Since, moreover, inclusion is the resolution of a dilemma, it will, where it appears, be bought at the cost of the options and possibilities that were rejected in reaching this resolution. These may include other desirable outcomes – higher attainment, perhaps, or customised educational responses, or participation in a group of like peers. Likewise, where these other outcomes appear, they themselves may well be bought at the cost of inclusion. Learning how to be 'better' at inclusion – how, in other words, to develop practices and structures that are more likely to produce inclusive outcomes – will certainly minimise trade-offs of this kind. It will not, however, make them disappear.

This in turn might lead us to reflect on the future of the 'inclusive school'. Currently, the notion of inclusion is operating as a powerful means of articulating principles of equity and participation which, as we have seen, have long underpinned both the English comprehensive ideal and the American notion of the 'common school'. Likewise, the notion of the 'inclusive school', however crude it may be, is enabling us to build up a knowledge-base of those surface features of schools which make it more rather than less likely that they will deliver inclusive outcomes. To this extent, the move towards more inclusive education is acting as a positive force in bringing about more equitable and participatory responses to diversity.

However, we should not expect that this will always be the case. Just as our case-study schools were founded on contradictions which generated dilemmas, tensions and conflicts, so the whole inclusion 'movement' is subject to the same centrifugal tendencies. These are already evident in the different meanings which inclusion has for different groups in different contexts. Rather than a single, clear concept of inclusion to which all pro-inclusionists can sign up and with which all inclusive education policies could align, therefore, we have complex sets of theories and discourses (Dyson, 1999). While some see inclusion in terms of the rights of disabled children to be present in a common social institution, others stress the importance of using education to redress social and economic disadvantages for a wide range of marginalised groups. Similarly, while some argue for the right of certain groups to opt out of an inclusive system, others argue for the importance of the participation of all in a microcosm of an inclusive society.

This is not surprising. If we see 'inclusion' as a principle through which we can attempt to resolve the fundamental 'dilemma of difference', then we should expect that different groups and individuals in different contexts will arrive at somewhat different resolutions. So long as the term 'inclusion' acts as an umbrella under which all of these groups and individuals feel able to shelter, there will continue to be an 'inclusion movement' which will operate as a community of researchers, advocates and practitioners who can engage productively with each other. However, it is to be expected that various members of this band of fellow-travellers will branch off in different directions from time to time.

Moreover, it is inevitable in due course that the processes which thrust inclusion to its current position of dominance will reduce its influence and bring forward some other means of responding to diversity. Elsewhere (Clark *et al.*, 1997), we have suggested that resolutions of educational dilemmas emerge as a result of the interaction of three factors – prevailing social and educational values, social, political and educational contexts, and available educational technologies. As these change, so existing resolutions begin to fragment and new resolutions emerge. Viewed in this way, a number of factors might be seen as instrumental in the rise of inclusion (see also, Gerber, 1996; Kauffman, 1995; Vislie, 1995): long-standing liberal values of equity and participation, sharpened by an increasing concern with the civil rights of marginalised groups; an increasingly individualistic social and political system in respect of which inclusion is both a reaction and a reflection; a technology of schooling which made more participatory responses to diversity in ordinary schools and classrooms possible; an economics of education which made segregated provision seem wasteful; and theories of governance which stressed the autonomy and self-sufficiency of the school.

It is not difficult to see how some or all of these factors might change and, as they did, how current resolutions would come to seem unattractive or non-viable and new resolutions would begin to present themselves. What impact might there be, for instance, from an economic slump, significantly reducing the resources in the education system, or an economic boom significantly increasing them? What if the promise of information technology to deliver radically new opportunities for learning outside schools and classrooms were fulfilled? What if the recurrent moral panics of recent years about 'standards' and behaviour gave way to panics about social disintegration, or disillusion with democratic processes, or the discipline of the workforce? What if the education market established in the 1980s were to be abolished? What, on the other hand, if it were to be extended by the mass privatisation of schools and education services?

These possibilities may seem like 'mere' speculation in contrast to the firm principles on which the move towards inclusion is currently based. It may, indeed, seem that the principles of inclusion would hold good even if these changes were to become realities. However, we wish to suggest that, whatever *may* happen in future, changes already *are* happening in the present and these changes are beginning subtly to reshape the ways in which the education system responds to diversity. This process of reshaping, we suggest, may well take us 'beyond inclusion' and it is this possibility which we shall address in the next, and final, chapter.

10

Beyond Inclusion?

In the last chapter, we attempted to explain what we found in our case-study schools in terms of 'dilemmas' and 'contradictions'. In particular, we argued that decision-makers at all levels of education systems face a 'dilemma of difference' in terms of responding to the substantive differences between students within a common educational framework. Such a view leads us to see the history of educational responses to diversity in a very particular way. That history is neither an uninterrupted progress towards unequivocally 'better' forms of provision, nor is it a continual cycling through new ways of reproducing the old relations of power and advantage. Rather, it is an episodic succession of dilemmatic resolutions – resolutions which emerge from time to time, find a temporary stability and then disintegrate as the conditions which produced them change as their own inherent centrifugal forces cause them to fall apart.

Our four schools represent different resolutions of this kind and we can, therefore, already detect the forces within them that were beginning to destabilise them. However, they also form part of a wider resolution across the education system which saw a number of schools in the 1990s using their new-found autonomy and the possibilities inherent in a common curriculum for all to develop responses to diversity emphasising equity and participation (Clark *et al.*, 1995b). This in turn is part of the succession of resolutions which we traced in Chapter 1 and which, from the late 1970s, certainly – and arguably from before then – have been founded on these 'liberal principles' (Clark *et al.*, 1997).

However, our schools are also, perhaps, rather late flowerings of this liberal tradition. As we have seen, they were struggling to realise these principles in a national policy context which was anything but favourable. As they continued to emphasise equity and participation, central government emphasised competition, standards and public accountability – and the stresses this caused were obvious in the schools. Moreover, the advent of the National Curriculum, of regular inspection and, in the field of special needs education, of the Code of Practice meant that central government, for the first time, began to exercise real control over some of the *details* of what was happening in schools. The disjuncture, therefore, between the espoused policy of the schools and the policies pursued nationally became all the more significant.

Whatever the fate of these particular schools, therefore – and we have already seen how two of them fell foul of the inspection process – it seems likely that, as time wore on, the sustainability of liberal and participatory approaches to diversity in schools generally was set to become more and more open to question. Had national education policy continued in the same direction after the 1997 General Election, the outcome may simply have been a progressive erosion of such approaches in favour of a return to more segregated forms of provision within and beyond ordinary schools. Certainly, the rise in numbers of statements (DfEE, 1997a) and of disciplinary exclusions (Parsons and Castle, 1998; Parsons and Howlett, 1996) in this period would indicate that this might be the case, not to mention the tenacity with which many schools continued to hold onto their distinctly non-inclusive special needs practices (Croll and Moses, 2000b).

However, national policy did not continue in the same direction. The 1997 election was won by 'New' Labour on a promise of placing education at the top of its agenda. What followed was a veritable whirlwind of activity which, although retaining many features of Conservative education policy, also took it in new directions. Indeed, 'modernisation' became a key term in the marketing of government policy, with the clear implication that there was to be no simple continuation of previous policy and certainly no return to the traditional approaches of either previous Conservative or previous Labour administrations (DfEE, 1997b). Moreover, the new government rapidly increased the level of central intervention in the detail of schools' work, most notably – though by no means exclusively – in introducing Literacy and Numeracy 'Hours' in primary schools (with some subsequent roll out to secondary schools) which provided teachers with a detailed teaching programme that they were effectively required to follow (National Literacy Task Force, 1997; Numeracy Task Force, 1998).

This 'modernising' tendency and interventionist stance meant that schools inevitably began to feel the impact of central government policy on their daily work in a way, it is arguable, which has not previously been the case in the English education system. What makes this impact significant from our point of view, however, is that, as befits a government with a socialist tradition (whatever its current ideological stance), 'New' Labour's education policy was explicit both in its acknowledgement of the significance of student diversity and in its avowed intent to address that diversity on the basis of principles – however 'modernised' – of equity and participation. It is for this reason that its initial White Paper, *Excellence in Schools* (DfEE, 1997b) was rapidly followed by a Green Paper on special needs education, *Excellence for All Children* (DfEE, 1997a), which, as we saw in Chapter 1, committed the government to the principle of inclusion. It is for this reason, too, that there has been a constant succession of measures from the government aimed at addressing issues of disadvantage and 'social exclusion' as they impact on the education system.

It is our contention that this combination of modernisation, high levels of intervention and the foregrounding of student diversity as an issue constitute a new resolution of the 'dilemma of difference' at national policy level and are beginning to facilitate new resolutions at school level. In the remainder of this chapter, therefore, we want to outline some of the features of these emerging resolutions. They are, we believe, significant in themselves since they are likely to achieve some level of stability in at least the medium term. However, our real purpose for including them here is that we believe that, just as we can say what sorts of responses to diversity preceded those of our case study schools, so we are now beginning to see what responses may succeed them. In so doing, we can understand more fully the dynamic process which generates and erodes resolutions and can, therefore, begin to see what sorts of questions we should be asking if we are to play some part in guiding that process.

New Labour, new inclusion?

As we pointed out in the first chapter, one of the earliest acts of the incoming 'New' Labour government in 1997 was to align its education policies with the Salamanca Statement (UNESCO, 1994) and declare itself to be committed to the principle of inclusion (DfEE, 1997a). In so doing, it was, of course, building on the liberal principles which informed our case-study schools, and moreover have informed the development of special needs education over the past twenty-five years and more. Indeed, it is arguable that it extended those principles insofar as it presented inclusion as part of a wider movement towards establishing the civil rights of disabled people (Disability Rights Task Force, 1999). Anecdotal evidence also suggests, at the time of writing, that the government's use of Education Development Plans and LEA inspections offers practical mechanisms whereby the commitment to inclusion in principle can be translated into action, at least at LEA level.

However, this simple extension of existing principles is by no means the whole story. First of all, the commitment to inclusion is equivocal in the extreme. Both the Green Paper (DfEE, 1997a) and the subsequent Programme of Action (DfEE, 1998a) on special needs education made it abundantly clear the government saw a continuing role for special schools and intended to adopt a 'practical, not dogmatic' (DfEE, 1997a, p. 45) approach to inclusion. The subsequent Bill (DfEE 2000b) seems likely to confirm that, in legislative terms at least, the time-honoured resolution – a presumption in favour of mainstream placement for most alongside segregated special education for some – is the government's preferred option.

More significantly, the government's commitment to inclusion within the field of special needs education has to be seen in the context of other, equally – if not more – powerful commitments. The Secretary of State for Education, David Blunkett, has taken recently (1999a and b, 2000) to setting out the government's overall education agenda under four headings: 'firm foundations', which is about enhancing the quality of early years and primary education; 'improving all schools', which is about raising standards of pupil and institutional performance; 'inclusion'; and 'modernising comprehensive education', which is about creating secondary provision which is more diverse and more achievement-oriented than 'traditional' comprehensive schools are taken to be.

These policy strands in turn are given coherence by what appear to be two overarching concerns. The first is the 'crusade for standards' promised in the 1997 White Paper (DfEE, 1997b) and operationalised through, amongst a whole range of other strategies, institutional target-setting (DfEE, 1997c and d, 1998b), the National Literacy and Numeracy Strategies (National Literacy Task Force, 1997; Numeracy Task Force, 1998) and the reform of the teaching profession (DfEE, 1998c). The second is a concern with 'social exclusion', signalled in the early establishment of a Social Exclusion Unit in the Cabinet Office and operationalised in terms of strategies targeted particularly at children, families and schools in areas of chronically low educational attainment, expectation and participation. Such strategies include Sure Start (DfEE, 1999e) aimed at supporting young children and their families, Education Action Zones (DfEE, 1999d) and Excellence in Cities (DfEE, 1999b) aimed at vulnerable areas and groups of schools, and the ConneXions strategy (DfEE, 2000a) aimed (particularly) at supporting 'at risk' young people into further education, employment or training.

Underlying these concerns is a 'third way' (Blair, 1998; Giddens, 1998) analysis of the role of education. This analysis starts from the assumption that, if Britain is to compete successfully in a global economy, it can only do so by developing a knowledge-based economy of its own, serviced by a workforce with a high level of skills. This in turn means that it has to:

> create a truly world class education service, which matches, or exceeds, the standards of our international competitors.
>
> (Blunkett, 1999a, p. 3)

This, of course is the driving force behind the 'crusade for standards'. However, it also informs the social inclusion agenda. If, Blunkett argues, we are to create this world-class service,

> we must have high expectations of everyone, regardless of background or circumstances.
>
> We must target support to those who need most help to reach those high standards. And we must change the culture. The tradition of blaming everyone else for failure is being replaced with a culture in which everyone, not least the Secretary of State, accepts responsibility for improving pupil performance.
>
> (Ibid.)

On this analysis, the concern for social inclusion is not something separate from the crusade for standards, informed by a charitable, or even rights-based, concern for the underprivileged. On the contrary, social inclusion is the aegis under which those students who are most at risk of educational failure are brought within the overall standards project. This has interesting implications for the way in which Blunkett uses the term 'inclusion'. He does, indeed, use it to refer to the presence of students with special educational needs in mainstream schools. However, such references are set in the context of more extended accounts of the government's strategy for reducing truancy and disciplinary exclusions, or for addressing the issue of 'looked-after' children, or of moving young people into further education or employment. Here again, the message is clear. Inclusion is not separate from social inclusion – and social inclusion is not different from the 'crusade for standards'. As the Secretary of State puts it:

> The goal is that every pupil should leave secondary school equipped for the challenges of the 21st century, and as many as half should take advantage of the academic challenges of higher education. Those with different aspirations will all need the

knowledge, skills, understanding and attitudes to equip them for
a place in a job market which will make ever higher demands.

As business leaders know better than anyone, the days of opportunity for unskilled or semi-skilled people are long since over.
The education system needs to change to reflect that.

Success for a few was an option in the past. Success for all is the
challenge now.

(Blunkett, 1999a, p. 6)

Success for all: a new resolution?

Whatever the rights and wrongs of this policy position, it marks, we
suggest, a new resolution of the 'dilemma of difference'. Like the
resolutions we saw in our case-study schools, it is based on notions of
equity and entitlement; all students, regardless of their characteristics
and of the disadvantages they experience, are entitled to a high-
quality education. It also implies some notion of participation, at least
in the sense that students are pushed to ever-higher levels of the
education system – into higher education, if possible, into further
education and training where this is not possible and from special into
mainstream school where applicable. There is, therefore, a real sense
that educational disadvantages are to be attacked vigorously. Since
'success for a few' is no longer an option, low attainment and educational 'failure' cannot be tolerated. *Everyone* has to be successful.

It is at this point where the new resolution diverges from the old.
There is no sense here of 'valuing difference', at least insofar as that
means accepting low attainment. Moorgate's 'comprehensive ideal' in
which teachers do their best for students but accept their inherent
limitations, or Lakeside's 'community' in which all are equally valued
and those with significant disabilities participate alongside their
highest-attaining peers may not be overtly rejected, but they are made
to seem somewhat irrelevant. Indeed, one of the government's first
acts on taking over responsibility for education was effectively to
outlaw 'ideologically-driven' mixed-attainment grouping (DfEE,
1997b). In practical terms, students whose attainments are low, for
whatever reason, can expect to be the subject of vigorous intervention:
they and their families will be targeted for support in the early years;
they will be moved out of cosy special schools into a standards-
oriented mainstream; the Literacy and Numeracy Strategies will drive
up their attainments in the 'basics'; their schools will push them towards their individual targets and towards helping the school to meet
its own institutional targets; they will participate in the attainment-

oriented initiatives of an Education Action Zone and/or be mentored towards higher attainments as part of an Excellence in Cities initiative; and, finally, a personal adviser will, under the 'ConneXions' strategy, ensure that they do not fall through the education and training net at age 16.

As we might expect, given our previous analyses, some of the more obvious fracture lines within this policy position are already beginning to surface. The more all students are driven towards ever-higher standards, the more the difficulties which some students experience in reaching those standards become obvious. Likewise, the more mainstream schools become driven by the notion of 'standards', the more inimical they are likely to become to such students. It is not too difficult to see how, in the long term, this resolution will itself begin to fragment. What matters now, however, is to understand that this is indeed a new resolution, related to but different from those which have preceded it.

This is perhaps most obvious if we supplement the four case studies around which this book is largely centred with two further – though less detailed – studies which illustrate what this new resolution might mean in practice.

Newgrange Community School

Newgrange School is a small comprehensive located in an inner-city area beset with multiple social and economic problems. The attainments of its students are the lowest of those in any school in the city – and levels of attainment in the city as a whole are well below national norms. Indeed, many of its students would be regarded as having special educational needs in most other schools. That they are not so in Newgrange is simply because the SENCO could not possibly cope with managing provision for such large numbers. After years of declining pupil rolls, declining funds and indifferent management, the school finally went into special measures after 'failing' its Ofsted inspection. It was only saved from closure by a vigorous campaign by local politicians and the appointment of a new headteacher who came fresh from another school in difficulties which he had 'turned round'.

The changes introduced by the new head were extensive. They included:

- a heavy emphasis on literacy in Key Stage 3 (i.e. for students aged 11–14), including literacy lessons each day in addition to their ordinary English lessons and extensive use of an IT-based interactive learning system;

- a vocational curriculum at Key Stage 4 (i.e. for students aged 14–16), particularly for the many students who were unlikely to do well in public examinations;
- intensive additional tuition for the relative small number of students who were likely to perform well in public examinations;
- a policy of setting by attainment, including the creation of a small 'bottom stream' for the lowest-attaining students;
- a policy of zero exclusions on disciplinary grounds, supported by an internal 'time-out' room, an off-site (but school-managed) 'unit' for the most difficult students and a series of inter-agency team meetings to plan strategies for managing those students and supporting their families;
- a new community policy, involving the creation of a community base in the school and the provision of an extensive programme of community education;
- a vigorous attack on truancy, including persuading parents of habitual non-attenders to withdraw their children from the school;
- an emphasis on innovative approaches to engaging disaffected students in learning, including the deliberate importation of many ideas from US urban high schools.

The Citadel initiative

The Citadel initiative is located in a small city which has significant pockets of social and economic deprivation. Its originator was the former head of a special school for secondary-aged students with 'moderate learning difficulties'. As part of the LEA's policy of establishing more inclusive provision, the school had been scheduled for closure for many years, but the head, with the more or less explicit support of the heads of local comprehensive schools, had fought a powerful rearguard action. In particular, he had established a 'sixth form' for older students offering a vocational curriculum, with a large measure of supported work experience and leading to nationally-recognised vocational qualifications.

Eventually, the LEA won the battle and closed the school – reopening it immediately as a 'pupil referral unit' (PRU) for students excluded from their schools for disciplinary reasons. However, as the government increased pressure on schools to reduce such exclusions (DfEE, 1999a), the PRU became a less attractive option to local headteachers. Seeing an opportunity, the former special school head established a scheme which offered to make provision for students at risk of exclusion. He entered a partnership with a national charity, the local FE College and a consortium of local comprehensive schools which enabled him to put together customised 'packages' of provision for individual students. Typically, such packages would comprise a day or two per week in an off-site centre where the students would work on 'basic' skills and personal development, a day's vocational training in the FE College, a day or two's work experience and a day back in school where they would work towards national examinations in one or two 'academic' subjects.

The scheme was immediately popular with local headteachers, who were prepared to fund places for their most difficult students. Disciplinary exclusions and the use of the PRU, therefore, fell dramatically.

Inclusion redefined?

Both Newgrange and the Citadel initiative are, we suggest, forms of inclusive provision. In both cases, some of the most highly problematic students in their areas are maintained and educated in mainstream settings. In particular, both are pursuing policies of zero exclusions and are seeking innovative ways of re-engaging disaffected students in the process of learning.

However, there is little doubt that the meaning of inclusive education – or, indeed, of the 'comprehensive ideal' – in these schools is quite different from that in our four case-study schools. The focus of the work at Newgrange and the Citadel, for instance, is not – or at least not exclusively – on students formally identified as having special educational needs. Instead, the target groups are those who are disaffected and disengaged – those who can be seen as at risk of 'social exclusion' – regardless of what other educational labels they may carry. As a result, inclusion as presence and participation in mainstream schools and classrooms is less important than action to re-engage students in learning. Certainly, they are maintained on the roll of mainstream schools, but this does not mean that they necessarily have to spend their time in such schools, much less that they have to be taught in mixed-attainment groups within mainstream classrooms. Moreover, the notion of a 'common curriculum' has disappeared from these schools. Since the aim is no longer participation but engagement and attainment, the curriculum is driven by considerations of 'relevance' – relevance, that is, both to what students are likely to perceive as their needs and to what professionals believe they will need if they are to flourish in the labour market and in society in general after they have completed statutory schooling.

Given what we learned from our four main case studies, of course, it will not surprise us to find ambiguities and tensions within this new construction of inclusion. The shift of emphasis away from the common curriculum and the mainstream classroom means that the initiatives at Newgrange and the Citadel can also be read as reductions of opportunities for participation and hence as moves towards greater exclusion. The Citadel initiative is a means whereby local schools can off-load their most problematic students, just as, in a wider sense, Newgrange is a means whereby the city as a whole can confine its most problematical children to a 'ghetto' provision. Moreover, the reconstruction of the curriculum is highly ambiguous. On the one hand, the emphasis on 'basic' skills and vocational education in both settings is an inclusive move aimed at re-engagement and hence at enhancing the life chances of marginalised students; on the other, it is an exclusive move aimed at directing those students into 'learning to labour' (Willis, 1977) and thus at reproducing existing patterns of social and economic disadvantage.

It will also not be surprising that the tensions and conflicts which characterised our four case-study schools are also beginning to emerge at the Citadel and in Newgrange. These are particularly marked in the latter setting, which is the longer established of the two. The school has failed to have the impact on levels of attainment which had been anticipated. As a result, it remains stubbornly at the bottom of the local school 'league table' and is coming under scrutiny from Ofsted. A recent inspection, moreover, suggested that the significant structural changes in the school had failed to impact on teaching and learning in the classroom, which remained highly variable. These difficulties, combined with some adverse publicity in the media, have kept the recruitment of new students low, with consequent threats to the school budget. Staff have become progressively more disenchanted as the promise of a radical new start for the school dissolves in the face of familiar and intractable problems. In particular, the head's policy of zero exclusions provoked increasing hostility as teachers faced the daily reality of highly disruptive – and sometimes dangerous – behaviour from their students. At one point, a teachers' strike was threatened and the head, brought in so recently to 'save' the school, has now resigned to take up a post elsewhere. The school is now in limbo, without a headteacher and with its future uncertain.

What we have then, is both new and yet familiar. At Newgrange and the Citadel, we can see in operation some new resolutions of what we have called the 'dilemma of difference'. In comparison with our four major case study schools, the aspects of difference to which attention is directed, the aims and priorities for action and the form that action takes have all changed. Newgrange and the Citadel are inclusive in ways which the other schools were not and exclusive in ways which those other schools fought desperately to avoid. On the other hand, the tensions, ambiguities and conflicts which characterised the first four schools also characterise Newgrange and the Citadel. The new approaches to difference and diversity have brought about a different resolution, but one that appears no more stable.

Shifting sands: what can we learn?

Given what we said in the previous chapter about the constant dialectical resolutions of the 'dilemma of difference', we should not be surprised to see these processes of redefinition, reconstruction and deconstruction under way once more. The processes in Newgrange and the Citadel are, we might predict, likely to be typical of what will happen to the whole thrust of government education policy. Just as the notion of inclusion as participation in mainstream schools and a common curriculum constantly encountered those aspects of student diversity which made that participation problematic, so we might now expect the government's notion that inclusion can be equated with the achievement of standards to fall foul of the stubborn failure of some students to attain those standards. Whether schools begin to crack under the strain, as at Newgrange, whether they find means of reducing the strain by off-loading their most problematic students, as in the Citadel initiative, or whether some other fracture line begins to appear in response to local circumstances, it remains certain that the resolution which currently seems to offer so much promise will ultimately begin to erode and fragment.

This somewhat depressing scenario, however, begs some fundamental questions. If any resolution of the 'dilemma of difference' is doomed ultimately to failure in this sense, is there any possibility of educational progress? Is it ever possible to say that one resolution is better than another, or that it is possible to learn anything useful from the past? Above all, is there anything that practitioners and policymakers can take from our analysis which might help them to act in ways which are more effective or more equitable in the future?

Certainly, at the level of the 'technology' of education there is something to learn. Over the past twenty-five years, we have, it seems to us, discovered means of enabling a greater diversity of students to participate more fully in mainstream schools and classrooms. Our four case-study schools, for instance, were operating in ways that would have been out of the question when we ourselves entered teaching in the early 1970s. What they and schools like them have developed by way of techniques for support, differentiation and the management of more inclusive forms of provision is, in that sense, a genuine technological development.

Where we stop short of committing ourselves to a straightforward notion of 'progress' is in the realisation which emerges from our analysis of the interdependence of technological change such as we have described with prevailing values and contexts which are themselves susceptible to change (Clark *et al.*, 1997). It is not so much that we engage in a linear quest to do the same things better as that our views of what we should be doing change. We learn, therefore, to do new and different things in different contexts and for different purposes. Moreover, a commitment to the notion of dilemmas and resolutions indicates that new and different ways of acting cannot escape the fundamental contradictions out of which they emerge. Likewise, an awareness of conflicts around interest and power warns us, in Skrtic's (1991a) term, to look 'behind' any resolution that is proposed in order to understand who really benefits from it and whether it does not further disadvantage children and young people who are already marginalised.

However, this capacity for doubt and critical interrogation is, in itself, we suggest, something to be valued. The more we can deconstruct the resolutions that are currently on offer to us, the more we understand whose interests they serve, what values they embody, what compromises and trade-offs they involve, the less we are their prisoner. The position we have outlined in this book is not one of naïve optimism which commits us to believe that change is a process of continual betterment leading eventually to the best of all possible responses to diversity. On the other hand, neither is it a determinist position which condemns us perpetually to reproduce the situation in which we find ourselves.

Rather, as resolutions rise and fall, spaces open up in which new resolutions become possible. The continual changes of technologies, the shifts in social and educational values, the reconfigurations of social, political and educational contexts make such new resolutions possible. In turn, these resolutions themselves impact on the complex situations out of which they emerge. Amidst such fluidity and turbulence, the scope for choice, and therefore for meaningful action is, if not unlimited, then at least real and significant. Moreover, although the choices and actions of policy-makers at the centre of the education system may appear to have the greatest impact, similar choices have to be made at every level of the system and at every point where action is called for. The choices made, therefore, by the heads of our case-study schools and by every teacher in every classroom of those schools, are significant. In the sort of dynamic situation our analysis has revealed, every choice has impact.

This means that, in the final analysis, what can be learned from this study is only partly about 'technology'. In contrast to many commentators, our concern is not with identifying and describing an unequivocally better way of responding to diversity. It is, rather, a concern with identifying and developing a better process for making choices and deciding on action to formulate such responses. As a matter of fact, from our particular location in history and from the perspective of the values we hold and the possibilities we can envisage, we do indeed see the resolutions arrived at by our case-study schools as 'better' than many other alternatives. However, what really matters to us is the continuing, principled interrogation of these and other resolutions as the only means of opening up possibilities which will accord more fully with those principles. To this extent, whilst we doubt some of his other conclusions, we share Skrtic's (1995a) view that the critical deconstruction and reconstruction of proposed responses to diversity are essential processes within democratic societies.

However, calling upon democratic principles in this way begs the final question of who participates in a democracy and whose voice prevails in democratic decision-making. Throughout this chapter and this book, we have used the pronoun 'we' to indicate both ourselves as authors and a loosely-structured community of like-minded researchers, policy-makers and practitioners to which we see ourselves belonging. We make no apology for this. Historically, it is precisely this community which has had the greatest power to shape all levels of the education system. This alone argues for the need for its members to be able to engage in principled analysis and debate so that their power is exercised in accordance with those principles. However, in recent years, there has been a growing tendency for governments to centralise more power to themselves and, in particular, to discourage any meaningful dialogue with the wider education community. The need, therefore, for the constant reaffirmation of the importance of analysis and debate is more urgent than ever.

Nonetheless, that community, however wide, is only ever going to constitute a minority of those with a stake in the direction which the education system takes. Governments recently have tended to emphasise the role of parents. Other groups, however, have begun to assert their own rights to be involved in the debate. In particular, disabled people and others who are marginalised in the education system have begun to question the legitimacy of the hitherto dominant educational voice in decision-making (Ballard, 1997; Barton, 1994; Oliver, 1992a and b). Whatever contribution, therefore, this book makes to the debate that 'we' must have, it is essential that 'we' remember the wider context within which that debate must be set.

Retrospect and prospect

As long ago as 1976, Ian Galletley issued a challenge for Remedial Departments (as they were then called) in mainstream schools to 'do away with themselves' (Galletley, 1976). In Lakeside, Moorgate, St Joseph's and Seaview, we have seen how that challenge was taken up some twenty years later. We have seen how those schools sought to develop responses to diversity which were, they believed, more equitable and more inclusive than traditional forms of special needs education. We have seen how far they succeeded and how much is to be learned from their endeavours. We have also seen, however, the difficulties they encountered and come to understand the dilemmas they faced and the contradictions which their responses embodied.

It is no longer possible to believe, as we once may have done (Dyson, 1990), that some technological advance or organisational restructuring will, at a stroke, resolve what we have called the 'dilemma of difference'. Our four schools, therefore, cannot serve as beacons to guide us to some unequivocally better way of doing things – any more than can the powerful arguments of Ainscow, Skrtic or their like. However, what they can do, and have done, is to challenge old preconceptions, open up new possibilities and – through their failures as much as through their successes – help us to understand more fully the situation in which we find ourselves. That understanding may not point us unequivocally towards the future, but, if nothing else, it increases our ability to find our own way.

Appendix: A Methodological Note

A common problem with books on inclusive education is that, even where they are based on primary research, the detail of the research methods used remains hidden. This appendix, therefore, sets out the methods we used in our case studies so that readers can form their own judgements about the trustworthiness of our findings. This appendix may prove particularly useful to those readers who are themselves involved in research, perhaps as part of a programme of study.

Design

The aim of this study was to investigate the relationships between espoused approach (the 'policy'), actual practice and practitioners' understandings in emerging approaches to special educational needs in ordinary secondary schools. In particular, it sought to study these relationships in schools which were seeking to dismantle traditionally segregated forms of special needs provision and 'embed' their responses to special needs in ordinary classroom practice.

Our previous research (Clark *et al.*, 1995a) had suggested that policy-practice-understandings relationships in this area of schools' activities were likely to be complex. For this reason, a case-study design was adopted, permitting fine-grained analysis. Linked case studies in a number of different sites were undertaken in order to be able to differentiate as far as possible between site-specific features and common features across sites. The latter might then illuminate the characteristics of policy-practice-understandings relationships more generally in this field.

From the start, the investigation had a theoretical orientation. It set out, not simply to *describe* policy-practice-understandings relationships, but to test the models current in the literature (notably those of Ainscow and Skrtic) in terms of their adequacy for accounting for these relationships and, if possible, to develop better models. It follows that the desirability of extensive data-gathering and of producing thick descriptions of school life in classic ethnographic mode had

187

to be balanced against the imperatives of this testing and development process. In the event, we discovered that the notion of 'models' – insofar as this implied schematic representations of relationships between aspects of the schools we were studying – was itself overly simplistic. It was only by bringing to bear a range of theoretical tools that we were able to make full sense of what we were finding. In particular, the literatures on dialectical analysis of organisations and on dilemmas in education were helpful in this respect (see Chapter 9). This, of course, cost us the ability to produce simple models which would yield straightforward prescriptions for practice. However, we believe it added considerable complexity and depth to our interpretations.

The theoretical intent of the investigation from the start is one reason why we opted for a multi-site rather than single-site design; whilst 'thick description' might have called for us to concentrate our resources in one school, theory-building seemed better served by the range of tests and challenges which arose from four schools. It also explains why we opted for a two-stage design. Phase 1 took the form of a 'mapping' exercise in which we collected similar data across all four schools in order to delineate the principal features of policy-practice-understandings. The maps we produced (which were both diagrammatic and textual) constituted 'local theories' which provisionally explained those relationships in each school.

Phase 2 was much more exploratory and purposive in design as we gathered data in order both to elaborate those maps in individual schools and to develop a theoretical account which would explain those relationships across all four schools. In phase 2, therefore, we engaged in an iterative process of fieldwork and theory-building, where the one directly informed the other.

The following sections describe in some detail how this design was implemented.

Sample

Data were collected in four comprehensive schools. These were selected according to the following criteria:

1. There was *prima facie* evidence both that the schools were adopting 'embedded' approaches to special needs education and that the detail of those approaches was different in each case.
2. They displayed a range of contextual features (size, numbers of pupils with statements, demography of intake).
3. They were accessible from the research team's base.

The *prima facie* evidence for the schools' approaches came partly through their participation in previous research undertaken by the team (Clark *et al.*, 1995b) and partly from other contacts with the schools (school-based in-service events, participation of staff in university courses, regional meetings and conferences, etc.).

Access to schools

A series of meetings was held with the senior management teams from the participating schools in the preparatory period of the investigation where the nature of the research and its implications for the schools were discussed. Prior to its commencement a staff meeting was held in three of the schools where the implications of the research were explained. In each of these schools the project was fully endorsed by the senior management teams and at the staff meetings no serious reservations were raised and no individual members of staff indicated their reluctance or unwillingness to participate. In the fourth school ('Seaview'), agreement was reached with senior managers, but it was their view that no staff meeting should be held. In the event, this caused some difficulties for the research team since some staff felt that they were being imposed upon and were mistrustful of the researchers. The significance of this in terms of management style within the school is commented on in Chapter 6.

Once agreement had been reached with senior managers and/or staff, a formal written invitation to participate was issued which effectively constituted a contract between the school and the research team, setting out the obligations and safeguards on both sides.

Data collection and analysis

The investigation was organised into two broad and interlinked phases.

Phase 1.
Phase 1 consisted of the following activities, which took place from May to October 1996:

1. Documentation either directly relevant to the school's approach to special needs education or providing information on its context within the school was collected. This comprised: SEN policy, staff handbook, school development plan, school brochure, SEN staff timetables, relevant job descriptions, latest annual governors' report, list of staff roles and responsibilities and any

other documentation judged by the head and research team to be relevant.

2. The documentation was analysed under the following headings:
   - statistical information (size of school, number of statements, number of staff, etc.)
   - context (e.g. catchment area, competitor schools)
   - mainstream structures (e.g. departmental organisation, staffing structure)
   - SEN strategy (e.g. SENCO role, SENCO background, numbers and roles of specialist teachers)
   - budget (e.g. size and construction of budget; SEN allocation)
   - environment (e.g. site layout, physical access issues).

3. A preliminary interview was carried out with the headteacher and/or the SENCO (or equivalent) in order to clarify the information provided and the broad parameters of the school's approach to special needs.

4. A 25 per cent sample of teaching and allied (i.e. learning support assistant) staff in each school was constructed for interview. The sample was selected in order to be representative of the staff as a whole in terms of the following characteristics:
   - gender
   - subject department affiliation
   - role (e.g. head of department, subject teacher, head of year)
   - teaching experience.

5. An interview schedule was prepared and semi-structured interviews lasting between 30 and 60 minutes were conducted with this sample. Interviewees were asked:
   - to describe their teaching experience, length of stay in this school and current role and responsibilities;
   - to say what they understood by special educational needs and their own approach to meeting such needs;
   - to describe the school's approach to special educational needs and its rationale as they understood it;
   - to outline what they saw as the main strengths and weaknesses of that approach and the way in which it impacted on their own teaching.

6. A total of 84 interviews were undertaken in this phase, all of which were taped and transcribed. Interviewers also kept field notes to record their initial responses to the interviews and relevant contextual information (e.g. mood, comments outside the interview).

7. The following procedures were used for analysing the transcripts. All members of the research team read all of the interviews to sensitise themselves to emerging themes. They then met

to discuss these themes and agree a strategy for further analysis. As a result of this discussion, the detailed analysis of each school was allocated to a pair of team members. This analysis took place through standard procedures of coding and categorisation:

- each team member read the transcripts separately and developed a set of inductive codes;
- pairs then met to compare, justify and modify their coding systems;
- the full team met to compare their coding systems and consider the extent to which these could be harmonised across the schools. (In the event, apart from minor harmonisations, the decision was made to preserve separate coding systems for each school in order to prevent premature closure in the interpretation of the data as a whole.)

8. On the basis of the categorised and coded data, each pair produced a provisional 'map' of the relationships between policy, practice and understandings in each school. The complexity of the analysis at this stage proved a significant challenge since the investigation was considering not merely the congruencies and disjunctures between policy, practice and understandings but also the ways in which these manifested themselves differently across different staff groups. The solution was twofold:

- The 'maps' were produced in diagrammatic form so that the complexity could be represented visually and more easily manipulated by the researchers.
- The 'maps' were also articulated as extended analytic memos, with supporting evidence, so that they could be interrogated critically by other team members.

9. The 'maps' produced by each pair were presented to the full team and discussed critically, with the intention of challenging the interpretations they contained and exploring common findings across the four schools. The maps were modified in the light of these discussions, though again the decision was taken for the most part to avoid harmonising the themes across schools in order to prevent premature closure.

10. In order to check the provisional 'maps' against respondents' perceptions, they were presented to the headteacher and other staff nominated by the headteacher in each school. These individuals were invited to clarify any missing or incorrect information and to comment critically on the interpretations of policy-practice-understandings relationships embodied in these maps. In each school, the maps were perceived as broadly acceptable working hypotheses worthy of further testing.

Phase 2

The following activities were undertaken in the second phase of the investigation which lasted from October 1996 to September 1997 (though contact with the schools was maintained for some time after this date):

1. The 'maps' produced in phase 1 formed the basis for data collection in phase 2. This phase was concerned with elaborating and refining the accounts of policy-practice-understandings relationships embodied in those maps. Data collection therefore took the following forms:

    *   The headteacher and SENCO (or equivalent) were identified as 'key players' in the school's approach to special needs education and were interviewed on a recurrent basis. These interviews typically took the form of 'briefings' on current developments and issues at the start of each of the four or five periods of fieldwork in each school which constituted this phase, with more substantial interviews towards the end of the investigation.

    *   Purposive samples of staff were constructed with a view to elaborating the 'maps' formulated in phase 1. Although these interviews were similar to those conducted in the earlier phase, the construction of these samples and the precise questions asked depended on the nature of the hypotheses emerging from that phase. For instance, where there was evidence from phase 1 that particular subject departments took distinctive views on the school's approach to special needs education, further interviews were conducted with members of these departments. Where salient issues emerged from phase 1 (for instance, the issue of students' behaviour), phase 2 interviews explored these issues in greater depth. Altogether, some 27 interviews of this kind were conducted across the schools.

    *   In order to explore the relationships between espoused policy and actual practice, lesson observations were undertaken where major elements in the school's approach were being implemented. The observations were sensitised in terms of the emerging interpretations of policy-practice relationships generated in phase 1 and were recorded in the form of narrative field notes. In Moorgate, for instance, lessons where support teaching was in progress were observed. In Lakeside, lessons where students with severe learning difficulties were included were observed. After each observation, focused interviews were conducted with the staff involved in order to explore their aims, the rationales for their actions and their perceptions of the successes and problems

of those actions. Altogether, some 38 observations and interviews of this kind were undertaken.

- Additionally, in each school, the SENCO (or equivalent), as key implementer of the school's approach, was tracked for a day in order to illuminate how far her/his work reflected the espoused approach and/or other factors. Further observations were undertaken of meetings (e.g. staff meetings, training days, management team meetings) in which issues relevant to the school's espoused approach were under discussion. The imminence and relevance of these meetings were signalled principally in the briefing interviews with 'key players'. The observations were sensitised through the provisional accounts generated in phase 1 and were recorded in the form of narrative field notes. Altogether, some eight further days of observation were undertaken in this way.

2. The analytical procedures for phase 2 data were essentially the same as those used in phase 1, though with modification to take into account the greater range of data types and the greater flexibility of sampling in this phase. A crucial element of these procedures was that analysis had to be undertaken on a recurrent basis so that a process of progressive focusing on salient issues could be undertaken as the 'maps' produced in phase 1 were elaborated and refined. In order to facilitate this, the team met on a frequent (at least fortnightly) basis to review new data and decide on future data collection strategy. These meetings were informed by analytic memos and other working papers as necessary, amending and elaborating the 'maps' produced in phase 1 and based on the principle of 'challenge' used there. The challenge was increased by the involvement of an independent judge in commenting critically on emerging findings towards the end of this process. At each meeting, decisions were taken regarding which themes to pursue as hypotheses were elaborated or new hypotheses emerged.

3. Decisions about how much data to collect in each school were determined partly by the available research resources and time and partly by using the principle of 'saturation'. In each school, a point was reached where the research team was confident that the further data that was then being gathered was not adding substantially to the process of developing the 'maps' of each school.

4. A degree of respondent validation was sought for the investigation's emerging findings. The research team prepared brief summaries of their findings in each school. Seminars (open to all staff) were then held in the schools in which the team's accounts of policy-practice-understandings relationships were reported to

staff, who were invited to comment critically on these accounts. In order to test the team's findings further and to explore their policy implications, a national policy seminar was organised for representatives of the LEAs in which the schools were located, DfEE, Ofsted and other researchers. An overview of the project's findings was presented and critical comment invited. The accounts of the case-study schools were amended in the light of feedback from these school and national seminars (though there was, in fact, a large measure of agreement that the accounts were accurate) and were written up as final working documents.

References

Abberley, P. (1987) The concept of oppression and the development of a social theory of disability, *Disability, Handicap and Society*, 2(1), 5–19.

Abberley, P. (1992) Counting us out: a discussion of the OPCS disability surveys *Disability, Handicap and Society*, 7(2), 139–156.

Adey, P. and Shayer, M. (1994) *Really Raising Standards: Cognitive Intervention and Academic Achievement* (London, Routledge).

Ainscow, M. (1991) Effective schools for all: an alternative approach to special needs in education, in: M. Ainscow (ed.), *Effective Schools for All* (London, David Fulton).

Ainscow, M. (1994) *Special Needs in the Classroom: A Teacher Education Guide* (London, Jessica Kingsley Publishers/UNESCO Publishing).

Ainscow, M. (1995) Special needs through school improvement: school improvement through special needs, in: C. Clark, A. Dyson and A. Millward (eds), *Towards Inclusive Schools?* (London, David Fulton).

Ainscow, M. (1998) Would it work in theory? Arguments for practitioner research and theorising in the special needs field, in: C. Clark, A. Dyson and A. Millward (eds), *Theorising Special Education* (London, Routledge).

Ainscow, M. (1999) *Understanding the Development of Inclusive Schools* (London, Falmer Press).

Ainscow, M. (ed.) (1991) *Effective Schools for All* (London, David Fulton).

Ainscow, M. and Tweddle, D. A. (1979) *Preventing Classroom Failure: An Objectives Approach* (Chichester, Wiley).

Ainscow, M. and Tweddle, D. (1988) *Encouraging Classroom Success* (London, David Fulton).

Ainscow, M., Hopkins, D., Southworth, G. and West, M. (1994) *Creating the Conditions for School Improvement* (London, David Fulton).

Altrichter, H. and Salzgeber, S. (2000) Some elements of a micro-political theory of school development, in: H. Altrichter and J. Elliott (eds) *Images of Educational Change* (Buckingham, Open University Press).

Artiles, A. J. (1998) The dilemma of difference: enriching the disproportionality discourse with theory and context, *Journal of Special Education*, 32(1), 32–36.

Ball, S. (1997) Policy sociology and critical social research: a personal review of recent education policy and policy research, *British Educational Research Journal*, 23(3), 257–274.

Ball, S. J. (1987) *The Micropolitics of the School: Towards a Theory of School Organisation* (London, Routledge).

Ball, S. J. (1994) *Education Reform: A Critical and Post-Structural Approach* (Buckingham, Open University Press).

Ballard, K. (1995) Inclusion, paradigms, power and participation, in: C. Clark, A. Dyson and A. Millward (eds), *Towards Inclusive Schools?* (London, David Fulton).

Ballard, K. (1996) Inclusive education in New Zealand, *Cambridge Journal of Education*, 26(1), 33–45.

Ballard, K. (1997) Researching disability and inclusive education: participation, construction and interpretation, *International Journal of Inclusive Education*, 1(3), 243–256.

Ballard, K. (ed.) (1994) *Disability, Family, Whanau and Society* (Palmerston North, NZ, Dunmore Press).

Ballard, K. (ed.) (1999) *Inclusive Education: International Voices on Disability and Justice* (London, Falmer Press).

Ballard, K. and Macdonald, T. (1998) New Zealand: inclusive school, inclusive philosophy?, in: T. Booth and M. Ainscow (eds), *From Them to Us: An International Study of Inclusion in Education* (London, Routledge).

Barton, L. (1994) Disability, difference and the politics of definition, *Australian Disability Review* (3), 8–22.

Barton, L. (1997) Inclusive education: romantic, subversive or realistic?, *International Journal of Inclusive Education*, 1(3), 231–242.

Barton, L. (ed.) (1988) *The Politics of Special Educational Needs* (London, Falmer Press).

Barton, L. and Oliver, M. (1992) Special needs: personal trouble or public issue?, in: M. Arnot and L. Barton (eds), *Voicing Concerns: Sociological Perspectives on Contemporary Education Reforms* (Wallingford, Triangle Books).

Barton, L. and Tomlinson, S. (ed.) (1981) *Special Education: Policy, Practices and Social Issues* (London, Harper and Row).

Barton, L. and Tomlinson, S. (ed.) (1984) *Special Education and Social Interests* (London, Croom Helm).

Benn, C. and Simon, B. (1972) *Half Way There: Report on the British Comprehensive School Reform* (2nd edn) (Harmondsworth, Penguin Books).

Benson, J. K. (1977) Organizations: a dialectical view, *Administrative Science Quarterly*, 22, 1–21.

Benson, J. K. (1983) A dialectical method for the study of organizations, in: G. Morgan (ed.), *Beyond Method: Strategies for Social Research* (London, Sage).

Bines, H. (1986) *Redefining Remedial Education* (Beckenham, Croom Helm).

Bines, H. (1995) Special educational needs in the market place, *Journal of Education Policy*, 10(2), 157–172.

Blagg, N., Ballinger, M. and Gardner, R. (1991) *Somerset Thinking Skills Course* (Oxford, Basil Blackwell in association with Somerset County Council).

Blair, T. (1998) *The Third Way: New Politics for the New Century* (London, Fabian Society).

Blase, J. (ed.) (1991) *The Politics of Life in Schools* (Newbury Park, CA, Sage).

Blunkett, D. (1999a) *Excellence for the Many, Not Just the Few: Raising Standards and Extending Opportunities in our Schools. The CBI President's Reception Address by the Rt Hon. David Blunkett MP 19 July 1999* (London, DfEE).

Blunkett, D. (1999b) *Social Exclusion and the Politics of Opportunity: A Mid-Term Progress Check. A Speech by the Rt Hon. David Blunkett MP* (London, DfEE).

Blunkett, D. (2000) *Raising Aspirations in the 21st Century. A Speech by the Rt Hon. David Blunkett MP Secretary of State for Education and Employment 6th January 2000* (London, DfEE).

Booth, T. (1995) Mapping inclusion and exclusion: concepts for all?, in: C. Clark, A. Dyson and A. Millward (eds), *Towards Inclusive Schools?* (London, David Fulton).

Booth, T. (1996) A perspective on inclusion from England, *Cambridge Journal of Education*, 26(1), 87–99.

Booth, T. and Ainscow, M. (eds) (1998) *From Them to Us: An International Study of Inclusion in Education* (London, Routledge).

Booth, T., Ainscow, M. and Dyson, A. (1997) Understanding inclusion and exclusion in the English competitive education system, *International Journal of Inclusive Education*, 1(4), 337–354.

Booth, T., Ainscow, M. and Dyson, A. (1998) England: inclusion and exclusion in a competitive system, in: T. Booth and M. Ainscow (eds), *From Them to Us: An International Study of Inclusion in England* (London, Routledge).

Bowe, R. and Ball, S. J., with Gold, A. (1992) *Reforming Education and Changing Schools* (London, Routledge).

Bowles, S. and Gintis, H. (1976) *Schooling in Capitalist America* (London, Routledge and Kegan Paul).

Burrell, G. and Morgan, G. (1979) *Sociological Paradigms and Organisational Analysis* (Aldershot, Gower).

Canter, L. and Canter, M. (1976) *Assertive Discipline: A Take Charge Approach for Today's Educator* (Seals, CA, Canter and Associates).

Carroll, H. M. C. (1972) The remedial teaching of reading: an evaluation, *Remedial Education*, 7(1), 10–15.

Carroll, T. G. (1992) The role of anthropologists in restructuring schools, in: G. A. Hess (ed.), *Empowering Teachers and Parents: School Restructuring through the Eyes of Anthropologists* (Westport, CT, Bergin and Garvey).

Central Advisory Council for Education (England) (1967) *Children and their Primary Schools. Volume 1: Report* (London, HMSO).

Centre for the Study of Inclusive Education (CSIE) (1996) *Developing an Inclusive Policy for Your School: A CSIE Guide* (Bristol, CSIE).

Clark, C., Dyson A. and Millward, A. (eds) (1995a) *Towards Inclusive Schools?* (London, David Fulton).

Clark, C., Dyson, A. and Millward, A. (1995b) Towards inclusive schools: mapping the field, in: C. Clark, A. Dyson and A. Millward (eds), *Towards Inclusive Schools?* (London, David Fulton).

Clark, C., Dyson, A., Millward, A. and Skidmore, D. (1995a) Dialectical analysis, special needs and schools as organizations, in: C. Clark, A. Dyson and A. Millward (eds), *Towards Inclusive Schools?* (London, David Fulton).

Clark, C., Dyson, A., Millward, A. and Skidmore, D. (1995b) *Innovatory Practice in Mainstream Schools for Special Educational Needs* (London, HMSO).

Clark, C., Dyson, A., Millward, A. and Skidmore, D. (1997) *New Directions in Special Needs: Innovations in Mainstream Schools* (London, Cassell).

Clough, P. and Barton, L. (eds) (1995) *Making Difficulties: Research and the Construction of SEN* (London, Paul Chapman Publishing).

Clough, P. and Barton, L. (eds) (1998) *Articulating with Difficulty: Research Voices in Inclusive Education* (London, Paul Chapman Publishing).

Collins, J. E. (1972) The remedial education hoax, *Remedial Education*, 7(3), 9–10.

Corbett, J. and Slee, R. (2000) An international conversation on inclusive education, in: F. Armstrong, D. Armstrong and L. Barton (eds), *Inclusive Education: Policy Contexts and Comparative Perspectives* (London, David Fulton).

Croll, P. and Moses, D. (1985) *One in Five – The Assessment and Incidence of Special Educational Needs* (London, Routledge and Kegan Paul).

Croll, P. and Moses, D. (2000a) Ideologies and utopias: education professionals' views of inclusion, *European Journal of Special Needs Education*, 15(1), 1–12.

Croll, P. and Moses, D. (2000b) *Special Needs in the Primary School: One in Five?* (London, Cassell).

Daniels, H. and Garner, P. (1999) Introduction, in: H. Daniels and P. Garner (eds), *World Yearbook of Education 1999: Inclusive Education* (London, Kogan Page).

Department for Education (DfE) (1994) *Code of Practice on the Identification and Assessment of Special Educational Needs* (London, DfE).

Department for Education and Employment (DfEE) (1997a) *Excellence for All Children: Meeting Special Educational Needs* (London, The Stationery Office).

Department for Education and Employment (DfEE) (1997b) *Excellence in Schools* (London, The Stationery Office).

Department for Education and Employment (DfEE) (1997c) *From Targets to Action: Guidance to Support Effective Target-Setting in Schools* (London, (DfEE)).

Department for Education and Employment (DfEE) (1997d) *Targets for our Future: A Consultation Document* (London, DfEE).

Department for Education and Employment (DfEE) (1998a) *Meeting Special Educational Needs: An Action Programme* (London, DfEE).

Department for Education and Employment (DfEE) (1998b) *Supporting the Target Setting Process: Guidance for Effective Target Setting for Pupils with Special Educational Needs* (London, DfEE).

Department for Education and Employment (DfEE) (1998c) *Teachers Meeting the Challenge of Change. Cm 4164* (London, The Stationery Office).

Department for Education and Employment (DfEE) (1999a) *Circular 10/99. Social Inclusion: Pupil Support. The Secretary of State's Guidance on Pupil Attendance, Behaviour, Exclusion and Re-integration* (London, DfEE).

Department for Education and Employment (DfEE) (1999b) *Excellence in Cities* (London, DfEE).

Department for Education and Employment (DfEE) (1999c) *Meet the Challenge: Education Action Zones* (London, DfEE).

Department for Education and Employment (DfEE) (1999d) *Sure Start: Making a Difference for Children and Families* (London, DfEE).

Department for Education and Employment (DfEE) (2000a) *Connexions: The Best Start in Life for Every Young Person* (London, DfEE).

Department for Education and Employment (DfEE) (2000b) *SEN and Disability Rights in Education Bill: Consultation document* (London, DfEE).

Department of Education and Science (DES) (1978) *Special Educational Needs: Report of the Committee of Enquiry into the Education of Handicapped Children and Young People (The Warnock Report)* (London, HMSO).

Department of Education and Science (DES) (1989) *A Survey of Pupils with Special Educational Needs in Ordinary Schools: A Report by H.M. Inspectorate* (London, DES).

Dessent, T. (1987) *Making the Ordinary School Special* (London, Falmer).

Disability Rights Task Force (1999) *From Exclusion to Inclusion: A Report of the Disability Rights Task Force on Civil Rights for Disabled People* (London, DfEE).

Dyson, A (1990) Special educational needs and the concept of change, *Oxford Review of Education*, 16(1), 55–66.

Dyson, A. (1999) Inclusion and inclusions: theories and discourses in inclusive education, in: H. Daniels and P. Garner (eds) *World Yearbook of Education, 1999: Inclusive Education* (London, Kogan Page).

Dyson, A. and Millward, A. (1999) Falling down the interfaces: from inclusive schools to an exclusive society, in: K. Ballard (ed.), *Inclusive Education: International Voices on Disability and Justice* (London, Falmer Press).

Dyson, A., Millward, A. and Skidmore, D. (1994) Beyond the whole school approach: an emerging model of special needs practice and provision in mainstream secondary schools, *British Educational Research Journal*, 20(3), 301–317.

Edelman, M. (1964) *The Symbolic Use of Politics* (Urbana, IL, University of Illinois Press).

Feurstein, R., Rand, Y., Hoffman, M.B. amd Miller, R. (1980) *Instrumental Enrichment: An Intervention Program for Cognitive Modifiability* (Baltimore, MD, University Park Press).

Franklin, B. M. (1994) *From 'Backwardness' to 'At-Risk': Childhood Learning Difficulties and the Contradictions of School Reform* (Albany, NY, State University of New York Press).

Fuchs, D. and Fuchs, L. S. (1994) Inclusive schools movement and the radicalization of special education reform, *Exceptional Children*, 60(4), 294–309.

Fulcher, G. (1993) Schools and contests: a reframing of the effective schools debate?, in: R. Slee (ed.), *Is There a Desk With My Name On It? The Politics of Integration* (London, Falmer Press).

Fullan, M., with Stiegelbauer, S. (1991) *The New Meaning of Educational Change* (2nd edn) (London, Cassell).

Galletley, I. (1976) How to do away with yourself, *Remedial Education*, 11(3), 149–152.

Galloway, D. and Goodwin, C. (1979) *Educating Slow-Learning and Maladjusted Children: Integration or Segregation* (London, Longman).

Garner, P. and Sandow, S. (1995) Towards the inclusive school, in: P. Garner and S. Sandow (eds), *Advocacy, Self-Advocacy and Special Needs* (London, David Fulton).

Gerber, M. (1996) Reforming special education: beyond 'inclusion', in: C. Christensen and F. Rizvi (eds), *Disability and the Dilemmas of Education and Justice* (Buckingham, Open University Press).

Gewirtz, S., Ball, S. J. and Bowe, R. (1995) *Markets, Choice and Equity in Education* (Buckingham, Open University Press).

Giddens, A. (1998) *The Third Way: The Renewal of Social Democracy* (Cambridge, Polity Press).

Golby, M. and Gulliver, R. J. (1979) Whose remedies, whose ills? A critical review of remedial education, *Remedial Education*, 11(2), 137–147.

Gold, A., Bowe, R. and Ball, S. (1993) Special educational needs in a new context: micropolitics, money and 'education for all', in: R. Slee (ed.), *Is There a Desk With My Name On It? The Politics of Integration* (London, Falmer Press).

Gross, J. (1996) The weight of the evidence: parental advocacy and resource allocation to children with statements of special educational need, *Support for Learning*, 11(1), 3–8.

Gulliford, R. (1979) Remedial work across the curriculum, in: C. Gains and J. A. McNicholas (eds), *Remedial Education: Guidelines for the Future* (London, Longman for the National Association for Remedial Education).

Hanko, G. (1995) *Special Needs in Ordinary Classrooms: From Staff Support to Staff Development* (3rd edn) (London, David Fulton).

Hargreaves, A. (1991) Contrived collegiality: the micropolitics of teacher collaboration, in: J. Blase (ed.), *The Politics of Life in Schools* (Newbury Park, CA, Sage).

Harris, A. (2000) What works in school improvement? Lessons from the field and future directions, *Educational Research*, 42(1), 1–11.

Hart, S. (1992) Differentiation – way forward or retreat?, *British Journal of Special Education*, 19(1), 10–12.

Haug, P. (1998) Norwegian special education: development and status, in: P. Haug and J. Tossebro (eds), *Theoretical Perspectives on Special Education* (Krsitiansand, Norway, Hoyskoleforlaget AS – Norwegian Academic Press).

Her Majesty's Inspectorate of Schools (HMI) (1990) *Special Needs Issues: A Survey by HMI* (London, HMSO).

Heydebrand, W. (1977) Organizational contradictions: toward a marxian theory of organizations, *The Sociological Quarterly*, 18, 83–107.

Hopkins, D., Ainscow, M. and West, M. (1994) *School Improvement in an Era of Change* (London, Cassell).

Hopkins, D., West, M. and Ainscow, M. (1996) *Improving the Quality of Education for All: Progress and Challenge* (London, David Fulton).

Hoyle, E. (1986) *The Politics of School Management* (Sevenoaks, Hodder and Stoughton).

Jeffs, T. (1992) The state, ideology and the community school movement, in: G. Allen and I. Martin (eds), *Education and Community. The Politics of Practice* (London, Cassell).

Jones, N. (1983) The management of integration: the Oxfordshire experience, in: T. Booth and P. Potts (eds), *Integrating Special Education* (Oxford, Blackwell).

Jordan, L. and Goodey, C. (1996) *Human Rights and School Change* (Bristol, CSIE).

Kauffman, J. M. (1995) The Regular Education Initiative as Regan-Bush education policy: a trickle-down theory of education of the hard-to-teach, in: J. M. Kauffman and D. P. Hallahan (eds), *The Illusion of Full Inclusion: A Comprehensive Critique of a Current Special Education Bandwagon* (Austin, TX, PRO-ED).

Lawton, D. and Chitty, C. (ed.) (1988) *The National Curriculum* (London, Institute of Education, University of London).

Lewis, I. and Vulliamy, G. (1980) Warnock or warlock ? The sorcery of definitions: the limitations of the report on special education, *Educational Review*, 32(1), 3–10.

Lipsky, D. K. and Gartner, A. (1997) *Inclusion and School Reform: Transforming America's Classrooms* (Baltimore, Paul H. Brookes).

Lipsky, D. K. and Gartner, A. (1999) Inclusive education: a requirement of a democratic society, in: H. Daniels and P. Garner (eds), *World Yearbook of Education 1999: Inclusive Education* (London, Kogan Page).

Lovell, K., Johnson, E. and Platts, D. (1962) A summary of a study of the reading ages of children who had been given remedial teaching, *British Journal of Educational Psychology*, 32, 66–71.

Luscombe, J. (1993) Rethinking the role of the special needs co-ordinator: devolving the remedial department, in: A. Dyson and C. Gains (eds), *Rethinking Special Needs in Mainstream Schools: Towards the Year 2000* (London, David Fulton).

Mintzberg, H. (1979) *The Structuring of Organizations* (Englewood Cliffs, NJ, Prentice-Hall).

Mintzberg, H. (1983) *Structure in Fives: Designing Effective Organizations* (Englewood Cliffs, NJ, Prentice-Hall).

Montacute, C. (1993) The self-destructing SEN department, *Managing Schools Today*, 2(9), 44–45.

Morgan, G. (1997) *Images of Organization* (2nd edn) (London, Sage).

Mortimore, P., Sammons, P., Stoll, L., Lewis, P. and Ecob, R. (1988) *School Matters: The Junior Years* (Wells, Open Books).

National Curriculum Council (NCC) (1989a) *Curriculum Guidance 2: A Curriculum for All* (York, NCC).

National Curriculum Council (NCC) (1989b) *Circular Number 5: Implementing the National Curriculum – Participation by Pupils with Special Educational Needs* (York, NCC).

National Literacy Task Force (1997) *The Implementation of the National Literacy Strategy* (London, National Literacy Task Force).

Norwich, B. (1994) Differentiation: from the perspective of resolving tensions between basic social values and assumptions about individual differences, *Curriculum Studies*, 2(3), 289–308.

Numeracy Task Force (1998) *The Implementation of the National Numeracy Strategy* (London, DfEE).

Oliver, M. (1988) The social and political context of educational policy: the case of special needs, in L. Barton (ed.), *The Politics of Special Educational Needs* (London, Falmer).

Oliver, M. (1990) *The Politics of Disablement* (London, Macmillan).

Oliver, M. (1992a) Changing the social relations of research production?, *Disability, Handicap and Society*, 7(2), 101–114.

Oliver, M. (1992b) Intellectual masturbation: a rejoinder to Soder and Booth, *European Journal of Special Needs Education*, 7(1), 20–28.

Ozga, J. (2000) *Policy Research in Educational Settings: Contested Terrain* (Buckingham, Open University Press).

Parsons, C. and Castle, F. (1998) The cost of school exclusion in England, *International Journal of Inclusive Education*, 2(4), 277–294.

Parsons, C. and Howlett, K. (1996) Permanent exclusions from school: a case where society is failing its children, *Support for Learning*, 11(3), 109–112.

Persson, B. (1996). The culture of special education: a means of sustaining educational barriers? in: Seminar on Culture, Difference and Inclusion, Sheffield, 16–19 February 1996.

Persson, B. (2000) Special education in today's Sweden – a struggle between the Swedish model and the market, in: F. Armstrong, D. Armstrong and L. Barton (eds), *Inclusive Education: Policy, Contexts and Comparative Perspectives* (London, David Fulton).

Pickup, M. (1995) The role of the special educational needs co-ordinator: developing philosophy and practice, *Support for Learning*, 10(2), 88–92.

Pijl, S. J. (1994a) Denmark, in: C. J. W. Meijer, S. J. Pijl and S. Hegarty (eds), *New Perspectives on Special Education: A Six-Country Study of Integration* (London, Routledge).

Pijl, S. J. (1994b) United States, in: C. J. W. Meijer, S. J. Pijl and S. Hegarty (eds), *New Perspectives in Special Education: A Six-Country Study of Integration* (London, Routledge).

Pijl, S. J., Meijer, C. J. W. and Hegarty, S. (eds) (1997) *Inclusive Education: A Global Agenda* (London, Routledge).

Porter, G. (1997) Critical elements for inclusive schools, in: S. J. Pijl, C. J. W. Meijer and S. Hegarty (eds), *Inclusive Education: A Global Agenda* (London, Routledge).

Reynolds, D. (1995) Using school effectiveness knowledge for children with special needs – the problems and possibilities, in: C. Clark, A. Dyson and A. Millward (eds), *Towards Inclusive Schools?* (London, David Fulton).

Reynolds, D., Teddlie, C., with Hopkins, D. and Stringfield, S. (2000) Linking school effectiveness and school improvement, in: C. Teddlie and D. Reynolds (eds), *The International Handbook of School Effectiveness Research* (London, Falmer Press).

Riddell, S. and Brown, S. (eds) (1994) *Special Educational Needs Policy in the 1990s : Warnock in the Market Place* (London, Routledge).

Riddell, S. and Brown, S. and Duffield, J. (1994a) Conflicts of policies and models: the case of specific learning difficulties, in: S. Riddell and S. Brown (eds), *Special Educational Needs Policy in the 1990s: Warnock in the Market Place* (London, Routledge).

Riddell, S., Brown, S. and Duffield, J. (1994b) Parental power and special educational needs: the case of specific learning difficulties, *British Educational Research Journal*, 20(3), 327–344.

Rizvi, F. and Kemmis, S. (1987) *Dilemmas of Reform* (Geelong, Deaking Institute for Studies in Education).

Rosenholtz, S. J. (1991) *Teachers' Workplace: The Social Organization of Schools* (New York, Teachers College Press).

Rouse, M. and Florian, L. (1996) Effective inclusive schools: a study in two countries, *Cambridge Journal of Education*, 26(1), 71–85.

Rouse, M. and Florian, L. (1997) Inclusive education in the market-place, *International Journal of Inclusive Education*, 1(4), 323–336.

Rutter, M., Maughan, B., Mortimore, P. and Ouston, J. (1979) *Fifteen Thousand Hours: Secondary Schools and Their Effects on Children* (London, Open Books).

Sampson, O. (1975) *Remedial Education* (London, Routledge and Kegan Paul).

Sayer, J. (1994/1987) *Secondary Schools for All? Strategies for Special Needs* (2nd edn/1st edn) (London, Cassell).

Scheerens, J. (1992) *Effective Schooling: Research, Theory and Practice* (London, Cassell).

Sebba, J. and Sachdev, D. (1997) *What Works in Inclusive Education* (Ilford, Barnardo's).

Sharp, R. and Green, A. (1976) *Education and Social Control: A Study in Progressive Primary Education* (London, Routledge and Kegan Paul).

Simpson, J. (1993) Rethinking the role of the special needs co-ordinator: the quality assurer, in: A. Dyson and C. Gains (eds), *Rethinking Special Needs in Mainstream Schools: Towards the Year 2000* (London, David Fulton).

Skidmore, D. (1998) Divergent pedagogical discourses, in: P. Haug and J. Tossebro (eds), *Theoretical Perspectives on Special Education* (Kristiansand, Hoyskoleforlaget Norwegian Academic Press).

Skidmore, D. (1999) Divergent discourses of learning difficulty, *British Educational Research Journal*, 25(5), 651–663.

Skrtic, T. M. (1985) Doing naturalistic research into educational organizations, in: Y. S. Lincoln (ed.), *Organizational Theory and Inquiry: The Paradigm Revolution* (Beverly Hills, CA, Sage).

Skrtic, T. M. (1991a) *Behind Special Education: A Critical Analysis of Professional Culture and School Organization* (Denver, CO, Love).

Skrtic, T. M. (1991b) Students with special educational needs: artifacts of the traditional curriculum, in: M. Ainscow (ed.), *Effective Schools for All* (London, David Fulton).

Skrtic, T. M. (1991c) The special education paradox: equity as the way to excellence, *Harvard Educational Review*, 61(2), 148–206.

Skrtic, T. M. (ed.) (1995a) *Disability and Democracy: Reconstructing (Special) Education for Postmodernity* (New York, Teachers College Press).

Skrtic, T. M. (1995b) The functionalist view of special education and disability: deconstructing the conventional knowledge tradition, in: T. M. Skrtic (ed.), *Disability and Democracy: Reconstructing (Special) Education for Postmodernity* (New York, Teachers College Press).

Stainback, W. and Stainback, S. (eds) (1990) *Support Networks for Inclusive Schooling* (Baltimore, MD, Paul H. Brookes).

Stakes, R. and Hornby, G. (1997) *Change in Special Education: What Brings It About?* (London, Cassell).

Stradling, R. and Saunders, L., with Weston, P. (1991) *Differentiation in Action: A Whole-School Approach for Raising Attainment* (London, HMSO).

Stringfield, S. (1995) Attempts to enhance students' learning: a search for valid programs and highly reliable implementation techniques, *School Effectiveness and School Improvement*, 6, 67–96.

Swann, W. (1985) Is the integration of children with special educational needs happening?, *Oxford Review of Education*, 11(1), 3–18.

Swann, W. (1988) Trends in special school placement to 1986: measuring, assessing and explaining segregation, *Oxford Review of Education*, 14(2), 139–161.

Swann, W. (1992) *Segregation Statistics* (London, Centre for Studies on Integration in Education).

Tansley, A. E. and Gulliford, R. (1960) *The Education of Slow Learning Children* (2nd edn) (London, Routledge and Kegan Paul).

Thomas, G. and Dwyfor Davies, J. (1999) England and Wales: competition and control – or stakeholding and inclusion, in: H. Daniels and P. Garner (eds), *World Yearbook of Education 1999: Inclusive Education* (London, Kogan Page).

Thomas, G., Walker, D. and Webb, J. (1998) *The Making of the Inclusive School* (London, Routledge).

Thousand, J. S. and Villa, R. A. (1995) Managing complex change towards inclusive schooling, in: R. A. Villa and J. S. Thousand (eds), *Creating an Inclusive School* (Alexandria, VA, Association for Supervision and Curriculum Development).

Tomlinson, S. (1982) *A Sociology of Special Education* (London, Routledge and Kegan Paul).

Tomlinson, S. (1985) The expansion of special education, *Oxford Review of Education*, 11(2), 157–165.

Udvari-Solner, A. and Thousand, J. (1995) Effective organizational, instructional and curricular practices in inclusive schools and classrooms, in: C. Clark, A. Dyson and A. Millward (eds), *Towards Inclusive Schools?* (London, David Fulton).

UNESCO (1994) *Final Report: World Conference on Special Needs Education: Access and Quality* (Paris, UNESCO).

Villa, R. A., Thousand, J. S., Stainback, W. and Stainback, S. (eds) (1992) *Restructuring for Caring and Effective Education: An Administrative Guide to Creating Heterogeneous Schools* (Baltimore, MD, Paul H. Brookes).

Villa, R. and Thousand, J. S. (eds) (1995) *Creating an Inclusive School* (Alexandria, VA, Association for Supervision and Curriculum Development).

Vincent, C. (1993) Education for the community?, *British Journal of Educational Studies*, 41(4), 366–380.

Vincent, C., Evans, J., Lunt, I. and Young, P. (1995) Policy and practice: the changing nature of special educational provision in schools, *British Journal of Special Education*, 22(1), 4–11.

Vincent, C., Evans, J., Lunt, I., Steedman, J. and Wedell, K. (1994) The market forces? The effect of local management of schools on special educational needs provision, *British Educational Research Journal*, 20(3), 261–278.

Vislie, L. (1995) Integration policies, school reforms and the organisation of schooling for handicapped pupils in western societies, in: C. Clark, A. Dyson and A. Millward (eds), *Towards Inclusive Schools?* (London, David Fulton).

Vislie, L. and Langfeldt, G. (1996) Finance, policy making and the organisation of special education, *Cambridge Journal of Education*, 26(1), 59–70.

Vlachou, A.D. (1997) *Struggles for Inclusive Education: An Ethnographic Study* (Buckingham, Open University Press).

Ware, L. (1998) USA: I kind of wonder if we're fooling ourselves, in: T. Booth and M. Ainscow (eds), *From Them to Us: An International Study of Inclusion in Education* (London, Routledge).

Weston, P. (1992) A decade for differentiation, *British Journal of Special Education*, 19(1), 6–9.

Wheal, R. (1995) Unleashing individual potential: a team approach, *Support for Learning*, 10(2), 83–87.

Willis, P. (1977) *Learning to Labour* (Farnborough, Saxon House).

Zeitz, G. (1980) Interorganizational dialectics, *Administrative Science Quarterly*, 25, 72–88.

Index

208